Hardcore Horror Cinema in the 21st Century

EDITED BY JAMES ASTON AND
JOHN WALLISS

To See the Saw *Movies:*
Essays on Torture Porn and Post–9/11 Horror
(McFarland, 2013)

Hardcore Horror Cinema in the 21st Century
Production, Marketing and Consumption

JAMES ASTON

McFarland & Company, Inc., Publishers
Jefferson, North Carolina

ISBN (print) 978-1-4766-6888-8 ♾
ISBN (ebook) 978-1-4766-3353-4

LIBRARY OF CONGRESS CATALOGUING DATA ARE AVAILABLE

BRITISH LIBRARY CATALOGUING DATA ARE AVAILABLE

© 2018 James Aston. All rights reserved

No part of this book may be reproduced or transmitted in any form or by any means, electronic or mechanical, including photocopying or recording, or by any information storage and retrieval system, without permission in writing from the publisher.

Front cover images © 2018 iStock

Printed in the United States of America

*McFarland & Company, Inc., Publishers
Box 611, Jefferson, North Carolina 28640
www.mcfarlandpub.com*

For Kirsten and Angharad,
Dorothy and Barbara

Acknowledgments

Hardcore horror films are not easy to watch, but the book has been slightly more of an enjoyable experience due to the help and support of colleagues at the University of Hull and individuals from within the horror community. In particular, I would like to thank Shane Ryan for giving up so much of his time and providing such illuminating answers to my questions. I would also like to thank Eric Stanze and Lucifer Valentine for their time and for supplying invaluable material regarding their films. Thank you also to the two anonymous readers who offered useful and constructive feedback on the draft version of this book. Thanks to Linnie Blake and Xavier Aldana Reyes for granting permission to include previously published material.

My family has provided unstinting support ever since I started on my circuitous route back into academia. Most of all, I would like to thank Kirsten and Angharad: Kirsten for everything we share about film and Angharad for being my future partner-in-crime when it comes to watching horror films!

Table of Contents

Acknowledgments   vi

Introduction: Beyond Videodrome—*An Archaeology of 21st-Century Hardcore Horror*   1

ONE. "Not like how Hollywood shows us": A Definition of Hardcore Horror in the 21st Century   15

TWO. The Genealogy of Extremity in North American Film   30

THREE. Global Currents of Extreme Horror   55

FOUR. "A malignant, seething hatework": The Films of Hardcore Horror in the 21st Century   80

FIVE. The Realist Aesthetic of Hardcore Horror   110

SIX. "These movies have brought me many problems": Performance and the Traumatized Self Within Hardcore Horror   131

SEVEN. Hardcore Horror Production: An Interview with *Amateur Porn Star Killer* Director Shane Ryan   153

EIGHT. "I'll pay you in cash to slip this thread into the purge": Navigating Fandom in Hardcore Horror   172

Conclusion: "It has no redeeming features whatsoever that I could discern"—The Cultural Value of Hardcore Horror   198

Chapter Notes   205

Bibliography   221

Index   229

Introduction: Beyond *Videodrome*— An Archaeology of 21st-Century Hardcore Horror

> HARLEN: There's no plot, it just goes on like that for an hour.
> MAX RENN: Goes on like what?
> HARLEN: Like that. Torture. Murder. Mutilation.
> MAX RENN: You never leave that room?
> HARLEN: No. It's real sicko. Perverts only.
> MAX RENN: Absolutely brilliant. I mean, look, there's almost no production costs. You can't take your eyes off it. It's incredibly realistic. Where do you get actors who can do this?
> —*Videodrome* (David Cronenberg, 1983)

David Cronenberg's provocative and prophetic sci-fi–horror hybrid *Videodrome*, which imagines a technological landscape merged to human consciousness, is a horrific and disturbing treatise on the mass media and its modes of reception and effects. Early on, in a narrative strand where burned-out TV exec Max Renn (James Woods) searches for violent and sexual product to satisfy his jaded audience, he comes across a seemingly real snuff "subterranean TV" program acquired by his colleague Harlen, the self-proclaimed "prince of pirates." In this illicit, pirated footage of torture and murder, Renn has finally found a program that will jolt a desensitized audience out of the stupor of their regular TV viewing habits. In its "real" displays of extreme and unexpurgated violence, the program *Videodrome* offers the possibility of sensation to viewers no longer affected by television's tame diet of sex and violence. In fact, *Videodrome* offers much more than just emotional effect. The low-grade footage has an insidious ability to open up the "neural networks" of the viewer, whereby the minds and reality of those watching are subjugated to the warped ideological message of the program. Renn's descent into this nightmarish and hallucinogenic dystopian world delineates an intricate and hidden-from-view power structure of the mass media: The film suggests that the only possible outcome is to merge the body with the electronic resonance of the "great cathode ray tube" to transform into the "new flesh." Such a re-programming of consciousness offers a pessimistic example of Louis Althusser's theory of interpellation in how the viewer becomes symbiotically attached to the television and accepts the destructive ideological and social forces as their own.[1]

Thus, *Videodrome* offers an ominous glimpse into the future with its warning of a loss of identity brought about by the pervasive nature of contemporary media and the contaminant developments in technology. Hidden within this cautionary tale of media effect and a debased televisual future, there's an illuminating conversation between Renn and Harlen over the merits of *Videodrome*. During this short interchange, the film offers an intuitive assessment as to the future direction of violent imagery in visual media productions. That is, in terms of the content described by Harlen ("Torture. Murder. Mutilation.") and Renn's reaction to it ("no production costs" and "incredibly realistic"), the conversation could be describing exactly the subgenre of hardcore horror in the 21st-century. With its descriptions of a sense of static, confined space; a spectacularization of extreme representations of violence over the necessities of the plot; low-fi production practices, and the focus on realist horror, *Videodrome* anticipates precisely the formal stylistics and thematic strategies of 21st-century hardcore horror.

Although there has been a proliferation of hardcore horror alongside more mainstream horror cinema in North America during the new millennium, the majority of the academic and popular discussion has been on the latter.[2] Perhaps, if we see the narrative of *Videodrome* as a correlative to our present time, such forms of horror test the boundaries of acceptable and legitimate forms of cinema and thus act as unpalatable and dangerous markers. The danger here is the notion of getting too close to the taboo of death rather than through a physical contact or media-effects arguments about the impact of viewing violent films. Here, the viewer knows the scene(s) are fabricated, but the verisimilitude of the representation posits the reaction that if it was real, then this is what it would look like, and thus interpellates the viewer to a forbidden and dangerous arrangement. In turn, it connects to a powerful affective charge surrounding violence and its association with the dead body. The optical arrangements are thus structured to direct the horror *at* the viewer and provide another aspect which further pushes hardcore horror to the margins of film discourse and into the subterranean recesses of film production.

It is not surprising then that the contemporary focus has been on "sanctioned" forms of extreme horror circulated in mainstream outlets, such as through theatrical distribution or release via DVD and Blu-ray platforms. A convergence of attention has centered on the hugely successful *Saw* franchise (2004–) and the violent remakes of 1970s horror which have been classified as torture porn—a term that has become a synecdoche for 21st-century extreme horror.

Steve Jones (2013) has provided an insightful evaluation of the phrase torture porn in a way that highlights how empty and misapplied the phrase has become when attached to films such as *Saw* (James Wan, 2004) and *Hostel* (Eli Roth, 2005). In fact, torture porn has been utilized as a pejorative term to denigrate the films and their viewers as well as acting as a lurid marketing gimmick to entice battle-weary viewers with the promise of explicit sex and violence. In both cases, the term resists critical discussion and provides an understanding of horror which is incorrect and/or reductive. What fills this critical and artistic void is precisely hardcore horror—the type of program *Videodrome* vaunts—a subgenre of 21st-century North American horror which has experienced a growing prevalence in the new millennium with its intense and immediate depiction of violence. Thus, hardcore horror can reposition discussions of the genre back toward a complete critical framework to better understand the role of horror in the landscape of contemporary cinema. Renn may have identified a televisual product that would appeal to the jaded audience of *Videodrome*'s fractured society, but its prophetic nature today is in the position of the program as unsanctioned and transgressive footage, which challenges the restrictive product, viewing experiences and predominant discussions within dominant culture. A program ignored at one's peril.

In this respect, hardcore horror can provide a vital reassessment of modern accounts of contemporary North American horror bringing together its production, exhibition and reception to recoup its critical and academic exclusion. In doing so, it will be possible to integrate this marginalized horror subgenre into the general discourse surrounding the contemporary horror film.

The "hidden" adjunct of hardcore horror to the mainstream represents a conspicuous absence in academic discourse during a period exhibiting a wide-ranging and eclectic scholarship on extreme, challenging and confrontational horror. Chief among these are Adam Lowenstein's *Shocking Representation: Historical Trauma, National Cinema, and the Modern Horror Film*; Linnie Blake's *The Wounds of Nations: Horror Cinema, Historical Trauma and National Identity*; Brigid Cherry's *Horror*, and Kevin J. Wetmore's *Post-9/11 Horror in American Cinema*. Within the above texts, examples of hardcore horror are not to be found though criticizing these approaches for not covering films which exist, to use Carol Clover's famous phrase for the slasher film, "[d]own in the cinematic underbush"[3] is perhaps unnecessarily punitive. But it does represent an omission which contributes to an overall account of contemporary horror that is partial. Even texts specifically dealing with extreme cinema, such as Phil Russell's *Beyond the Darkness: Cult, Horror and Extreme Cinema* (2013), omit any traces of hardcore horror's marginal film practices. Instead the focus is on extreme horror that has been brought into official culture (via cinematic exhibitions, approval from the Classification and Ratings Administration [CARA] or British Board of Film Classification [BBFC], and DVD and Blu-ray formats) and can thus be seen to compromise the label of being genuinely extreme. Russell's work is indicative in how it diminishes the cultural status and value of hardcore horror despite how the films have undergone a contemporary, post-millennial boom.

The outcome is to marginalize the films as being illegitimate which leads to their indifferent treatment as worthless by critics and scholars. Indeed, the "unlikable" and extremely violent nature of these films leaves them as nothing more than a debased spectacle for the prurient spectator. Yet, recent scholarship has begun to address what Jeffrey Sconce might see as the paracinema of hardcore horror and has, either directly or indirectly, provided ways in which to define the films as related to but discreet from other extreme horrors such as torture porn.[4]

Recent texts such as Jones' *Torture Porn* (2013), the Neil Jackson-Shaun Kimber-Johnny Walker-Thomas Joseph Watson collection *Snuff: Real Death and Screen Media* (2015) and David Kerekes and David Slater's meticulously researched and significantly updated *Killing for Culture—From Edison to Isis: A New History of Death on Film* (2016) have all addressed in some manner the aesthetic components, thematic strategies and socio-historical context of various essential hardcore horror films that include *August Underground* (Fred Vogel, 2001) and *Amateur Porn Star Killer* (Shane Ryan, 2006). Jones' book provides the most relevant treatise with regards to hardcore horror as it contains the chapter "You Will Not Believe Your Eyes … or Stomach: Hardcore Horror," the only academic treatment thus far to put forward a working definition and marks an origin point at looking at films such as *August Underground* and *Slaughtered Vomit Dolls* (Lucifer Valentine, 2006) as a whole, connected subgenre strand of horror. The term has undoubtedly been used previously in fandom and popular criticism and the prefix "hardcore" is most commonly aligned with pornography and certainly carries a pervasive cultural footprint. Nevertheless, Jones is the first to ossify the term to formalize criteria and here the use of "hardcore" is purposeful due to the focus on explicit levels of representation in both categories: the sex act in pornography and the act of violence and death in hardcore horror. Furthermore, Jones makes clear reference to the interconnected nature of the two forms when he initially states that hardcore horror encompasses an independent filmmaking sensibility and financial status, which combines the "narrative facets and aesthetic practices"[5] of pornography and horror.

Thus, for Jones, the intersection of hardcore horror and hardcore pornography provides three characteristic elements which distinguish the films from other 21st-century North American horror. Namely, an explicit focus on depictions of sexual violence, a privilege of violence over the basic mechanics of plot and a realist aesthetic which depicts violence as "spontaneous and genuine rather than performed and contrived."[6] Jones suggests that one of the central threads that run through these films is how the majority of "contemporary American hardcore horror adheres to a visual style that is fashioned after the mythic 'snuff' film."[7] Jones takes the lead from Kerekes and Slater's imperious 1993 first edition of *Killing for Culture* and in which the authors mapped out the growing aesthetic utilization of the pseudo-snuff film in the representations of extreme horror. But it is Alexandra Heller-Nicholas' book *Found Footage Horror Films: Fear and the Appearance of Reality* (2014) which provides both an excellent foundation and most relevant analysis of the snuff film for the study of hardcore horror. She traces a critical history of the found footage horror and how it has appropriated codes and conventions of the snuff film demonstrated in the highway safety films of the 1950s and 1960s and the mondo documentaries of the 1960s and 1970s. Heller-Nicholas puts forward a detailed definition of the formal properties and thematic strategies of found footage horror post–*The Blair Witch Project* (Edward Myrick and Eduardo Sánchez, 1999), which have subsequently been adopted and developed by key hardcore horror filmmakers.

Therefore, following Jones and Heller-Nicholas, this study will discuss and situate hardcore horror within the contours of the larger cultural field of 21st-century North American horror. The bridge between these two studies and hardcore horror is the use of snuff aesthetics and its cultural appropriation from historical antecedents such as the shockumentary, mondo cinema, the safety film, horror films such as *Cannibal Holocaust* (Ruggero Deodato, 1980) and *Henry: Portrait of a Serial Killer* (John McNaughton, 1986) and filmmakers such as Nick Zedd, Hideshi Hino and Jorg Buttgereit. What this highlights is that hardcore horror is not a phenomenon located exclusively in the 21st-century (or indeed in North America) but one that has a long, convoluted and controversial history. It has, however, crystallized into a particular strand of North American horror post-millennium and post–9/11 where the utilization of snuff is central to each film's representational strategy. The conventions of snuff tend to center on the visual qualities and arrangement of the film and include amateur filmmaking techniques, degraded film stock and at least the inclusion of either violent death or sexual violence. The form and content of snuff are typically used for three interrelated reasons:

firstly, to situate the film as illicit and unsanctioned and similar in this respect to Renn's interpretation and reception of the pirate footage of *Videodrome*; secondly, to utilize and exploit the "mode's ostensible unmediated spontaneity, which is antithetical to studio horror's typically glossy professionalism"[8]; and lastly, to disrupt the boundary between the real and the imitative so that a "snuff-fiction" can emerge that challenges the notion of the separateness of reel and real horror.

These tenets attest to the outlaw and marginal status of hardcore horror and how they are used both as a representational and marketing tool. As such, the focus will be on three filmmakers who have come to exemplify the resurgence of extreme horror in the contemporary period and its utilization of the snuff film, but who remain largely overlooked in academic horror discourse.

Firstly, Fred Vogel can be seen, through his *August Underground* trilogy (*August Underground, August Underground: Mordum* [2003], *August Underground: Penance* [2007]) to be the pioneer filmmaker of 21st-century hardcore horror and to exemplify many of the practices associated with this horror subgenre. Secondly, Shane Ryan continues Vogel's extreme aesthetic but develops it more toward the avant-garde and pornography in his *Amateur Porn Star Killer* trilogy (*Amateur Porn Star Killer, Amateur Porn Star Killer 2* [2008], *Amateur Porn Star Killer 3: The Final Chapter* [2009]). Lucifer Valentine will act as the final case study; his "vomit gore" films (*Slaughtered Vomit Dolls, ReGOREgitated Sacrifice* [2008], *Slow Torture Puke Chamber* [2010], *Black Mass of the Nazi Sex Wizard* [2015]) act as a bridge between the realm of hardcore horror and that of affective performance art to offer new ways to experience horror. All three filmmakers provide clear examples and developments of hardcore horror regarding how technological, cultural and sociohistorical contingencies have impacted on their making.

With regards to these case studies, Jones and Heller-Nicholas' work provide important analysis with which to interpret the films along the contours of their formal properties and thematic strategies. However, to use their work as the beginning and end of this study will invariably mean that the outcomes gained will always remain partial and unformed. As hardcore horror operates outside of normative filmmaking practices, such as the use of commercial precepts, the official marketing and exhibition formats, and the spaces of mainstream fandom, it is essential to account for an archaeology of horror. Here, a wider examination of the cultural field of North American horror and the horror genre in the 21st-century can be provided, both regarding how it is made and experienced. Thus, to situate the analysis of the films within this larger sphere, the work will be indebted to Antonio Lázaro-Reboll's approach to an "archaeology of horror" put forward in his book *The Spanish Horror Film* (2013). In doing so, it will be possible to "reintegrate marginal filmic and cultural practices"[9] into 21st-century North American horror by also looking at the production, marketing and consumption of the liminal filmic spaces of hardcore horror.

The parallels between *Hardcore Horror* and Lázaro-Reboll's *The Spanish Horror Film* are clear in that both attempt to recoup marginal horror practices into dominant accounts: 21st-century North American horror and Spanish cinema respectively. For Lázaro-Reboll, this means arguing for a "more inclusive cultural geography of horror which takes into account the institutions and technologies, genre users and consumers that shape and participate in the process of genre classification and (re)configuration."[10] In turn, this leads to his formation of an "archaeology of horror" that accounts for the discursive practices and structures in which the horror film is "produced, circulated and consumed."[11] Regarding *Hardcore Horror*, such an approach is vital to achieve a complete archaeology of the films and to position them within the existing academic discourses on contemporary horror.

Chapter Breakdown

As outlined above, the volume organizes a holistic treatment of hardcore horror in the 21st century to provide an account of the broad social processes of North American horror film classification. In examining how particular "users," to cite Lázaro-Reboll's term for people who produce, evaluate and consume a particular genre, it will be possible to align hardcore horror with the larger cultural history of extreme cinema and with the general practices of post-millennial North American horror.

Therefore, Chapter One will take the need for a comprehensive account of the definition of hardcore horror as a starting point with which to discuss the ossification of its industrial, technological, aesthetic, thematic and consumptive practices. The supply of an extensive chronological account of the scholarly work into the historical and contemporary study of extreme cinema locates the book within the wider discourse on extreme or hardcore horror and provides a comprehensive and relevant definition. Therefore, forming a definition initially provides an exploration of why hardcore horror is designated as extreme, an essential aspect of its study if the films are going to be integrated into wider horror discourses and if the contribution of the films or their cultural value to horror studies is to be adequately positioned. For instance, the films included as case studies in this volume do not directly present offensive material for the sole purpose to affront, horrify or disgust. In fact, as Jones has pointed out, "the status 'hardcore' … discloses little about the films themselves."[12] Thus, to fully understand the mechanisms at play, the codes and conventions of hardcore horror need to be analyzed. Therefore, a detailed and working definition can account for the formal properties, thematic strategies, audience consumption and the production practices evident and recurrent throughout each film.

Chapter Two provides an expansion of the pre-history of extreme cinema to carefully adduce how previous manifestations have influenced, negotiated, reinforced and contested the various strands of hardcore horror. The chapter begins with a brief outline of the pre-history of cinema to stress the importance of situating extremity in film (or visual projection) within its socio-historical context. An account of early forms of visual presentation from the magic lantern to the Kinetoscope will present the notion that affective images and shocking content have always been a part of visual projections. Indeed, as the chapter moves through key historical periods such as the Universal horror films of the 1930s and standalone examples like *Blood Feast* (Herschell Gordon Lewis, 1963), *Snuff* (Michael and Roberta Findlay, 1976) and *Henry: Portrait of a Serial Killer*, it can be possible to trace how the myriad formations of extreme cinema run through these various examples and, in turn, into the contemporary form of hardcore horror. While the horrors on display in the films of *Dracula* (Tod Browning, 1931) and *Blood Feast* might seem tame by today's standards, they nonetheless provide insight into the "what" of extreme cinema. That is, the definition of hardcore horror in the 21st century has its antecedent in earlier films such as *Dracula*'s affective charge which terrorized audiences in the early 1930s and *Blood Feast*'s intensive focus on the spectacle of violence. Furthermore, *Snuff* outlines the potential for unconventional marketing and distribution patterns of marginal and underground films showcasing extreme and controversial material while *Henry*'s controversial content allows for an examination of how the film challenges standards of acceptability and taste. Both of these latter films again delineate basic criterions of hardcore horror and what the chapter aims to position is that the discursive practices of hardcore horror did not emerge in a socio-cultural vacuum and are in fact just the most recent manifestation in the continuum of extreme film in North America.

Chapter Three continues from the previous section in accounting for international examples of extreme film to ossify the contention that hardcore horror is located within the ebbs and flows of historical and global contingencies. Looking at the global precedents of extreme film is another essential foundation with which to situate an examination of hardcore horror's "archaeology" more effectively. The global exemplars under discussion in this chapter are *Salò, or 120 Days of Sodom* (Pier Paolo Passolini, 1975), *Cannibal Holocaust, Man Bites Dog* (Rémy Belvaux, André Bonzel and Benoît Poelvoorde, 1992) and *Srpski Film/A Serbian Film* (Srdjan Spasojevic, 2010). These films are connected to the national case studies of Germany and Japan, both of which have a rich and detailed history of extreme filmmaking. The purpose is to engage with national practices, film-horror conventions, regulatory and legal frameworks, and taste cultures to emphasize the transnational aspect of extreme film and how different national contexts engage with controversial and boundary testing cinema. It is not to say that films such as *Salò* or *A Serbian Film* replicate the examples of hardcore horror precisely, but that they nonetheless illustrate how hardcore horror is not an ahistorical phenomenon, nor a completely new, unprecedented advent of extreme film. The global examples are connected to the historical trajectory of North American film in that they present a clear framework of the intricate practices tied up in the criteria for a definition of hardcore horror. For example, the connection between cinematic realism and the affective power of extreme cinema is particularly well illuminated, especially by *Salò*, *Cannibal Holocaust* and *A Serbian Film*. The films also test the thresholds of social and legislative structures and how audience and institutional modes seek to negotiate the social impact of violent material. The recurring elements to emerge surround realism, reception and impact and show that the archaeology of hardcore horror is inextricably bound up in existing and historical permutations of extreme imagery found in global examples.

Chapter Four follows on from the historical and worldwide contours of extreme film mapped out in the previous two chapters. It begins by situating North American horror which partially fulfills the criteria stipulated as essential to being considered as hardcore to provide another important facet in how hardcore horror overlaps with different arrangements of horror. The definition provided in Chapter One can be further tested against these films, such as *Murder Set Pieces* (Nick Palumbo, 2004) so that it is possible to delineate hardcore horror from other forms. With the definition and the historical and contemporary context of extreme film in place, it will be possible to finally move onto the films of Vogel, Ryan and Valentine. A general "archeology" is critically applied to the films which solidifies their position as examples of hardcore horror and point to themes picked up in the following chapters. Running concomitant to the critical overview is a situating of the films within the socio-technological-industrial-historical context of the time in which they were made. The importance is that socio-historical contingencies impact significantly on not only the form and content of extreme films but in how they are disseminated and consumed. From the early examples of *Dracula* and *Blood Feast* to the contemporaneous *A Serbian Film*, an understanding of context facilitates a critical and comprehensive reading. Therefore, events such as 9/11, the restrictive homeland surveillance of the Patriot Act, torture and atrocities committed in Abu Ghraib and Guantanamo Bay, and the wars in Iraq and Afghanistan provide a focus for hardcore horror in terms of how they understand, work through and act out the "unsettling and disorientating present"[13] they are part of.

Alongside these traumatic and psychically damaging events were the increases in portable recording technology and social media platforms with which to show and air subsequent footage, the rise in surveillance culture, and a palatable sense of fear surrounding the use of these very recording devices. In the contemporary period, rather than "being rendered obsolete by the changing faces of information and media distribution," films utilizing these new digital technologies have instead become inexplicably linked with our understanding of the world around us and have "managed to continue the tradition of transgressive reality."[14] It is in this climate that the "real" of hardcore horror has established a disturbing, powerful and liminal presence. The corpus of hardcore horror addressed in Chapter Four includes case studies along with other notable examples. For example, Eric Stanze's progenitor of contemporary North American hardcore horror *Scrapbook* (2000) serves as the first example and includes the direct and intensive horror films of Adam Rehmeier (*The Bunny Game*, 2010), James Cullen Bressack (*Hate Crime*, 2013), and Stephen Biro (*American Guinea Pig: Bouquet of Guts and Gore*, 2014). Thus, the chapter provides a filmic, technological and socio-historical context with which to analyze the case study films and to provide much of the thematic material to be considered in-depth throughout the volume.

Chapter Five picks up on the major recurrent aesthetic convention of hardcore horror—the pursuit of realist horror and the purposeful attempt to break down the barrier between the real and mimesis. Fred Vogel's *August Underground* films and Shane Ryan's *Amateur Porn Star Killer* series act as case studies in this chapter regarding how they approached the changing precepts of realist horror in the contemporary period. Despite hardcore horror's marginal and under-analyzed status, they are prominently positioned to explore the convoluted and complex area of the "real" which has become a conspicuous feature in debates and commentary on modern horror cinema. The changes to recording technology, the rise of social media sites, and the capture and dissemination of atrocity footage from 9/11 to the death videos of terrorist networks have meant that our understanding of the real has been continually in flux. Vogel's *August Underground* trilogy provides an unexpurgated document of violence and death, and the films deploy the "home video," snuff aesthetic of long takes, inferior audio-visual quality and amateurish camerawork. The rationale for Vogel was to produce an almost "found" document that he hoped would dupe people into thinking it was the real thing. In doing so, Vogel highlights the importance of the formal characteristics such as *mise en scène* and special effects, but also social and economic aspects in determining how contemporary horror films position themselves as "real." Although Vogel was unable to eradicate the boundary between the real and mimesis, the *August Underground* films serve as a fascinating marker of how realism in cinema has undergone profound changes post-millennium in an age categorized by an amateur aesthetic, accessible recording technology and "unmediated" access to atrocity. Conversely, Shane Ryan picks up on Vogel's snuff aesthetic but not to produce a realist horror that could pass for the real thing. Ryan's films engage in-depth with the cultural mythology of snuff and have provided a particular focus on the manipulation of the real toward a more technically sophisticated and entertaining format. Therefore, Ryan offers a realist aesthetic in line with Vogel and hardcore horror but purposefully manipulates his footage to emphasize how if snuff footage did (or, indeed, has) become available, it will likely be changed by a distribution–production company to make a more dramatic, accessible or subjective version. In this case, Ryan's films demonstrate how reality further recedes from our grasp in a post–9/11 and post–YouTube world where even the real would be questioned if not mediated through various stylistic or ideological filters.

Chapter Six discusses the second strand of realism in hardcore horror which focuses on the authenticity of the performance of Ameara La Vey in Valentine's "vomit gore" films and Rodleen Getsic in *The Bunny Game*. The credibility of the performances is paramount to the notion of receiving the film as authentic and is an essential criterion, along with special effects and the production design, in formulating the real within the *mise en scène* of hardcore horror. The performance of actors can receive less attention than other formal elements of contemporary horror such as narrative, sound design, special effects, décor or thematic strategies. However, performance provides an essential formal layer of realist horror in how it opens up entry points into realism by addressing the conflation and overlap of "real" human action and the imaginary realm of filmic performance. The categorization of performances in hardcore horror is threatening to a safe and in-control (self) identity, with many actors within the subgenre finding themselves unable to continue in their roles or to be associated with the films due to the breach between actor and performer. Therefore, by focusing on aspects of the traumatized self in hardcore horror, it is possible to analyze how performance contributes to notions of the real and develops new representational and experiential engagements with horror. The central theoretical strand in this investigation is Gilles Deleuze's term of affective-performativity as picked up and developed by Elena del Río in her book *Deleuze and the Cinemas of Performance: Powers of Affection* (2008). This allows us to see if affective acts such as vomiting and sadomasochistic play can not only provide an unprecedented realist horror but disrupt normative viewing positions with regards to identity and gender and the power dynamics built into their representations.

Chapter Seven looks at the alternative production practices, marketing initiatives and distribution networks of hardcore horror. The chapter includes an extended interview with Shane Ryan as an accessible and first-person report of how low- and no-budget underground horror filmmakers struggle to produce their films and the unconventional means that are utilized to get them made and shown. Ryan covers many salient areas about the production practices of hardcore horror such as the rise of new media technologies, the availability of accessible, portable recording equipment, and the impact of the Internet in shaping narrative direction and content. Ryan's interview attests to the problems and issues incorporated in some filmmakers working within hardcore horror, and thus his answers serve as a testimony to the larger filmmaking practices as he talks about the problems of funding, promotion and reception. Despite the myriad constraints impacting upon his filmmaking, Ryan has provided a successful strategy which has seen him bring the films to a large and favorable market. Therefore, Ryan articulates adeptly the alternative production practices and thematic strategies that filmmakers of hardcore horror have explored and exploited to get their marginal and transgressive films marketed and distributed.

Chapter Eight completes the archaeology of hardcore horror by looking at the expansive nature of audience reception and the modalities of fan interaction. In doing so, the chapter discusses examples of verbal and visual fan practice; forums, such as *Rue Morgue* and *Bloody Disgusting*, and the video-sharing site YouTube. Through an examination of these sites, the chapter interrogates Matt Hills' (2005) work on the pleasures of horror regarding connoisseurship and affect of horror cinema; Sara Thornton's (1995) work on subcultural capital, and Mark Jancovich's (2000) work on cult texts and the nature of distinction. Finally, Patricia Lange's (2009) work on "videos of affiliation" is used and YouTube fansites, to show how meaningful connections can be formed between fans over the disparate and wide-reaching platform encapsulated by YouTube's surfeit of user-generated content. As one would expect from any study into horror fandom, there are definite similarities between horror fans in general and those specifically engaged in hardcore horror fandom. The alignment between connoisseurship–distinction–(sub)cultural capital is a dominant structuring element in much of horror fandom studies. Therefore, by including hardcore horror fandom and reception into horror fan studies, we can provide a more comprehensive set of parameters that work toward Lázaro-Reboll's "inclusive cultural geography" and account for the wide-ranging "genre users and consumers" of horror. The purpose of this chapter, therefore, is to recoup the fans as a social group who were previously overlooked but who help provide a complete picture of how contemporary horror is received, acted upon and disseminated.

In *Videodrome*, the prospect of hardcore horror, the snuff film within a film, is used as a disturbing device that begins to fracture the narrative of the film as well as the psychological state of Max Renn. Reality and fiction become indistinguishable. The television program *Videodrome* offers a stark attack on the existing staid and homogeneous TV product which offers viewers the cut-price, leaden thrills of "commercial" entertainment. *Videodrome* is dangerous and even fatal as Renn's reality becomes so unraveled that he ends up murdering his co-workers, shooting the producer of *Videodrome* and finally committing suicide so that he can leave his body and become the "new flesh." Hardcore horror has a similar effect on the terrain of contemporary North American horror when given space to co-exist alongside the commercial ventures *Saw*, *Paranormal Activity* (Oren Peli, 2007), *The Conjuring* (James Wan, 2013) and *Freddy vs. Jason* (Ronny Yu, 2003). The extreme nature of the films offers a troubling and "dangerous" presence, one that challenges and threatens the center. For that reason, by bringing the filmmakers and their films into larger discourses on horror, it enables us to account for a more inclusive landscape of the genre. In this case, hardcore horror of the contemporary period moves away from the apocalyptic scenario mapped out in Cronenberg's film. Here, hardcore horror may well be and remain a marginalized and unpalatable adjunct to mainstream and commercial horror, but that does not mean it should be seen as damaging to a critical treatment of the contemporary horror genre as it provides much cultural worth in its rich detail and developments of the major horror strands and practices. Hardcore horror *is* marginal, *is* repugnant, *is* threatening, yet it *is* a valuable addition if appreciation and understanding of the contemporary North American horror film are to be fully realized.

ONE

"Not like how Hollywood shows us"[1]
A Definition of Hardcore Horror in the 21st Century

The proliferation of horror films emanating from North America in the 21st century has engendered an increase in critical and academic response which has almost exclusively focused on the conventions of established horror cinema.[2] The selection of these films has been predicated on the tenets of mainstream acceptability; certification via organizations such as CARA, the attachment of mid- to high-level production companies, and limited to full theatrical release schedules. Despite the commercial popularity of 21st-century horror (the *Saw* franchise has grossed more than $870 million worldwide; *Paranormal Activity* more than $900 million)[3] and its related academic discourse, there has not been a corresponding interest in hardcore horror. This omission is certainly conspicuous when one considers that it has also undergone a contemporary, post-millennial boom. Hardcore horror in the present period can be seen to originate in Eric Stanze's *Scrapbook* and developed through Fred Vogel's *August Underground* trilogy toward Lucifer Valentine's recent cycle of "vomit gore" films. Micro-budgets, a strong realist aesthetic, and alternative distribution, marketing and exhibition strategies characterize these examples. Furthermore, the use of violence in hardcore horror dominates the narrative and is often interconnected with extended and explicit sequences of sexual abuse.

Despite this, hardcore horror still lacks a clear and precise definition as the citation of extreme filmic examples are often located elsewhere in the more acceptable forms found within European art cinema, East Asian film or mainstream horror. Indeed, one of the key factors surrounding the absence of hardcore horror within disciplinary discourses is the porous nature of its form. For example, there has been a sizable application to a protean variety of horror films and inter-genre strands of terms such as hardcore, underground and extreme. Such an indiscriminate use of terminology dilutes the category of extreme cinema by placing the title on examples far removed from the content permeating the landscape of hardcore horror. Prevailing writing on horror forwards a more acceptable and accessible conception of extreme in that they focus squarely on films within the remit of official or legitimate markers. For example, in the numerous "Most Extreme" film lists circulating on the Internet, such as from Horrornews.net and Tasteof cinema.com, they tend to cite either the revered art-house filmmaker Pier Paolo Pasolini and his *Salò, or 120 Days of Sodom*, the contemporary French extremity of *Irreversible* (Gaspar Noé, 2002) and *Martyrs* (Pascal Laugier, 2008), or infamous horror classics in the vein of *Cannibal Holocaust* and *Nekromantik* (Jorg Buttgereit, 1987). While these examples can certainly be considered controversial regarding the material represented and in the themes explored, they do still conform to an understanding of "extreme" as legitimate. That is, the critics, writers and websites all validate their selections through the inclusion of institutional factors. Established norms such as the award of a rating certification, broad exposure through cinematic release to flagship DVD or Blu-ray editions, and critical reverence regarding the director as auteur all act as unofficial selection criteria. It is therefore unusual to find on these lists any films adhering to an illicit, illegitimate status. For Taste of Cinema's "The 30 Most Extreme Movies of the 21st-Century So Far," the harrowing political allegory *A Serbian Film* resides at the number one position, yet there is no mention of any hardcore horror films within the list.[4] Horrornews places a Japanese pseudo-snuff series, the *Guinea Pig* collection (various directors, 1985–1988), as the most disturbing films of all time, but examples such as *Scrapbook* (tied at 11), Valentine's "vomit gore" trilogy (#12) and Vogel's *August Underground* films (#15) are all mentioned outside of the Top Ten.[5] In these lists, the notion of extreme cinema oscillates between foreign titles ranging from the prominent and well-known (*Salò*) to the obscure and hard-to-find (*Melancholie der Engel* aka *The Angels' Melancholia*, Marian Dora, 2009).

In looking briefly at the Internet's "most extreme films of all time" lists, a convoluted and broad understanding and application of extremity in film are utilized. In other spheres, we see a similar perspective emerge. A link between the popular "best of" sites and syndicated publications was a 2004 article published in *ArtForum*, "Flesh and Blood: Sex and Violence in Recent French Cinema" by James Quandt. It outlined a cycle of extreme French films due to their explicit examination (both in terms of their representations of sex and violence) of the psychological fears and anxieties circulating in French society at the end of the millennium. Filmmakers Gaspar Noé (*Seul contre tous*, 1998), Claire Denis (*Trouble Every Day*, 2001) and Bruno Dumont

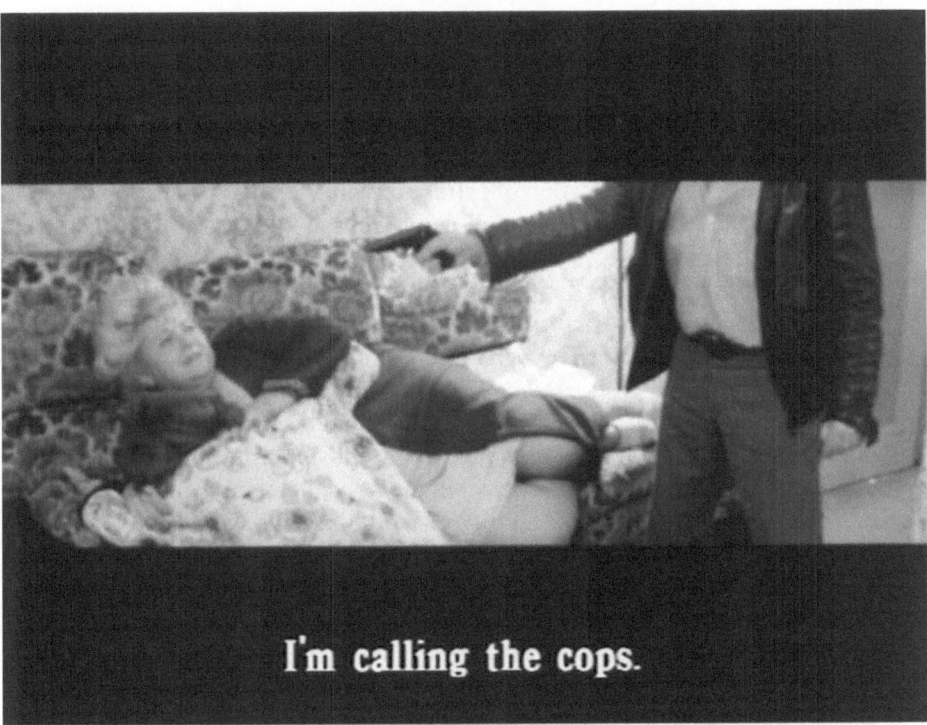

New French Extremism in *Seul contre tous* (*I Stand Alone*), Strand Releasing. The Butcher (Philippe Nahon) and his mistress (Frankye Payne).

(*Twentynine Palms*, 2003) put forward compelling and unsettling narratives to situate the viewer as more active. Particularly, in confronting issues such as French colonialism, the rise of far-right politics in France, sexual and gender politics, and issues of censorship, violence and why we watch extreme visual material. In this instance, the term "extreme" was once again used to categorize a particular strand of cinema which was considered "legitimate," and that was part of more conventional filmic practices of theatrical exhibition, auteurism, the studio system and the use of well-known actors.

Quandt's article positioned the rise of extreme cinema in France as an important indication of a more global trend post-millennium and post–9/11, especially in North America. The large circulations of the syndicated press (and their online presence) in the U.S. and Canada replicated Quandt's attention on a visceral and impactive cinema by providing a significant amount of coverage to the rise of extreme films in the 21st century. A majority of the discourse was on the franchises of *Saw* and *Hostel* (2005–2011) and the rise of what *New York Times* writer David Edelstein termed "torture porn."[6] In his article "Now Playing at Your Local Multiplex: Torture Porn," Edelstein cited Noé's *Irreversible* as a bridge between the "titillating and shocking"[7] extremity of contemporary French cinema and American films such as *Saw* and *The Devil's Rejects* (Rob Zombie, 2005). Edelstein lamented, "[T]hese movies are so viciously nihilistic that the only point seems to be to force you to suspend moral judgments altogether."[8] Indeed, the majority of film criticism mentioned the application of extreme cinema and its connection to torture porn as a way to disparage and denigrate the films and their fans. For example, wholesale rejection for the entire *Saw* franchise was provided by Mike Hale of the *New York Times* when he dismissed the films as "meretricious garbage."[9] Peter Howell, writing in *The Toronto Star* about director Dennis Iliadis' 2009 *The Last House on the Left*, singled out the gratuitous content of the film in terms of its extreme violence toward women before warning people off the movie altogether. Howell concluded his review by emphatically (and sarcastically) stating, "[D]o not go to this movie if you simply seek entertainment. If you're a sociologist tracking the decline of civilization over the past four decades, you're in for a night of solid research."[10] In fact, fans were often conceptualized as sadistic torture freaks who were willingly pushed to extremes in order to "feel something."[11] Peter Hartlaub of the *San Francisco Chronicle* provided one such example of positioning the audience as debased and deranged, suggesting, "It's the perfect movie [the *Saw* franchise] for people who spent their childhood pulling the wings off flies and incinerating ants with magnifying glasses."[12]

Although popular reception of extreme cinema in the 21st century tends to focus on recognized filmic examples while largely dismissing their content and audiences as corrupted, it has nonetheless conveyed an interest and popularization of challenging and confrontational cinema. As one would expect, the increase of contemporary films marked by a move toward the extreme has been picked up through film studies and scholarship. Indeed, academic studies into extreme horror have been evident since the late 1980s in an attempt to catalogue the move from the supernatural- and monster-motivated horror of classical Hollywood to the existent horror that emerged during the war in Vietnam. Andrew Tudor's delineation of secure to paranoid horror in U.S. cinema, Isabel Cristina Pinedo's writings on postmodern horror and Cynthia Freeland's seminal article on realist horror all provide possible criteria for which hardcore horror can be placed against.[13] For instance, the central features combined in these works are: a violent disruption of the everyday world; an internal threat; a transgression and violation of boundaries; the breakdown of good vs. evil; the repudiation of narrative closure; the lack of authority in and trust of central institutions; a destabilization of the border between mimesis and reality, and the integration of the realist aesthetics of news reports into the plot. Although these texts look at horror in a broad sense, they do provide criteria which have influenced and inflected many academic approaches to extreme cinema in the contemporary period and underscore the direction of 21st-century horror narratives. However, as we shall see, the majority of academic work in this area has moved toward discussions of extremity in art cinema or the perceived extremity of torture porn. Here, the examples draw from European film and the franchise horror of *Saw* and *Hostel*. In this respect, academic study replicates the popular press and Internet film sites in again providing a legitimate framework with which to conceptualize "extreme" cinema.

In the most recent edition of *The Oxford Dictionary of Film Studies* (2012, online 2015), the short definition for extreme cinema commences with "[a] group of films that challenge codes of censorship and social mores, in particular through explicit depiction of sex and violence, including rape and torture."[14] As a concise overview, it hews closely to a set of criteria that incorporate the contours of hardcore horror. The entry goes on to suggest an alternative term, "ordeal cinema," be also used, which "indicates that the viewer commits to watching a film that will take them through a horrendous experience in what seems like real time. The most extreme form of extreme cinema is the snuff film."[15] When the passage goes on to provide examples, it completely circumvents any discussion of horror cinema, despite these films legitimately providing decisive case studies of extreme cinema as laid out by the overview supplied.

The Oxford Dictionary for Film Studies entry does cite at length New French Extremism, and this has attracted the attention of numerous film scholars writing predominantly on the issues of content and affect. Martine Beugnet's *Cinema and Sensation: French Film and the Art of Transgression* (2007), Tanya Horeck and Tina Kendall's edited collection *The New Extremism in Cinema: From France to Europe* (2010), Asbjørn Grønstad's *Screening the Unwatchable: Spaces of Negation in Post-Millennial Art Cinema* (2012) and Mattias Frey's *Extreme Cinema: The Transgressive Rhetoric of Today's Art Film Culture* (2016) all provide detailed and insightful commentary on 21st-century extreme cinema. However, these texts focus on art cinema and include films such as *Shortbus* (John Cameron Mitchell, 2006), *Oldboy* (Chan-wook Park, 2003), *Irreversible*, *Trouble Every Day* and *À ma Sœur!* aka *Fat Girl* (Catherine Breillat, 2001) and filmmakers Michael Haneke and Catherine Breillat. In the introduction to *The New Extremism in Cinema*, Horeck and Kendall define "new extremism" along the same contours of *The Oxford Dictionary* when they state that the films provide "graphic and confrontational images of sex and violence [which] appear designed deliberately to shock and provoke the spectator."[16] Grønstad echoes and reinforces Horeck and Kendell in the confrontational nature of extreme cinema in that "these films appeared to pose some kind of challenge to the viewer" and that "each work want[s] to test our endurance."[17] Grønstad continues by highlighting the explicit nature of extreme cinema and how this is directed toward the corporeal frame: "[I]t put the body—more often than not in states of agony, ecstasy or abjection—center stage, and it seemed mischievously intent on triggering scandals."[18] Frei begins *Extreme Cinema* with an account of the Berlin premiere of Lars von Trier's *Nymphomaniac Vol. 1.* (2014) and how the ethical considerations surrounding the graphic material engendered "commentaries about how cinema today is too realistic and visceral in its depictions of sex and violence."[19] Frei goes on to explore how these manifestations of European art cinema are carefully staged events which manufacture interest in their "salacious" content through innovative marketing and promotional activities. Often the films are delineated as different from other forms of extreme cinema in terms of how far their material promises to go, yet are constrained by codes and conventions that use provocation as a marketable cinematic commodity. Frei's insightful examination of the industrial factors of extreme cinema point toward the misapplication of the term "extreme" as used by filmmakers and film writers though ultimately contains his scholarly work with the confines of European and U.S. independent cinema.

The definitions provided within these texts are useful and contribute to relevant ways of thinking about hardcore horror despite their film examples moving away from horror to the realm of European art cinema. While it is not necessarily the remit of individual texts such as those cited to include an in-depth treatment of horror or underground cinema, it does attest to the denigration and disregard of horror in discussions of extreme cinema. The issue is most notable as hardcore horror provides very specific case studies with which to engage, work through and think about the content and affect of extreme visual representations in film. Grønstad acknowledges this exact point when he writes that *Screening the Unwatchable* was to initially be called "Illicit Images" until a colleague mentioned that all the films under discussion were in fact "licit."[20] For Grønstad, the movement toward sanctioned filmic examples emphasizes a convoluted and contested engagement with extreme material. The images on display might appear forbidden (and the "why" is the crux of Grønstad's scholarly endeavor) but that there was always a "textual confinement" where "the violence, while grisly in itself, may have been staged *for* the viewer, but it was never directed *at* them."[21]

Academic journals have also concentrated on "art-horror" and extreme cinema from Europe and East Asia. *Jump Cut* has regularly discussed Asian extreme cinema ranging from the UK branding of Tartan "Asia Extreme" to problems associated with cross-cultural reception and critical analysis of extreme films.[22] *Jump Cut* has also published a number of articles on torture porn and U.S. extreme horror in the wake of 9/11. Articles such as "Torture Porn and Surveillance Culture" by Evangelos Tziallas and "*Hostel II*: Representations of the Body in Pain and the Cinema Experience of Torture-Porn" by Gabrielle Murray reinforce the importance of content and affect in examples of extreme cinema. Indeed, many of the *Jump Cut* articles surrounding torture porn focus on thematic issues such as torture, control and surveillance as a direct riposte to social and political contingencies post–9/11. As *Jump Cut* editor Chuck Kleinhans outlined with regards to these articles, they displayed "a new sophistication and complexity in discussing the genre and its political implications."[23] He goes on to combine the importance of considering the thematic content of these undervalued films with the "affective nature of this new stage of horror."[24] The purpose of such an approach is to investigate the "cultural and political anxieties" bound up in an audiences' "own bodily emotions—fear, anxiety, shock, surprise, revulsion, sympathy, disgust."[25]

Other journals focusing specifically on the horror genre have pressed the magnitude of examining films associated with torture porn because of the commentary they provide on the landscape of the U.S. following 9/11 and events such as Abu Ghraib. Similar to the popular press and *Jump Cut*, *The Irish Journal of Gothic and Horror Studies* has singled out *Saw* and *Hostel* as exemplars of the nexus between horror and social and political contexts. Julian Ponder's article "'To the Next Level': Castration in *Hostel II*" elevates one of the more extreme visual motifs in the film—castration—to a discussion over male power under threat whereby "castration may not signify ultimate loss as much as ultimate gain."[26] The connection between this new "castralbody" which has "cast aside the useless penis" and the failure of traditional male power in the light of the Bush administration's invasion of Afghanistan and Iraq is clear.[27] *The Irish Journal of Gothic and Horror Studies* has also covered extreme filmic content by again citing torture porn as extreme examples of horror in the 21st century alongside more archetypal texts such as *Cannibal Holocaust* and the recent politico-horror allegory *A Serbian Film*.[28]

The attention and interest in torture porn are also evident in numerous academic monographs and anthologies. Aston and Walliss' edited collection *To See the Saw Movies: Essays on Torture Porn and Post–9/11 Horror* addresses the socio-cultural, religious and philosophical underpinnings of the *Saw* films to examine how they operate as an often barbed commentary on America in the new millennium. For the authors, it is not their intention to necessarily mark *Saw* or torture porn out as extreme, but rather to recoup the stigmatism of the films by outlining how they offer keen insight into the time in which they were made. Likewise, Aaron Michael Kenner's *Torture Porn in the Wake of 9/11: Horror, Exploitation, and the Cinema of Sensation* picks up on the value of torture porn as providing a way of adducing the complicated relationship between films such as *Saw* and *Hostel* and American culture post–9/11. In Steve Jones' book *Torture Porn: Popular Horror After Saw*, he cogently discusses the etymological basis of the term torture porn to illuminate how limited it is as a descriptive label. Jones puts forward the basic contention

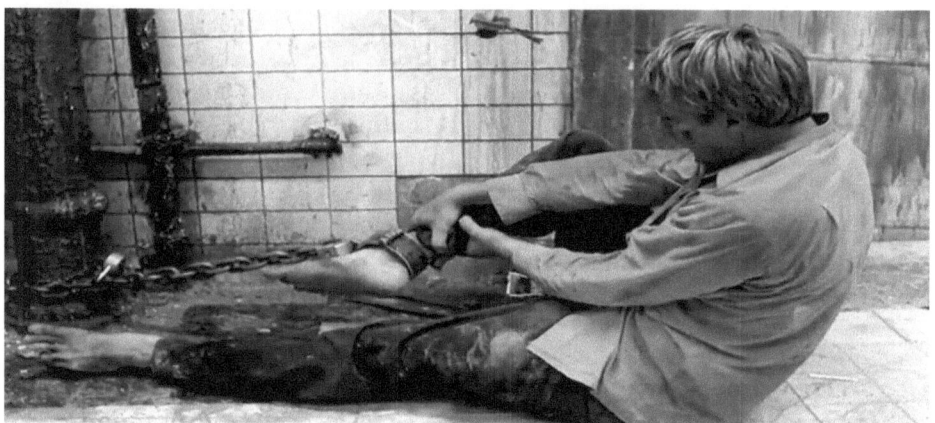

The mainstream extremity of torture porn. Dr. Lawrence Gordon (Cary Elwes), in *Saw* (Lions Gate Home Entertainment).

that the term "misrepresents the films themselves.... [T]he label has also been utilized to incriminate the subgenre's filmmakers and fans."[29] Indeed, Jones argues persuasively that the term has become a pejorative whereby it "replicate[s] various prejudices about popular violent cinema."[30] Torture porn represents the majority of academic work surrounding U.S. and North American extreme cinema, though when analysis does move away from this sphere, it does not necessarily touch upon the foundations of hardcore horror. Phil Russell's *Beyond the Darkness: Cult, Horror and Extreme Cinema* sets out to address the "darker side of film"[31] though circumvents any attempt to define what might constitute extreme horror. Instead, Russell states that the book is merely an introduction to the "controversial, the shocking, the disturbing" and suggests that it "serves as a gateway into extreme cinema rather than a complete guide." For Russell, the intention of the book "is to give readers an idea of what is out there, but by no means is the territory fully mapped-out in these pages."[32] Nor is a mapped-out definition. In fact, many of the examples of hardcore horror are conspicuously absent.

Therefore, in the majority of popular and academic discourse on extreme cinema in the 21st century, we can see two overlapping strands emerge. Firstly, a general, though relevant definition of extreme cinema is provided and then mapped onto European extremity or art-extremity from East Asia.[33] Secondly, extreme cinema is located in sanctioned and legitimate forms (that is, films successfully assigned a rating certification and released through limited or wide theatrical screenings) such as the torture porn franchises *Saw* and *Hostel*. Although there is an avoidance or disregard for hardcore, confrontational or underground horror in the mainstay of academic discourse into extreme cinema, there has been the emergence of work recently that has concentrated on the niche horror of found footage and snuff. These approaches have not dealt directly with hardcore horror but have incorporated numerous examples within their texts and have begun to suggest a precise working definition. The Cine-excess conference and affiliated eJournal, the insightful scholarship of Alexandra Heller-Nicholas' *Found Footage Horror Films: Fear and the Appearance of Reality*, David Kerekes and David Slater's 2015 updated volume of their seminal 1993 *Killing for Culture: An Illustrated History of Death Film From Mondo to Snuff*, now re-titled *Killing for Culture: From Edison to Isis*, and the 2016 anthology *Snuff: Real Death and Screen Media* begin to provide a specific definition of hardcore horror away from those found within the more "acceptable" cinematic examples of the extreme.

Started in 2007, the Cine-Excess Cult Film Conference and Festival has emerged as a high-profile international event bringing in horror luminaries such as Dario Argento, Ruggero Deodato and Roger Corman alongside world or UK premieres and academic and industry film panels. The mission statement of the conference organizers, passed on to their eJournal, is to provide a commercial, industry and academic space whereby the "usual, proper, or specified limits"[34] of previous film journals can be breached. In this context, the organizers can give attention to maligned films ranging from *House at the Edge of the Park* (Ruggero Deodato, 1980) to *The Human Centipede* (Tom Six, 2009) and which fall into the marginal subgenre of hardcore horror. Therefore, in their inaugural 2013 edition "Subverting the Senses: The Politics and Aesthetics of Excess," the coverage may have dealt with recurrent and existing areas of extreme cinema such as the launch of Tartan's "Asia Extreme" label, but it did move away from more traditional avenues of film scholarship with articles on *The Bunny Game*. Adam Rehmeier's controversial 2010 film, rejected by the BBFC (and not rated by CARA), features explicit representations of sexual violence. Jenny Barrett's "More than Just a Game: Breaking the Rules in *The Bunny Game*" engages with notions of the real in the film and identificatory practices. The article goes on to examine how the film forwards "an exploitative gaze at the objectified female" and undermines the filmmaker's assertion of the narrative being a "feminist text."[35]

Notions of the real have been at the center of Heller-Nicholas' *Found Footage Horror*, Kerekes and Slater's *Killing for Culture* and the *Snuff* anthology. The connecting thread between these texts and their subsequent importance for the study of hardcore horror is the snuff film. Kerekes and Slater examine the relationship between the visual image and representations (real or simulated) of death meticulously. Entwined with this prurient and complex attraction to the viewing of death is the faux-snuff film which trades on the dichotomy of "snuff as real and snuff as reality."[36] Faux-snuff exists somewhere in-between and, as Marina Warner points out, allows the viewer to look "at the most accurate representations of things which in themselves are too painful to see."[37] Thus for Kerekes and Slater, the faux-snuff film offers "a close proximity to death on film, the division very often being the simple understanding that we *know* it isn't real."[38] The authors then cite Fred Vogel and how his films forward "the illusion of authenticity"[39] which breaks down the boundary between the real and mimesis. Heller-Nicholas also examines the legend of the snuff film through its various manifestations of safety films, mondo documentaries and cinematic snuff in how they influenced the found footage horror of the contemporary period. In Heller-Nicholas' treatment, the real is central, and is achieved in found footage via its "brand of amateur aesthetics" which is "crucial to the construction of verisimilitude."[40] Heller-Nicholas forwards a definition that makes much use of "consumer grade technology"[41] in which an authentic style of low-fi and degraded audio-visual content is produced, often as "user-generated content"[42] which aligns it with "do-it-yourself" Internet sites such as YouTube. Other properties tend to be the "spectacle and affective qualities"[43] of the footage and the immediate and intensive imagery produced; the notion that if this was real, then this is how it would look.

The 2012 conference at Bournemouth University on Snuff: Real Death and Screen Media represented a similar battleground to Cine-Excess in its tackling of a subject shunned by academia. The result was the publication of an edited collection of the same name which sought to "evaluate fictional and reality-based media narratives that have informed our understanding of the snuff phenomenon since its origins."[44] The editors describe how faux-snuff and snuff-themed films, since the 1976 release of *Snuff*, have "infiltrated global popular culture as a recognizable and even commercially viable element"[45] from Hollywood through to the independent sector and underground productions. The formal properties of these films once again relate to a realist aesthetic and the importance of an amateur quality, yet the book also traces the thematic strategies linking these disparate films. Historically, the taxonomic approach has provided a limited framework of faux-snuff which outlines the centrality of the masculine gaze of these films and the murderous and often sexual proclivities of the (male) observer-camera operator over the female observee-victim. Here masculinity is in crisis: violent and perverse. However, with recent atrocity images on the Internet such as the beheading videos from the Islamic State, gang executions from Mexican drug cartels and individual psychopathic acts from the likes of the Dnepropetrovsk maniacs and Luca Magnotta, it is not so meaningful to see faux-snuff as only sexually violent and misogynistic. The redefinition of snuff along the axis of "social, cultural, and political significance"[46] means that filmmakers are becoming acutely aware of their real-world counterparts, and the ideological formations that snuff now provides.

The above texts have advanced scholarly work and appreciation into maligned and marginalized filmic subjects and have generated discursive structures through which hardcore horror can be addressed, such as the notion of the real and the DIY filmmaking aesthetic. Nevertheless, they all take as their foci of interest areas that necessarily move away from hardcore horror and toward other genres and elements such as European cinema, found footage and the snuff film. Once again, this leaves open a specific definition for hardcore horror. Rather ironically, we do find a working definition within a book focusing on the established and commercially successful torture porn subgenre. Returning to Jones' *Torture Porn*, he states how misapplied the term is and concludes that torture porn should not be considered as an extreme or hardcore example of horror as it exposes an "inattentiveness to horror that exists outside the mainstream."[47] For Jones, films such as Vogel's *August Underground* trilogy can be seen to espouse representational strategies of an extreme or hardcore nature legitimately. Thus, in the chapter "'You Will Not Believe Your Eyes ... or Your Stomach': Hardcore Horror," Jones outlines that there are three primary characteristics: an explicit focus on depictions of sexual violence, that there is a privilege of violence over narrative context and a realist aesthetic which depicts violence as impulsive and convincing. The full range of characteristics put forward by Jones are:

> An explicit focus on depictions of sexual violence
> A privilege of violence/spectacle over narrative
> A realist aesthetic
> Low-budget to no-budget
> Marginality and/or subcultural affiliation
> A grass roots outlook
> Not shown theatrically
> Word-of-mouth promotion
> Internet marketing
> Lack of certification
> Exclusivity of film—not for "most fans"
> Abduction, torture, rape motifs
> *Vérité*, first-person camera
> Fragmented set pieces
> Sex intertwined with rape, mutilation and murder
> Taboo
> An alternative ethos/films to revel in dissonance[48]

Jones' detailed and comprehensive definition includes and adapts many of the terms and dictates mentioned in existing discourse, from the notion of extreme cinema supplied by *The Oxford Dictionary of Film* as containing confrontational and shocking content surrounding explicit representations of sex and violence to found footage and snuff's utilization of realist codes and conventions. These characteristics of hardcore horror also connect to the more general developments of horror found in work by Tudor, Pinedo and Freeland. However, Jones' definition is complicated by the presence and development of pornographic films such as *Forced Entry* (Lizzie Borden and Rob Zacari, 2002), the custom shoots of Factory 2000 and the snuff-porn of Eyewitness Production. Both strands are examples of extremity, in the genres of horror and pornography respectively, which does position them as underground and marginal filmic practices. However, despite the overlap in aesthetics and themes (not to mention production practices and reception), an important distinction does exist in terms of their respective affective qualities. Freeland delineates one of the key methods of realist horror (which can be developed and mapped onto hardcore horror) as "violat[ing] our conceptual categories"[49] by presenting the monster as realist via the "foregrounding of gruesome spectacle over plot."[50] For Freeland, this differs from more conventional horror in removing the barriers between the audience and the monster-horror so that the film "perpetuates[s] a climate of fear and random violence where anyone is a potential victim."[51] Such an approach would strengthen the affective charge of the film, instilling a strong sense of fear or horror within the viewer. When contemplating a film like *Forced Entry*, which was promoted as a pornographic film and not as a horror movie, it is worth noting that barriers between the viewer and the acts on screen were removed to provide a more extreme experience. The film does utilize snuff aesthetics such as found footage, "real" violence and the breakdown of the real and mimesis. In doing so, the film inadvertently brought about a negation of sexual gratification and arousal at the expense of instilling fear and/or dread within the viewer. *Forced Entry* was received very negatively and rejected as a "legitimate" pornographic film due to the shift in its affective charge. To highlight how unpalatable the film had become, the industry trade journal *Adult Video News* (AVN) roundly denounced the film as a "horrible, unwatchable, disgusting, aberrant movie"[52] while viewers such as Nina Whett, writing for *Adult Industry News*, unequivocally rejected its mix of sex and violence when she said, "Promoting violence and or making (or trying to make) RAPE look sexy is very disturbing to me.... There is nothing sexy or cool about anyone Raping anyone else and if you think it is, you: #1 need to keep that fantasy off camera.... #2 you're deluded and you are in need of psychiatric help."[53]

Other North American pornographic films, such as the *Meatholes* series (Khan Tusion, 2004–2006) and the "extreme porn" films of Max Hardcore, similarly combine pornographic material with degrading treatment and physical abuse of the female performers. The excessive nature of some of the obscene acts in these productions can also be marked as repulsive and disgusting, especially when consensual acts move toward actual or fabricated displays of sexual violence. Certainly, this is a disturbing trend of contemporary pornographic film and is possibly a "result of relative cultural tolerance for sexual imagery in this period"[54] and perceived judiciary and media bias on prominent sexual assaults, rape and gender-based violence within North America.[55] Nonetheless, despite the emerging overlap between "extreme porn" and hardcore horror, the aspect of affect is much more centrally focused on violence in the latter films so that there remains a distinction between the two forms. Here, viewer expectation is crucial in how the film is received "if we accept the fundamental goal of pornography as the display of graphic sex acts for purpose of arousal."[56] For example, to return to *Forced Entry*, the film does utilize criteria found within hardcore horror and as such sublimates responses to the material toward being repulsive and horrific rather than as being sexually stimulating. Here the affective charge moves toward fear, dread and horror and as a result the film did not fulfill dominant pornographic conventions and expectations surrounding its content and its reception. Extreme Associates which produced *Forced Entry* was indicted in 2003 for distributing obscene, pornographic materials. The ensuing trial acted as a test case probing the public and legislative limits for pornography in North America. Mary Beth Buchanan, the federal prosecutor in the case, pointedly addressed the "violent and degrading material"[57] as a primary reason for the legal proceedings and the need to redraw legislation to limit what types of pornographic film should be sold and distributed.

From the example of *Forced Entry*, it can be seen that the issue of affect is worth expanding on in terms of providing a clear delineation between extreme pornography and hardcore horror. Misha Kavka talks about the affective charge of the snuff film in its staging of "real" death on screen.[58] In this case, a number of hardcore horror films can be seen to closely adhere to the formal properties of snuff in their verisimilitude of realistic and "unmediated" death. Films such as *August Underground*, *Amateur Porn Star Killer* and *American Guinea Pig* structure their narratives around the aesthetics of snuff while others such as *Scrapbook*, the "vomit gore" films and *The Bunny Game* provide discreet sequences which purport to show "real" unexpurgated violence, humiliation and degradation.

With this in mind, the work of Kavka provides a useful and illuminating treatment of affect which can be applied to horror and pornographic viewing positions. Kavka develops Vivian Sobchack's "charge of the real"[59] where documentary rubs up against the border of the fictional. At this point, where for example death and the real meet in snuff, the image becomes a paradox of the real and the imaginary that can only be resolved via the spectator's "distinctive subject relations"[60] to the world outside of the film. In the case of snuff or (hardcore) horror, it is our knowledge of the material to "shock, horrify, terrify or even gross out"[61] which gives it its affective charge and/or reality. It is clear that extreme pornography and hardcore horror (and horror in general) intersect but it is the intent and/or expectation of the affective qualities of hardcore horror which provides a demarcation with other powerful affective texts. An additional layer to demarcate the affect between hardcore horror and pornography is the work by David Church (2009) on reputation and viewing positions. For Church, expectation of extreme films such as *August Underground* is formulated through fan discourse which frequently marks them out as "sick films" that impart a "displeasurable affectivity."[62] Thus, the films are anticipated in advance by viewers to be of a specific affective quality linking them to extreme violence, transgressive content and emotional reactions of disgust, repulsion and horror. Combining Kavka with Church, we can see that a particular type of affect (horror, fear, anxiety) imposes itself on the viewer *before* as well as during and after the viewing experience. The placement of hardcore horror within the subcultural niche of horror fan discourse, therefore, generates a considerable affective expectation. Also, the proximity the films take to the tortured, degraded, broken and destroyed body further exacerbates the affective charge which is realized through the realist nature of the snuff aesthetics. Horror films directed more toward the mainstream tend to erect barriers to mitigate the affective impact, and extreme pornographic films emphasize at least a partial limning of sex as pleasurable. Conversely, hardcore horror attempts to remove any distancing mechanisms between the viewer and the film with the primary aim of creating an overall affective experience which engenders strong feelings of fear, dread and horror.

Taking into account the importance of affect is essential if a working definition is to be formed along the contours of hardcore horror's representational strategies and viewing positions. The other crucial area is realism and here Jones' inclusion of the realist aesthetic in his definition of hardcore horror has to be distilled in order to demarcate it from other horror films that produce an authentic and credible *mise en scène*. Realism in hardcore horror is its most distinctive and unprecedented quality and is pivotal to its content and affect. Therefore, the type of realist arrangement needs qualifying in terms of the arrangement of films under discussion. In this respect, hardcore horror taps into the postmodern condition over the collapse of the real/representation binary. So too have many contemporary films, both horror and non-horror, from *Natural Born Killers* (Oliver Stone, 1994) to *S&man* (J.T. Petty, 2006) and *Cloverfield* (Matt Reeves, 2008). Yet films such as *August Underground*, *Amateur Porn Star Killer* and *Slow Torture Puke Chamber* present their footage as if captured apart and away from the context of a conventional narrative film; as a video diary, a found object or a visual memento.

Therefore, the importance of convincing special effects, verisimilitude of the violence–sexual violence and authenticity of performance needs to be

Angela Aberdeen (Ameara La Vey) (*Slaughtered Vomit Dolls*, Unearthed Films).

framed as realist *within* this context. Rather than, for example, in a film like *Cloverfield* which presents a fantastical event in terms of "This is what it might look like if a monster attack on Manhattan were to happen." Doing so better places the realist codes of hardcore horror in how the violence is "directed *at*" the audience to return to Grønstad's acknowledgment of the limitations of "licit" examples of cinematic extremity. With the importance and contextualization of affect and realism in place, a revised definition that we can take forward to the films would be:

>   An explicit focus on depictions of sexual violence
>   A privilege of violence/spectacle over narrative
>   The construction of an unmediated, realist aesthetic
>   Explicit nature of violence/sexual violence and realistic depiction (of special effects)
>   Authenticity of performance
>   A strong affective charge of fear, dread and horror
>   Not shown theatrically;
>   Lack of certification

Two

The Genealogy of Extremity in North American Film

In the previous chapter, it was made clear that the critical and academic discourse on extreme cinema favored more "legitimate" examples, yet it still revealed how the term is discursively applied to a range of cinematic texts located across different national cinemas. Such an understanding and conception of the term "extreme" broaches the consideration that hardcore horror does not exist in a vacuum or that it is completely separate and removed from other extreme filmic examples. The intersection between films means that it is important to track historical and global trajectories of extreme cinema to highlight concurrent examples and ancestors of hardcore horror. Doing so provides a rich and more in-depth context to the emergence of these films in the 21st century and a strengthening of how and where the term "extreme" should be applied.

With this in mind, the next two chapters look back toward the genealogy of extreme cinema in North America as well as including exemplars of global film extremity. Therefore, from a vantage point of providing a transparent configuration of extreme film, the position of hardcore horror within these multifaceted contours can be situated and examined.

> Throughout the history of film, a prurient imbalance has existed between observer and observed, driving the spools in the shadowy projection box.[1]

Kerekes and Slater's opening to *Killing for Culture* maps out the long engagement film has had with images and representations of the horrific. From the turn of the century kinetoscope curios such as Thomas Edison's *Electrocuting an Elephant* (1903) and *The Execution of a Chinese Bandit* (1904) to the 21st-century atrocity videos of Isis, filmic images of death have pervaded our cultural landscape and disturbed and destabilized our normative viewing habits and experiences. Alongside these testimonies of real death as a form of cinematic spectacle has been the parallel development of a wide-ranging and diverse strand of an extreme and subversive horror film. It is a constituent of the broader church of horror that has evolved, transformed and mutated into various thematic forms and shapes. It posits a selection of films which, as Brigit Cherry (1999) points out, is dependent on the contract between the viewer and the film and the historical context in which the film is produced and viewed. Therefore, a necessary concession to make with regards to horror films, and more pointedly to extreme examples, is that "what might be classed as the essential conventions of horror to one generation may be very different to the next, and what one person considers to be the defining features of a horror film may be in total disagreement with another's classification."[2] The outrageous extremities of Herschell Gordon Lewis' *Blood Feast* (1963), with its disembowelments, dismemberments and human sacrifices, are now considered to be a gaudy, camp, Grand Guignol extravaganza, containing little to horrify or terrorize a contemporary audience. Similarly, Alan Shackleton's re-packaging of Michael and Roberta Findlay's sexploitation film *Slaughter* (1971) with a gory end coda of a "real" onscreen death and the new provocative title of *Snuff*, caused riots and demonstrations when initially released in 1976 but today is only met with incredulity and amusement. However, it is important to track the cycles, movements, historical archetypes and generic hybrids so that we can underline how the aesthetic and thematic strategies of 21st-century hardcore horror do not exist in a historical and cultural vacuum. Instead, in providing a brief summation of the chronology of horror films that were considered extreme when released, it is possible to trace over the conduits and contours that have fed into contemporary practices and the images and representations which continue to challenge, unsettle and horrify audiences.

The Phantasmagoric Kinetoscope and Early Images of the Extreme

The historical examination of American cinema will invariably commence with the period 1895–1907. Charles Musser covers the emergence of cinema in this 13-year period in his imperious study which traces the confluence of screen practices back to the 17th century. In *The Emergence of Cinema*, Musser takes as his focus the use of "projected images and their audio complement" and tracks it to the motion pictures which "includes not only cinema but forms of exhibition that did not involve projection."[3] Here, Musser allocates a considerable amount of time examining the technology of pre-cinematic exhibition to highlight the central overlapping practices between the motion pictures and earlier presentation formats such as the magic lantern and the peephole kinematoscope to show that cinema "was the culmination of long-standing efforts to present ever more lifelike moving images on the screen."[4] The magic lantern can be traced back to the 1600s and "provided suitable models for early screen practitioners"[5] regarding a portable projection system that enabled them to travel, first to exhibit to royal audiences throughout Europe and then later to more general audiences in the 1800s. During this latter period, Étienne Gaspar Robertson developed the "fictional narratives and documentary programs"[6] traditionally associated with the magic lantern exhibitions toward the phantasmagoria of ghostly and spectral apparitions. In Robertson's own words, these shows promised a "spectacle which man can use to instruct himself in the bizarre effects of the imagination.... I speak of terror inspired by the shadows, spirits, spells and occult work of the magician."[7] Robertson's shows were proceeded by various other practitioners dabbling in the illusory practices of phantasmagorical projections, which attest to the continued interest and early establishment of visual projections and their connection to extreme form, tone and effect.

The peephole kinematoscope developed in the middle of the 1880s from the elaborate projections of the magic lantern and variants such as the stereopticon by utilizing a lever or pulley system. The mechanism fashioned a short visual narrative via the advancing of single image slides. The viewing of these animated photographs usually took the form of mystical or comical scenes and provided a subversive destabilizing of the strange and the familiar to create uncanny spectacles such as replacing a man's head with that of a pig or donkey.[8] Continuing the illusory sense of movement achieved in these projection devices, as well as the shocking and provocative imagery, was Eadweard Muybridge and his advances in visual exhibition. Muybridge used multiple camera set-ups and innovative projection techniques to capture and screen the authentic motion of athletes and horses. In one particularly infamous screening in 1887, he initially projected multiple sequences of animal images until cannily switching to the movement of barely clothed people. The show proceeded up until a climactic scene featuring a series of dancing women "which called down repeated applause."[9] Muybridge was clear in his intentions as although he advances the technological achievements of projected visual images, he also sought to act as an *agent provocateur* in that he provides sensational imagery to challenge the values of conservative religious groups and the repressed environment of Victorian culture. One particular response to the show is indistinguishable from more contemporary reviews aimed at the harmful and damaging effects of violent or extreme film in that the article laments that the spectacle of Muybridge's scantily clad actors may "be entirely defeated by the shock to the delicate sensibilities" of the audience and in general that "among savages such exhibitions are entirely natural and expected, but in civilised society they are shocking to the moral sentiment, indecent and demoralizing."[10]

The pre-cinematic forms of the magic lantern, the kinematoscope and the groundbreaking work of Muybridge utilized rudimentary technological devices and crude (by our standards) visual projections. Nevertheless, they provided an extreme viewing experience often seized upon by the moral watchdogs of the age as incorrigible forms of entertainment liable to corrupt and harm the typical spectator. As the novelty of cinema became an established economic and commercial enterprise in the late 1880s and early 1900s, practitioners continued to develop innovative technological effects in rupturing the perimeter between the real and the fictional in their exhibitions. *The Execution of Mary, Queen of Scots* (Alfred Clark, 1895) deployed a stop-motion cut so that the decapitation of the queen would appear as if in one shot to the spectator. Thomas Edison developed a range of wide-format cameras to photograph actual and non-staged events such as boxing matches (*The Corbett-Fitzsimmons Fight*, Enoch J. Rector, 1897) and horse races (*Suburban Handicap*, James H. White, 1897). The focus on documenting reality, or at least providing an acceptably authentic and disarming construct, outlines the importance of the "real" in early incantations of cinema. Though seemingly at the other end of the spectrum to 21st-century digital recordings of actual and constructed scenes of horror, it does show for how long violent, but more importantly extreme and shocking, experiential forms of motion pictures have been a recurring element in the historical development of film in North America.

Subversive Monsters of the 1930s

The horror film cycle of the 1930s may have dealt in the fantastical with its recourse to supernatural entities such as vampires, werewolves and reanimated corpses but the decidedly non-realist stylistics of these films nonetheless provided a sensationalist, subversive and often sinister experience. The decade became a fertile era of horror where the high production values of the films meant that they often achieved the status of a wide-release class–A picture. The films utilized "sinister settings, expressionist lighting, evocative mood music, and specialized makeup" in their narrative directions which encompassed the "mad-scientist film...; vampire movies; monster movies; and metamorphosis movies."[11]

Universal exemplified the indelible stamp of 1930s Hollywood horror with its specialized focus on the genre and the company's intent to propel horror into the first-run picture houses. Their *Dracula* and *Frankenstein* (both 1931) harnessed the directorial talents of Tod Browning and James Whale, respectively, and cemented Universal's status as the most commercially successful and critically acclaimed horror studio during this time. Jon

Towlson in *Subversive Horror Cinema* argues that the output of films primarily between the years 1931 to 1936 represented "a sustained subversive output [which was the] result of a symbiosis of genre innovation, sympathetic producers and an alienated audience: a country in the grip of economic crisis and impending war."[12] While the political allegory contained in much of the horror cinema of the decade and found most prominently in Whale's *Frankenstein* and Browning's *Freaks* (1932) is not necessarily evident in the nihilistic narratives of 21st-century hardcore horror, there are still webs of confluence that link North America's first great cycle of subversive horror with the most recent. The formation of 1930s horror occurred in the historical context of the aftermath of World War I, the rise of fascism in Europe combined with increasing threat of further global conflict, and the economic hardship of the Great Depression. This period of crisis engendered a "national trauma and ideological conflict"[13] whereby horror films sought to provide a vent or release from fears and anxieties circulating in society. Furthermore, the social collapse often represented in these films cogently spoke to an age of trauma by "revealing [society] as ultimately untenable in terms of providing sustained social stability on a local, national, or international level."[14] America in the 1930s and America in the 21st century are both marked by traumatic events happening to the body politic, and in this environment of unease and uncertainty, there is the potential of a more subversive filmmaker to emerge, one whose radical aesthetic and thematic strategy is more likely to find an audience. The pseudo-snuff films of Vogel engender a fear of portable recording devices and what horrors they might capture that are inextricably linked to greater fears and anxieties over warfare and terrorism. Similarly, Browning and Whale channeled the trauma of war and socio-economic downturn into narratives of vampiric predators, out-of-control monstrous bodies and rogue scientists to critique dominant power structures which were deploying ever more oppressive practices to ensure authority was maintained.

Frankenstein became Universal's most successful film at the U.S. box office during 1932, underlining the impact and affect horror films were then having on audiences. The film initiated the mad-scientist trope and featured a monster, played by the iconic horror actor Boris Karloff, who affected "an augmented structure and a blood-curdling makeup that even a Lon Chaney would find it difficult to surpass in horrifying abnormality."[15] The film deployed Karloff's Monster as an allegory for the social problems circulating in America during the Great Depression, which discriminated against and persecuted marginalized people such as homosexuals, World War I veterans, the homeless and the criminal as the locus of all society's ills. In this context, the Monster became an "amalgam of all that society cast out and called 'monstrous' or 'other' in the 1930s."[16] Thus, *Frankenstein*'s subversive social commentary and obscene application of the deviant "other" in the form of a monster made from "human odds and ends"[17] provided much of the film's dramatic power and horrific countenance. Indeed, the film "was widely censored for its scenes of perceived blasphemy, sadism and child molestation"[18] including in the UK wherein the British Board of Film Censorship introduced the rating H for horrific due to the number of films (*Dracula*, *Dr. Jekyll and Mr. Hyde* [Rouben Mamoulian, 1931] and *Freaks*) released with extreme and disturbing content.

Similarly, *Freaks* garnered a significant amount of controversy when released by MGM in 1932. The story follows the exploitation of a touring circus of "freaks" by "normal" circus performers, particular Cleopatra, a trapeze artist, who marries Little Hans with the purpose of poisoning him for his money. When the "freaks" find out about Cleopatra's treachery, they chase her down during a stormy night and mutilate her into an almost unrecognizable form as a legless giant hen. The virulent reaction to *Freaks* was expressed as early as initial test screenings and prompted MGM to severely cut and re-edit the film from the director's original vision. Nonetheless, the film still provided an unparalleled horror experience in terms of visceral shock sequences and taboo thematic strategies visualized in an "environment rich with polymorphously perverse sexuality."[19] Browning attached viewer sympathy to the circus "freaks" and emphatically aligned audience identification to them during their uprising against Cleopatra, which made for a transgressive cinematic experience.

The film also provided a subversive commentary on the U.S. during the Depression as *Freaks* reverses the conventions of the horror film by engendering respect and sympathy with the so-called genetically deficient and abnormal circus performers. Browning's aim was to address the issues of injustice and social class in the U.S. during the Depression where many "outsider" groups were persecuted and often unfairly treated. Lauded today for its progressive elements, *Freaks* was received more as an exploitative and tasteless film at the time. The themes of "miscegenation and reproduction of the genetically unfit"[20] proved too subversive and troubling for the majority of cinemagoers, the MGM studio and moral watchdogs.

In 1932, after the first spate of horror titles appeared in American picture houses and of which *Frankenstein* and *Freaks* featured prominently, Colonel Jason S. Joy, a Production Code administrator, lobbied the Motion Picture Producers and Distributors of America (MPPDA). Colonel Joy's intention was to confront the head of the MPPDA Will Hays to see if "this [was] the beginning of a cycle that ought to be retarded or killed."[21] Many films were censored or banned outright attesting to their status as unpalatable creations of horror and terror. MGM edited 30 minutes of footage from *Freaks* as well as adding a more affirmative coda although it was still withdrawn from circulation and forthrightly banned after only a short, limited theatrical run.

Many more early 1930s horror titles tested the socio-cultural and political thresholds of what was considered tolerable including *Island of Lost Souls* (Erle C. Kenton, 1932), which provided one of the most extreme examples of Hollywood horror during the 1930s. Alison Peirse talks about how the film "explicitly worked towards a consistently horrific framework intended to strike fear into the viewer"[22] in its narrative of female monstrousness set against the bizarre and unsettling human-animal experiments of H.G. Wells' Dr. Moreau (played in wonderfully camp fashion by Charles Laughton). The "bestial link of animals and humans"[23] in *Island of Lost Souls* provided a horrifying and transgressive spectacle that initiated an international ban on the film and long delays in screening the film to general audiences (the UK did not show the film until 1967). Later additions to Hollywood's 1930s output similarly provoked audiences and regulatory bodies. Films such as *The Black Cat* (Edger G. Ulmer, 1934), *Mad Love* (Karl Freund, 1935) and *WereWolf of London* (Stuart Walker, 1935) provided unnerving horrors from the brutal modernist set design of *The Black Cat* to the sustained violence enacted on the male (monstrous) body in *WereWolf in London*. Horror films during the period were made both pre- and post-regulation of the Production Code in 1934 and maintained a consistent challenge to the dictum of the code which related to a moral commitment regarding "what was considered appropriate, proper and decent for audiences to watch at the movies."[24]

The 1950s and the Neutralization of the Extreme Image

The 1950s represented the next concerted cycle of horror films within Hollywood with examples that spanned the decade from *The Thing from Another World* (Christian Nyby, Howard Hawks, 1951) to *The Creature Walks Among Us* (John Sherwood, 1956) and *Return of the Fly* (Edward Bernds, 1959). A number of these films crossed over with science fiction conventions such as the threat of alien invasion, monstrous genetic mutations and dangerous experiments carried out by unhinged and obsessive scientists. Furthermore, the films imagined large-scale disaster narratives and apocalyptic scenarios in their engagement with Cold War anxiety during the decade. The policies of the U.S. government and fears about the permeability and ineffectual nature of national security protocols were downplayed or exorcised in many of these films or neutralized via intense spectacle and the aesthetics of destruction. Susan Sontag has commented that films like *The War of the Worlds* (Byron Haskin, 1953) and *Invasion of the Body Snatchers* (Don Siegel, 1956) can bring the fantastical into the realm of the quotidian and in doing so provide an "imagination of disaster" that neutralizes audiences' fears.[25]

For Sontag, the heavy dependence on spectacular narratives turns toward an "unremitting banality [which] normalize[s] what is psychologically unbearable, thereby inuring us to it."[26] Emptied out of any social criticism or transgressive material, the films offer a naïve and fallacious register of the fears surrounding nuclear Armageddon or Communist infiltration of the U.S.

Despite the pervasive hybrid nature of horror and sci-fi genres during the 1950s and their countenance of a less violent and unsettling horror, there were popular forms of the genre which attempted to reposition a more subversive critique of American society framed by the Cold War. Filmmakers Herman Cohen and Roger Corman released a number of horror titles toward the end of the decade that resonated with the emerging youth culture in America. For example, Cohen oversaw the productions of films aimed squarely at teen audiences with outlandish titles such as *I Was a Teenage Werewolf* (Gene Fowler, Jr., 1957) and *I Was a Teenage Frankenstein* (Herbert L. Strock, 1957). The films did not provide a shocking or transgressive visual arrangement in their teen-friendly focus on over-the-top monsters and alien invasions, yet did provide a subversive ideological commentary "marked by anxieties unique to America during the early years of the Cold War."[27] In fact, these films and studio pictures such as Paramount's *I Married a Monster from Outer Space* (Gene Fowler, Jr., 1958) sought to "delegitimise the normative forces of order in society,"[28] particularly those circulating in the tense standoff between the U.S. and Soviet Russia. The subthemes of paranoia over authority disseminated in these horror films explicitly framed the misgivings about whether the central institutions of America, such as the government and the military, could in fact "protect society from disorder."[29] With this in mind, Paramount's *I Married a Monster from Outer Space* puts forth an almost unprecedented pessimistic and paranoid narrative which explicitly draws a negative assessment of all "conventional authority"[30] to deal with the crisis at hand. Although a number of studio and independent features from this decade engaged in subversive ideological formations of contingent socio-historical events such as the Cold War, the visual content aimed toward screwball entertainment or the teen preoccupation with sex and sexual themes. The erotic film was in ascendance during the 1950s with a number of "ethnological" and "documentary" films made about exotic cultures or naturism and its proponents. Films such as Bettie Page's Burlesque trilogy *Striporama* (Jerald Intrator, 1953), *Varietease* (Irving Klaw, 1955) and *Teaserama* (Klaw, 1955), the incendiary, censor-baiting *Garden of Eden* (Max Nosseck, 1954) and Russ Meyer's soft-core sensation *The Immoral Mr. Teas* (1959) all challenged censorship laws and acceptable content relating to representations of sex and nudity. Violent films, on the other hand, did not find as much coverage or outlet as evidenced by the sci-fi–horror hybrid or the teen horror cycle emanating from film companies such as American International Pictures (AIP).

However, there were a number of exploitation movies released and exhibited in the U.S. during the 1950s whose purpose was "primarily to repulse with images of violence, carnage, or bloody ritual."[31] The often unpleasant and repellent nature of films such as *Half-Way to Hell* (Robert Snyder, 1953) and *Mau-Mau* (Elwood Price, 1955) in their respective inclusion of documentary footage of concentration camps and an exploitative marketing campaign sought to lure audiences with promises of "ghastly acts brought on by modern warfare, technology, and crumbling political systems."[32] The films attempted to actively engage the viewer in geopolitical events by making them complicit in acts of terror and violence committed around the world. Although these films often constructed and manipulated extreme "real" footage with narrative exposition, they failed to adequately provide enough blood and gore to "shock viewers sufficiently to question, and perhaps reject, aspects of postwar life"[33] such as secularism, commodity culture and political fundamentalism. However, these "atrocity films," despite their relatively unimpressive commercial impact, did engender a space within film production for a more effective and extreme interconnection of documentary and narrative filmmaking. The mondo film gained worldwide exposure a few years later with the Italian shockumentary *Mondo Cane* (Paolo Cavara, Gaultiero Jacopetti and Franco Prosperi, 1962) which directly led to the U.S.-based mondo films, and significant precursors of 21st-century hardcore horror, *Faces of Death* (John Alan Schwartz, 1978) and *The Killing of America* (Sheldon Renan and Leonard Schrader, 1981).

Atrocity movies can also be seen to have provided space, and appetite, for more fictional, narrative-based horror and initiated the 1960s boom in the gore film. The paradigmatic example and perhaps one of the seminal extreme-hardcore U.S. horror films was producer David Friedman and director Herschell Gordon Lewis' *Blood Feast*, a film where violence and gore were unashamedly central, explicit and intensive in their presentation. *Blood Feast* emerged as an "integrally primal and powerful movie"[34] with its narrative immediacy of extreme violence and lack of elision or suggestion in its many set-pieces of innovative and grisly carnage. For critics and viewers alike, it "provided the template for the adoption and presentation of gore"[35] which is still reverberating in the visual arrangement and framing of horror as we move into 21st century.

Nothing So Appalling in the Annals of Horror: Blood Feast *as the Hardcore Horror Prototype*

Herschell Gordon Lewis' ascension into the motion picture hall of fame as the infamous director of the notorious and seminal horror film *Blood Feast* was both circuitous and unconventional. Starting off his vocational life as a Mississippi State University English professor, Lewis soon moved, through the lure of money and creative enterprise, into advertising where he produced many television commercials and government films. When he met David Friedman, it was with the express intention of financially capitalizing on his experience in television and radio by producing feature-length films. Friedman was an established producer and distributor of exploitation films and provided a "hard-boiled, rock-em sock-em slam-bang"[36] style of film advertising and campaigning that complimented Lewis' technical experience of film production. Initially, Lewis and Friedman produced and distributed *The Prime Time* (Gordon Weisenborn, 1960) before moving on to their own projects such as *Living Venus* and *The Adventures of Lucky Pierre* (both Herschell Gordon Lewis, 1961). These films presented an innocuous and impotent addition to the nudie film market which by 1961 was becoming over-saturated. It meant Lewis and Friedman had to either strengthen the sexual content of their films so that they became "less and less socially acceptable"[37] and thus more distinctive, or find another disreputable, though still potentially lucrative, avenue to pursue. According to Lewis and Friedman, this took the form of simply sitting down and making a "list of the *kinds* of films the major companies either could not make, or *would not* make."[38] The result was simple and brief: gore.

Blood Feast was made for $24,000 and shot over six days while Lewis and Friedman were in South Florida shooting the stripper–nudist camp film *Bell, Bare and Beautiful* (Lewis, 1963). *Blood Feast* utilized the same locations used in the "official" film as well as crew and cast members and as such acted as a horror "flip-side," or repressed id, to the tame and uninspired content of *Bell, Bare and Beautiful*. That is, the narrative of the film follows an Egyptian caterer called Fuad Ramses (Mal Gordon) who is killing and dismembering young women to harvest their body parts in preparation for a ritual cannibalistic feast to summon the goddess Ishtar. He is eventually thwarted by the police while attempting to kill Suzie Fremont (June 1963 Playboy Playmate Connie Mason). The cops chase him into a local refuse site where he is finally crushed to death by a trash compactor. The form and style of the film are crude, garish and purposefully framed as a parodic schlock horror. The aesthetics of the film also confirm its hurried and low-budget production, from the often unconvincing performances to the inadequacies of technical set-ups in the lighting and framing of particular scenes. Yet the film compensates for these production shortcomings by providing an affective horror experience for audiences that can be seen to contribute a significant criterion for 21st-century North American hardcore horror. Lewis was correct in plainly pointing out that "nobody ever walked out of the theater because of a ragged pan"[39] due to *Blood Feast*'s affective power in how it presented and detailed its violent set-pieces. In fact, the use of gore in this respect provides another rationale for its use other than commercial in that it enabled the filmmakers to handle the scenes *intensively* rather than needing to create an extensive *mise en scène* or production to capture and contain the spectacle. Lewis' effective use of an affective and intensive horror is ultimately what the film has become (in)famous for, and certainly provides paradigmatic material for the future direction of horror which has culminated in the intimate and horrific narratives and visual arrangements of contemporary hardcore horror.

The ensuing publicizing and marketing of *Blood Feast* focused squarely on the emotional impact the film would have on audiences. Alongside the William Castle–esque gimmicks such as vomit bags which contained the inscription "You may need this when you see *Blood Feast*," Lewis and Friedman also generated interest in the affective power of the film through the design of the posters. These lurid promotional items promised "Nothing so awful in the annals of horror" in the "slaughter and mutilation of nubile young girls" now presented "more grisly than ever in BLOOD COLOR!" In these examples, Lewis and Freidman utilize their backgrounds in advertising to lure or lead audiences to the film by promising a unique quality of horror experience. One critic called it the "absolute nadir of exploitation cinema"[40] with *Variety* perhaps offering the strongest denouncement in its review: The Hollywood trade paper called out the film as a "totally inept shocker … incredibly crude and unprofessional from start to finish" and "an insult even to the most puerile and salacious of audiences."[41] Audience response was much more favorable as the film went on to gross more than $4,000,000, primarily at drive-in theaters in the southern and midwest states of the U.S. However, it is difficult to find empirical data on how audiences reacted to and engaged with *Blood Feast* other than from the impromptu canvassing carried out by the filmmakers while the film was being shown.[42] Jonathan Crane mentions that there was no cult or paracinematic audience in place during the early 1960s who would have viewed the film with an "ironic detachment that is now central to cult film and midnight viewing."[43] Audiences may not have been attuned to the oppositional qualities of alternative cinema in the face of Hollywood hegemony but it is likely that they were drawn to the film first by the promise, and then the actual delivery, of material that they would never see in a mainstream or Hollywood production. After its premiere screening in Peoria, Illinois, the film became a word-of-mouth sensation, according to Lewis. Audiences were keen to discuss and disseminate their hyperviolent movie encounter.[44]

Lewis often talked about trigger mechanisms in the making of a film which enabled him to "lead the audience"[45] toward an emotional engagement of the affective qualities and experiential nature of a film. With regard to *Blood Feast*, the audience was already preconditioned to anticipate and accept a viewing experience which held "no reverence for established procedures"[46] found in mainstream filmic practices. Gimmicks such as the vomit bags, fake paramedics and injunctions taken out against the film suggested a film whose content would be transgressive and taboo. Indeed, the general theme of cannibalism in the film is a seditious act in confronting an audience altogether unprepared for this type of thematic material. Yet it is the immediate and intensive representation of violence and murder which would have alerted viewers much more forcefully to the transgressive nature of the visual taboo on display. The opening scene perfectly accounts for Amos Vogel's notion of the "injunction not to look"[47] when confronted with forbidden and transgressive images. In *Blood Feast*, there is nothing else and nowhere else to look *but* at the "contagious"[48] taboo object. The pre-title sequence starts when a young, attractive woman enters her apartment and undresses, ready to take a bath. It is a tranquil scene aligned more with Lewis and Friedman's earlier nudie-cuties than with transgressive gore though the omin-

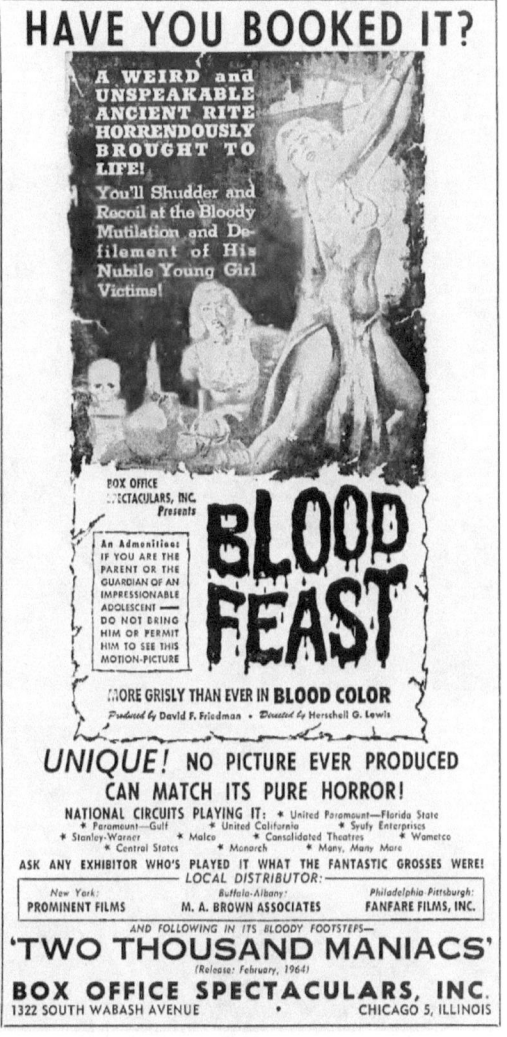

The exploitation marketing style of Lewis and Friedman (courtesy Regional Horror Film).

ous rhythmic beating of a kettle drum and a morbid radio announcement about a recently murdered woman whose "body was badly mutilated" alerts the viewer to the impending threat the woman faces. The visual arrangement of the sequence as the woman is attacked and killed by Fuad Ramses is determined through a spectacular composition which centers the violence as primary and essential. Everything else is relegated to the periphery or excluded

Above and left: **Nowhere to look *but* at the horror. Pat Tracey (Sandra Sinclair) in *Blood Feast* (Something Weird Video).**

from the frame. Lewis' camera provides various close-ups of Ramses deranged features as he gouges and dismembers with his knife, while the soundtrack consists solely of the piercing screams of the woman alongside extended, intensive images of her bleeding eye socket and dismembered leg. The entire sequence lasts 2:44 minutes and delivers the "shock of the new" in its treatment of violence in such a forthright and unapologetic manner. The affective charge of *Blood Feast* is horrifically announced and serves as an immediate introduction to what follows as a fundamentally powerful and genre-defining film.

Jonathan Crane has pointed out that due to the technical deficiencies in the film, "the spectacle had to be so compelling that it did not matter a whit that nothing on screen registered save for the regular eruptions of wonderful gore."[49] The pre-credit sequence establishes the repetitive structure of the film in that violent set-pieces punctuate the narrative at regular intervals in much the same way sex scenes do in pornographic features. Linda Williams' work on hardcore pornography also has some crossover with the gore films of Lewis and Friedman. In particular, with regards to Williams' idea of the "frenzy of the visible" in how "technologies of the visible" facilitate hardcore filmic bodies and "the enhanced vision of spectators"[50] toward pleasurable and affective experiences. *Blood Feast*'s treatment of violence in a direct, almost anatomical address utilizes the intimate visual technology of the movie camera to provide an emotional contract with the violent spectacle. As Mendik articulates, "[F]or those fortunate to see any of Lewis' productions it is specific (splatter) scenes rather than the narrative as a whole which imprints themselves on the viewer's memory."[51] Lewis' extreme attack on the body, the unflinching gaze of the camera, and the affective charge of repulsion, fear and horror is most clearly seen in the film's most controversial set-piece when a woman's tongue is removed as Ramses continues his human harvest for the goddess Ishtar. For the tongue scene, a mixture of fake blood, cranberries, gelatin and a real sheep's tongue were used, which added to both the visceral impact of the scene and the authenticity of its removal. Here Lewis arranges the *mise en scène* in terms of a primitive cinema with no dialogue, the return of the basic, monotonous cadence of the kettle drum, and the vaudeville-esque villainy of Ramses. However, the spectacle of violence is once again the primary, almost sole focus, as the viewer is presented with further close-ups of the gory dismemberment as the scene concludes.

The legacy of *Blood Feast* rests primarily in how it acts as a foundation for the slasher film in terms of its narrative development of a male killer who stalks and kills various female characters in a highly repetitive and ritualized way. Mikita Brottman has called the film the "*ur*-text for a long tradition of slasher and stalker films" and thus singles it out (as opposed to *Psycho* [Alfred Hitchcock, 1960]) as an important progenitor of films from *Halloween* (John Carpenter, 1978) to *Frankenhooker* (Frank Henenlotter, 1990).[52] Brottman clearly details the narrative similarities between *Blood Feast* and the slasher which add credence to the notion of it as the prototype of the latter. She goes on to claim that the "cinematic shock relating to body horror"[53] characterizes the slasher narrative. Here, the films are "distinguished by the opening up of the body and the shocking revelation of the taboo insides."[54] *Blood Feast* certainly forwards the unsettling spectacle of the material body with its dismemberments, eye gouging and brain removals but this does not necessarily apply to the slasher, particularly the first cycle from *Black Christmas* (Bob

Clark, 1974) to *Friday the 13th Part 2* (Steve Miner, 1981). In these films, violence is kept to a minimum and is rarely gory or prolonged in its duration. *Blood Feast*'s persistent, graphic and regular intrusion into the broken, mangled and mutilated body also provides a prototype for hardcore horror rather than being exclusively in the domain of the slasher. The challenging and extreme nature of hardcore horror is primarily directed toward the corporeal body: both of the human monster-killer, but more so the terrified victim. In the examples from *Scrapbook* to *Slow Torture Puke Chamber*, the body is center stage and its intensive and affective "opening up" and abject destruction reverts the spectator to the gory machinations of *Blood Feast*'s pre-credits sequence. It is in this respect, along with its affective horror, that the position of the film as a forebear of contemporary North American hardcore horror emerges.

Snuff: *The Film They Said Would Never Be Shown*

By the end of the 1960s and the beginning of the 1970s, Lewis' unique contribution to the horror film was waning and in danger of becoming obsolete in the landscape of emerging paranoid horrors such as *Last House on the Left* (Wes Craven, 1972) and *The Texas Chain Saw Massacre* (Tobe Hooper, 1974).[55] Lewis' *The Gore Gore Girls* (1972) staged a desperate last stand as the film ratcheted up the spectacle of violence along with abundant scenes of naked women. It represented a failure for Lewis, and the colorful and excessive visuals became camp and almost parodic compared to the disturbing "natural" or "pure" horrors ushered in by *Night of the Living Dead* (George Romero, 1968) and *Rosemary's Baby* (Roman Polanski, 1968). Indeed, for Crane, the only available development now for horror filmmakers after the intensive onscreen carnage of Lewis and to compete with the new, socially conscious horrors of George Romero and Wes Craven was "to leave off illusion and enter the real."[56] Although the pseudo-snuff narratives of hardcore horror have convincingly visualized the filmic forms, codes and conventions of realism, they were established during this period as filmmakers reimagined the monstrous. The main route taken was in terms of positing an explicit "challenge [to] the moral-social-political assumptions, production values and narrative strategies"[57] of existing horror found in the practices of production companies such as AIP and Hammer. The outlandish gothic architecture of Roger Corman's AIP Poe films and the erotic charge of Hammer monsters were replaced by the quotidian which existed at the edges of contemporary America. Violent mobs, psychotic teens and monstrous families encompassed the films that ushered in the modern era in North American horror and

Two. The Genealogy of Extremity in North American Film   45

which explicitly sought to engage with the socio-political contingencies of the U.S. riven by the tumult and trauma of the 1960s. Amidst the changing definition and redefinition of horror and the relationship between the monstrous and the everyday emerged an "old-fashioned act of cinematic hucksterism"[58] which promised that most taboo of forbidden images—death—to be finally given actual visual documentation via the process of killing somebody in front of the camera. The film was *Snuff* and it transformed the urban legend of real filmed murder into a "sociocultural *bete noire*"[59] of the 1970s. In doing so, the film acts as another significant precursor of 21st-century hardcore horror.

Snuff started out as the topical Manson family–inspired sex and death opus *Slaughter*, directed by prodigious sexploitation filmmakers Roberta and Michael Findlay (*Her Flesh* trilogy, 1967–68). Not uncommon for a low-budget exploitation film, *Slaughter* suffered numerous production issues but in this case, they were so severe that companies were reluctant to distribute the film. Monarch Releasing eventually purchased the film in 1975 and in a bold exploitation-carny display of ingenuity supplied an incendiary coda where the film "ends" only for the camera to continue shooting as the director mutilates and kills a female member of the crew. Monarch distributor Alan Shackleton devised and funded the additional section to *Slaughter* along with a promotional campaign attesting to the authenticity of the snuff ending. He also tapped into contemporary flashpoints with regards to extreme cinematic violence and the rise of hardcore pornography in the wake of the commercial success of *Deep Throat* (Gerard Damiano, 1972). Thus, *Snuff* provides a historical position crucial in the genealogy of the aesthetics, thematic strategies and marketing utilized by the filmmakers of 21st-century hardcore horror. That is, in the promotional direction taken by Shackleton, the approach addresses and further ruptures the border between the real and mimesis engendered in much of the discourse surrounding 1970s North American horror. It also cleverly exploited anxieties over the growing cultural phenomenon of pornography by inextricably connecting *Snuff*'s "explicit images of mutilation and defilement with hardcore sex."[60] Finally, and relating to the aesthetics of the snuff sequence, the film is shot, framed and performed in a decidedly amateur countenance, while all the time framing the material as if being found footage (in this case the footage is not "found" but presented as if actually taking place). Consequently, *Snuff* cogently spoke to the fears and anxieties surrounding the direction of the new modern breed of horror film and the disconcerting directions they may further take to satiate jaded audiences. It also provided, along with *Blood Feast*'s intensive displays of violence, another clear template for hardcore horror in how the film exploited the found footage aesthetic, destabilized the profilmic construction, and staged innovative and unconventional marketing strategies.

The marketing campaign of *Snuff* immediately brought into focus how important it was to present the notion of authenticity in terms of the provenance of the film. Often this was clouded in mystery and ambiguity and via purposeful actions taken by Shackleton in which he would inform authorities of snuff movies infiltrating picture houses and cinema clubs. The *Snuff* poster provides the first instance of establishing a platform so that the filmmakers can imply that the film may show real death and that snuff films may actually exist. Shackleton had self-imposed an X rating to the film connecting the aesthetic of violence in *Snuff* to the "real" sex of hardcore pornography. Furthermore, the poster featured an illustrated cut-up image of a naked, bloodied woman with the dramatic title underneath declaring "The film that could only be made in South America ... where Life is CHEAP!" The trailer also capitalized on the illicit, contraband nature of the film with warnings detailing that *Snuff* was "the movie they said could never be shown" and that it was obtained from South America in a clandestine manner so as to avoid seizure and prosecution from American authorities.

When the film premiered in January 1976, it was presented without credits and it was apparent that it had been (badly) dubbed into English (that is, the Findlays' film *Slaughter*), which again strengthened Shackleton's claim to possessing an authentic snuff film imported from outside of America. Thus, before any viewer got to the end of the film, and thus exposed to the reality that *Snuff* was in fact a hoax, the promotion and marketing of the film had shrewdly exploited growing public concerns over violent pornography and snuff. As a result, the film faced many pickets and protests and which led feminist groups such as NOW (the National Organization for Women) and WAVAW (Women Against Violence Against Women) to formulate a nationwide discourse on the subject of pornography and violence while initiating charges of obscenity and theater closures. In this respect, *Snuff* acts upon a "hyperactive theatricality of ambiguity, rumor and moral panic"[61] that provides a blueprint for hardcore horror concerning its promotional strategies.

Henry: He's Not Jason, He's Not Freddie, He's Real

The film they said "could never be shown" had now in fact been shown numerous times and had impacted on the popular imagination so much so that *Snuff* had "cultivated a whole new point of reference for death on film: Murder as entertainment."[62] For a brief time, "snuff" entered the mainstream with Paul Schrader's *Hardcore* (1978) where a devout, respectable and affluent father (George C. Scott) attempts to find his missing daughter. The search leads to the seedy and dangerous world of pornography in which he is exposed to a stag-snuff film. It is a dramatic and sobering moment for the father, who is repulsed by what he witnesses. The scene would have also provided a jolting moment for audiences as the snuff footage, the "embodiment of a diseased world,"[63] intrudes into the cinematic space of a respectable and high-profile film.

Yet it was the exploitation film which turned most effectively to the growing cultural phenomenon of snuff. Films such as *Emanuelle in America* (Joe D'Amato, 1976) and *Last House on Dead End Street* (Victor Janos [Roger Watkins], 1977) provided authentic (re)constructions of snuff in an unsettling and believable fashion considering that they were auxiliary features of fictional narratives. However, it was the American variations of the Italian mondo movie *Faces of Death* and *The Killing of America*[64] which most forcibly confronted the salacious aspects of *Snuff* in their controversial treatment of the taboo surrounding representations of real death.

Although both films were initially aimed at the Japanese market, they provide a significant North American context in both their focus on U.S.-based atrocities and influence on 1980s shock video compilations and horror films such as *Henry*. In turn, their influence has worked through and joined with these discursive media forms to continue into the snuff aesthetics of contemporary hardcore horror. They also provide key discussion points on the representation of real death which provides an important footnote along the way to the cycle of the 21st-century hardcore horror film. *Faces of Death* attempts to position itself as a "serious investigation into the mystery of death" but is nothing more than poorly fabricated "freak-show exploitation."[65] It starts with surgery and morgue footage which is authentic before introducing our wholly unconvincing narrator and pre-eminent pathologist, Francis Gröss, who provides a moralizing and didactic framework which accompanies the footage of plane and automobile crashes, constructed execution sequences, fabricated deadly animal attacks and amateurish stagings of human sacrifice and cannibalism. While the genuine footage is juxtaposed with constructed scenes, it does not have the unsettling power of *Cannibal Holocaust* or earlier Italian mondo movies due to the unconvincing performativity of the actors involved. At no point are they believable and this aspect of the film anticipates one of the key criteria required for hardcore horror in that the performances *must* seem genuine and believable. Ultimately, *Faces of Death* is an "insincere, cheaply commercial and cynically realised"[66] development of snuff in its crass appropriation of Italian mondo and extended purview of *Snuff*'s notorious coda. In fact, the film would not be considered a principal contribution to contemporary North American extreme horror were it not for its national success and the franchise it engendered, becoming "one of the most famous elements of shockumentary film history."[67]

Another less than salubrious outcome of *Faces of Death* shock-snuff aesthetics was that it gave rise to a more depraved and callous violent spectacle that informed future compilations such as *Death Scenes* (Nick Bougas, 1989) and *Executions* (David Herman, Arun Kumar and David Monaghan, 1995) as well as the Internet shock sites Rotten.com and Ogrish.

The Killing of America opens with these blood red words against a black background: "All of the film you are about to see is real. Nothing has been staged." Immediately the film promises a more authentic approach to that of *Faces of Death* and what follows is a litany of atrocity exhibits as the solemn narrator provides fear-inducing statistics relating to gun crime, mass murders and notorious serial killers: America is riven with murder and death. The film attempts to locate all this killing within the paradigm of the "evil within" thesis, popular in the growing paranoid horrors of the 1970s and brought to the fore here in an exposé of a divided America overwhelmed by violent people and brutal acts. Yet the film provides a limited engagement with the sociocultural contingencies such as racism, increasing social stratification, the obsession with violence and of violent criminals, and more tangential aspects regarding voyeurism. Instead, we see the violence as unavoidable, everywhere and spontaneous, and the lack of context does support the general structure of the film which seems to exist to "generate maximum unease"[68] in the viewer. *The Killing of America* features infamous events and archive footage from the 1960s and 1970s such as the Jonestown massacre, Charles Whitman's mass shooting from an Austin clock tower, candid interviews with serial killer Ed Kemper, courtroom footage of Ted Bundy and a range of documentary footage detailing explicit material relating to gun violence. The end result is a depressing and irresponsible treatment of gun crime in America which veers toward exploitation as much as *Faces of Death* did.

The film does posit real footage of murder and death and as such is significant in terms of the aesthetics connected to these representations. The scenes may be real and not fabricated but the grainy, amateurish footage of CCTV or the poorly framed recordings of news crews rushing in for a scoop shows how filmmakers can approach pseudo-snuff, realist horror so as to make their images authentic and believable. Another area of utmost importance is how people in these various segments react to the horror that unfolds around them. We can see how their reactions have informed the performativity of contemporary hardcore horror so that the "hyperactive theatricality of ambiguity" in *The Killing of America* is pushed into new directions far removed from the unconvincing representations of *Snuff* and *Faces of Death*.

With this in mind, the first American horror film to successfully incorporate these elements into its narrative and *mise en scène* was the unflinching, controversial and pivotal film to hardcore horror, *Henry: Portrait of a Serial Killer*. John McNaughton's first feature adopts an almost social realist approach in how it catalogues the banal everyday lives of two serial killers alongside sequences of spontaneous, unflinching and disturbing acts of violence, sexual assault and murder. *Henry* was based on the real-life exploits of Henry Lee Lucas and his accomplice Ottis Elwood Toole, who were sentenced to life imprisonment in 1983 for a series of sexual assaults and murders of young women. The commitment to providing a realist horror was evidenced in pre-production of the film as McNaughton was adamant that the "objective [be] to horrify an audience to the maximum degree possible"[69] by removing the barriers between them and the horror on display. In doing so, McNaughton provided a stark and extreme piece of transgressive cinema which tapped into a broad and complex array of socio-cultural discourses surrounding realist horror. In Cynthia Freeland's seminal article on realist horror, published in 1995, she uses *Henry* as a case study to map out a definition for films advancing a break from the distancing narratives of art horror where impossible monsters and stylistic aesthetics dominate. For Freeland, *Henry* encapsulated the three criteria essential for realist horror: The monster was real, the spectacle was privileged over plot, and the film diminished the clear boundary between the real and mimesis. McNaughton's intention to remove the "buffer of fantasy"[70] clearly addresses these three aspects in how the resulting film confronts audiences with an authentic formal aesthetic; a flat and ugly spectacle of violence; the monster as human and as real; a lack of moral certitude and/or resolution; and a withholding of audience identification or empathy with the killers and their victims. As such, the film provides a compelling—though repellent—horror which generated a great deal of controversy due to the authenticity of its realist horror tropes.

The contention surrounding *Henry* leads to considerations on how it impinges upon taste and classificatory boundaries and is not something directly addressed in Freeland's article. Yet doing so is an essential factor in providing a holistic examination of extreme horror and the value of a film like *Henry* in discussions of 21st-century hardcore horror. In North America, the film received an X rating from CARA; this generated a substantial amount of media buzz and free publicity but also meant that film companies were often reluctant to release the film due to the financial restrictions and limited distributional avenues an X-rated film would be afforded. In the UK, it was heavily cut and was not seen in an uncensored version until 2003. The strict regulatory practices applied to *Henry* were exacerbated by the burgeoning home video industry in both North America and the UK. The primary rationale was that of the growing moral panic over video nasties and the changing dynamic of film spectatorship from the communal and public space of the film auditorium to the "more personalized experience, [and] a wholly private one if required"[71] of the home. The draconian responses circulating the release of the film emanated mainly from the realist horror of *Henry* and in particular the notorious home invasion scene which has been "consistently flagged up

as the most controversial in the film."[72] The scene is a vital component with which to test the transgressive and extreme nature of *Henry* and how it has achieved the status of a critical historical exemplar of hardcore horror. That is, many points meet at Henry's home invasion scene in the historical trajectory of the extreme horror film; snuff-fiction aesthetics, authentic performativity, the immediacy and intensity of the violence; the affective charge of watching realist horror and the policing of violent material.

When the film was reviewed by regulatory bodies in both the U.S. and the UK, it was not just the horrific nature of the unexpurgated footage that was of concern but also how the scene succeeded in "making the viewer as voyeur complicit in it."[73] The sequence lasts little over three minutes and begins with Henry and Otis driving along a suburban road at night before stopping outside a house. They proceed to break into the house in a seemingly random and spontaneous manner and hold hostage an affluent, middle-class family before murdering the young son and father and sexually assaulting and then murdering the mother. All of this is captured on videotape by Henry, who is both the director and actor, along with Otis, in their own home video snuff movie. As the scene concludes, we abruptly shift to the living room of Henry and Otis as they sit watching (and re-watching) the footage on television. It is here that the audience becomes aware that they are not watching the footage in real time but after the event and *with* the two killers. Shaun Kimber describes this particular scene as an example of "strong" horror in that it provides an affective impact in terms of its film violence due to the formal properties and the downplaying of conventional filmmaking qualities. The footage is amateurish, badly shot and framed, carried out in one continuous take and is often blurry, grainy and of generally poor quality. The performativity from the actors, particularly the victims, is believable and leads to a *mise en scène* that is authentic, direct and realistic. Yet when *Henry* cuts to Otis on the couch saying that he wants "to see it again," the scene takes on a more significant countenance with regard to how it has influenced contemporary hardcore horror. Not only does the content provide a transgressive interplay between the diegetic violence and the viewer but it also becomes a troubling and potent cultural form as it taps into fears and anxieties circulating in the age of home video and the moral panic over video nasties.

The home invasion scene gives a discrete form to snuff. As Kerekes and Slater outline, and which the home invasion covers in most respects, snuff "was hidden; was select; was one room and one camera; was black and white; was silent; was grainy; was colour with bad editing."[74] The notion of the killer filming the violence and the accompanying lack of overtly stylized direction

Opposite: **Marketing in opposition to cinematic horror (poster of** *Henry: Portrait of a Serial Killer***, courtesy The Red List).**

features in large part or as an auxiliary feature in all of the hardcore films from Stanze's *Scrapbook* through to Valentine's last installment in the "vomit gore" films *Black Mass of the Nazi Sex Wizard*. Both Stanze and Vogel have cited the realism and authenticity of *Henry* as a major influence, with Vogel saying that the home invasion sequence had a lasting impact regarding influencing his later horror films. Particularly, in offering an oppositional arrangement to Hollywood horror, in that, for Vogel, *August Underground* had to be immature, dirty, ugly and of course real."[75] Yet the "home video" aspect to this scene also intensifies the realist horror by having the snuff footage "produced by and for the psychopathic serial killer"[76] in which the audience watches alongside, fully complicit in the killers' murderous actions. The affective charge engendered via the interface between the film/killer and the audience "encourages emotional and moral responses in the spectator"[77] with regards to the notion of violence as entertainment. However, in the age of home video, it presented a more problematic relationship to violence as viewers, similar to Otis, could rewind and watch over and over scenes of violence and murder. *Henry* overstepped the threshold of acceptable content and the home invasion proved difficult, if not impossible, to re-situate back within existing regulatory frameworks. In the UK, the scene was initially removed from the film and later re-cut due to its nature and in the U.S. the film company filed a lawsuit challenging the original X rating due to their unsuccessful attempts to lobby for the more legitimate and accessible R rating. In the end, *Henry* was released unrated, which restricted exhibition revenue though increased its underground and controversial status. Here, the double helix of content and reception, which underlines the controversy *Henry* generated, provides the lasting legacy of the film in how it intersects with the form, themes, taste, cultures and regulatory contours of 21st-century hardcore horror.

The Not-So-Extreme Coda: Splatterpunk and Charming Killers

Extreme horror cinema in the 1990s leading directly up to Stanze's release of *Scrapbook* in 2000 and the formation of the hardcore horror subgenre was sublimated to mainstream studio productions. The most prominent of these films were the multi–Oscar-winning *The Silence of the Lambs* (Jonathan Demme, 1991) and the box office successes of the self-referential, postmodern horror *Scream* (Wes Craven, 1996) and its acolytes. There were still additions and new entries to the shockumentary of extreme "mix-tapes" that had continued more or less unabated since the original *Faces of Death* in 1978. In 1990, the release of the fourth *Faces of Death* entry (John Alan

Two. The Genealogy of Extremity in North American Film 53

Schwartz) initiated a decade in which a more niche and specialist film for the "true 'reality death enthusiast'"[78] emerged. *Traces of Death* (Damon Fox, 1993), *Executions* and *Faces of Gore* (Todd Tjersland, 1998) all continued the format of *Faces of Death* in their attempt to provide a patina of legitimacy and officialdom to their atrocity exhibitions (though in these examples, the content descended into a cruel and sadistic exploration of crime and accident footage from around the world). By the end of the decade, the shockumentary film had reached its nadir and was to be replaced by 21st-century compilation tapes mixing sex and nudity with violence and the rise of Internet sites such as Necrobabes and Rotton.com. While films such as *Faces of Gore* did provide a shocking and repellent survey of "the human body in total devastation,"[79] they nonetheless represented a peripheral formation of extremity that did not, or did but only in less marginal cultural spaces, move over into narrative forms within a more mainstream film practice.

One such horror convention challenged the sanitized product of studio horror: splatstick, which Towlson describes as "surreal bad taste comedy horror."[80] The cycle arguably started in 1981 with *Evil Dead* (Sam Raimi) and *Basket Case* (Frank Henenlotter) and intersected with non–U.S. horror in the form of Peter Jackson's early New Zealand films *Bad Taste* (1988) and *Brain Dead* (1992) as it moved into the 1990s with examples such as *Society* (Brian Yuzna, 1989) and *Return of the Living Dead 3* (Yuzna, 1993). The use of splatter can be traced back further to Herschell Gordon Lewis' 1960s horror films and has always had a subversive accompaniment in place. In the 1980s and 1990s, splatstick addressed themes such as the lack of faith in central institutions (particularly the military and the medical establishment), anti-materialism in terms of body modification, and the growing social stratification in the Reagan and Bush Sr. political eras. While the themes provide a transgressive opposition to the gloss of *The Silence of the Lambs* and the pastiche of *Scream*, their use of extreme violence is offset by an excessive and over-the-top formal arrangement cut through with a lack of seriousness. The affective power is sublimated onto entertainment and enjoyment rather than engendering emotional responses in line with terror and fear. As such, they share many characteristics with the 1950s cycle of teen-orientated horror films in their subversive themes but safely distanced horror content. If they have influenced hardcore horror at all, it is in their placing of the distorted, malleable, mutated and transformed human body at the center of the narrative.

Despite the examples of extreme and subversive horror in the 1990s, the overriding impression is one of a legitimate and sanitized form. There is certainly more nuance to the decade than straightforwardly rejecting films as examples of Hollywood homogeneity and repetitive sequels and franchises, but the filmmakers associated with hardcore horror point to this uniformity, unoriginality and lack of a realist horror as a major reason for their respective approaches to the genre. Eric Stanze has often talked about pushing the boundaries with *Scrapbook* in terms of presenting the serial killer in an ugly and raw manner. For Stanze, the focal element for a successful characterization was to move away from Anthony Hopkins' affectation of Hannibal Lecter as a mythical and high cultural figure toward the disturbing pathology and "realism" of Henry. The outcome was a less distinguished anti-hero and a more unhinged, violent psychopath, which precipitated more of a horrific affective charge and realist horror for which "a lot of people would consider not an appropriate movie to make."[81] Fred Vogel also explicitly indicted the 1990s horror landscape as stultifying and uninspired when he said that he "wanted to show the real nasty side"[82] of horror and that he "was tired of all the serial killer movies that didn't show you what's really going on."[83] *August Underground*'s meticulous and drawn-out attention to the processes of torture and murder in a graphic and unexpurgated visual documentation is the legacy of Vogel's anti-stance to what he saw as the sterile nature of 1990s horror and the "charming" figure of the serial killer.

Hardcore horror, while acting as a distinct break from the preceding decade and the films that came to dominate the critically and commercially successful part of the genre, also continues many of the historical precedents of horror. That is, examples of mondo, snuff-fictions, the intensive horror of *Blood Feast* and the affective horror of 1930s Universal films which, in turn, can be traced back all the way to the phantasmagoria of the magic lantern shows. By providing a genealogical overview of extreme horror, a long, complex and interconnected history within the cultural landscape of North American horror can be evidenced. Twenty-first century hardcore horror thus emerges as representative of its latest incantation and, although providing some abrupt discontinuities with previous exemplars, also taps into, develops and reinforces many tributaries of extremity existing in film.

Three

Global Currents of Extreme Horror

The previous chapter outlined the North American antecedents that formed multiple avenues into the contemporary landscape of 21st-century hardcore horror. The influences of *Snuff* and *Henry* provide a clear imprint over the general production practices, formal properties, thematic strategies, regulatory frameworks and viewer reception of films such as *Scrapbook* and the *August Underground* trilogy. In doing so, an important and useful background can be produced to acknowledge such connections and enrich the analysis of contemporary extreme horror. Furthermore, in an age defined by the opening-up of borders within filmmaking (and academia), global cinemas have also impacted on hardcore horror (as they have in all fields of film) along the contours of "industrial practices, working practices, historical factors, aesthetics, themes and approaches, audience reception, ethical questions and critical reception."[1] Indeed, foreign examples of cinematic extremity can also be traced via a historical trajectory as well as connected to contemporary formations. Global cinema as a synchronic and diachronic entity can provide another indispensable adjunct to the understanding, critical analysis and reception of North American 21st-century hardcore horror. Therefore, the chapter covers three main points. The first deals with the historical examples of *Salò, or the 120 of Sodom, Cannibal Holocaust* and *Man Bites Dog*, which have all had the most influence on the archaeology of hardcore horror. The second takes Japanese and German cinema as case studies due to the historical legacy both countries have in producing extreme film and how, in the contemporary period, they have provided archetypal examples such as *Grotesque* (Shiraishi, 2009) and *The Angels' Melancholia*. These latter two films in particular offer global examples of how the formal and thematic aspects associated with hardcore horror have fed into the production practices in other national contexts.

It is with the third point viewed from the contemporary case study of

A Serbian Film, that the merging of North American extreme horror with other national examples is most pronounced. *A Serbian Film* not only delineates the thematic and formal properties of extreme film content, but also provides a means with which to examine the strict and heavily regulated social and legislative mechanisms at play in the policing of the production and dissemination of extreme film content. This is a crucial element in exploring a full and critical positioning of audiences and their ethical concerns with regards to the extreme content of hardcore horror.

A Theorem of Death: The Deliberate Transgression of Salò, or 120 Days of Sodom

Pier Paolo Pasolini's final film delivers one of the most notorious and controversial spectacles in all of cinema. Since the time of its release, *Salò* has infuriated and repulsed audiences in equal measure. Vincent Canby, writing in the *New York Times* in 1977, called the film a "demonstration of nearly absolute impotency, if there is such a thing. Ideas get lost in a spectacle of such immediate reality and cruelty,"[2] while Richard Brody, writing in *The New Yorker* in 2016, talks about how "its representation of depravity may be unsurpassable."[3] Severe censorship afflicted the film; it was rejected by the BBFC in 1976 on the legal basis of gross indecency. (The definition in British law: "[A]nything which an ordinary decent man or woman would find to be shocking, disgusting and revolting," or which "offended against recognised standards of propriety."[4]) That is to say, at the time, any artistic merit or thematic relevance could not be legitimized or taken into serious consideration due to the extreme content of the film.

The critical reception to *Salò* has equally positioned the extremity of the film in a troubling and controversial space with many contemporary critics lambasting the "disgusting on screen debauchery."[5] *Time Out* called it "undeniably a thoroughly objectionable piece of work … very hard to sit through…. Nasty stuff," while BBC.com dismissed Pasolini's project as "[g]rim and pointless in equal measure."[6] Another significant indicator of its incendiary nature is its relational positioning against hardcore horror in the Internet's numerous "Most Extreme Films of All Time" sites. Hardcore horror examples such as *August Underground* and *Slaughtered Vomit Dolls* are not found at or near the top of these lists, but *Salò* often is. Both Horror News and Truly Disgusting put it in second place (behind the Japanese *Guinea Pig* films and *A Serbian Film* respectively) and forthrightly announced that it cannot be watched "without the expected kneading in your stomach brought on by pure disgust…"[7] "[It] will test your limits and challenge you in ways you would've never thought you could be challenged by a film."[8] *Salò* pushes at the threshold of acceptable filmic representations and not surprisingly engendered a vehement response in audience members, most of whom were scathing in their reactions.

Despite the strong negative feelings surrounding the film, there has been a gradual move of its socio-cultural position toward a center of legitimacy and quality highlighting a conflicted trait at the heart of the discourse. For example, Salò remained prohibited in the UK until 2000 when the implementation of new guidelines allowed the film an 18 certificate. In light of the new parameters which redefined the regulatory boundaries and thresholds of extreme cinema, the BBFC now "considered that although the film was undeniably—and intentionally—shocking, it did not contain anything that would 'deprave and corrupt' viewers."[9] The BBFC reclassification of the film from a legislative and social angle acted as one of the first cultural re-evaluations of the film which now began to emphasize Salò as an "essential work"[10] due to its newfound thematic importance of speaking to the authoritarian abuses of twentieth-century history. Filmmakers such as Michael Haneke, Catherine Breillat and John Waters, who saw Salò as a "beautiful film" in how "it uses obscenity in an intelligent way,"[11] have all since championed the film, while Criterion and the BFI have released high-end Blu-ray editions complete with academic essays and filmmaker testimonies. Despite the move toward a cultural sanctioning and acceptable status, the film *still* provides a challenge to conventional representations *and* existing markers of extreme film. Therefore, Salò's affective charge and unsettling viewing position can offer a crucial insight into what is an essential criterion of hardcore horror.

Pasolini's film begins near the Northern Italian town of Marzabota before moving toward Salò. The region where the director sets his film was a place of terrible violence and atrocities, including the extermination of an entire village, by Mussolini's Fascist Party toward the end of World War II. In this respect, the film explicitly chimes with the "particular historical phenomenon of Nazism-Fascism"[12] associated with the war. Yet Pasolini's Salò is also a symbolic location in which four male Fascists govern a retreat and "whose occupations link them with the foundations of society: a magistrate, a bishop, a duke and a banker."[13] From this position of privilege and authority, they organize a sadistic and sexually transgressive revelry of their most base and perverse desires. Furthermore, the idea of the retreat and the actions that proceed to unfold between the four fascists and the young male and female victims is taken from the Marquis de Sade's *120 Days of Sodom* and is structured in a circular form reminiscent of Dante's *Inferno*. With these differing literary and historical antecedents, Pasolini creates an incredibly bleak treatment of the deindividuation and dehumanization of the innocent through the power dynamics of the exploiter and the exploited. At once it is an annihilative denunciation of fascism, an apocalyptic view of modernity riven by rampant consumerism and bourgeois mentality, and a severe indictment on spectatorship and scopophilic pleasure. However, in taking the film, in Pasolini's words, "so far beyond the limits"[14] experienced by critics and film viewers previously (certainly with regards to Pasolini's existing body of work), the despairing thematic content is exacerbated by a Brechtian formal aesthetic and a contradictory arrangement of representational and allegorical strategies. The former provides a cold, alienating distance between the viewer and the events on the screen which problematizes the boundary between the real and mimesis. The authentic and drawn-out horrors on display in the fascist's sadomasochistic torture of the young, barely adult victims take on the countenance of the decidedly unnatural and the unreal while the latter constructed an uneasy "parallel between the imaginary sadism of the libertines and the all-too-real phenomenon of Italian Fascism."[15] Both approaches produce an ambiguous spectatorship and one which works to implement the viewer in the unfolding atrocities and to align them with the actions of the fascists so that the film takes on an unsettling, even horrific countenance.

Salò articulates the ambiguity at the heart of the narrative by providing repetitious shots of the picturesque natural world of outside before gradually moving to the meticulously organized and choreographed inside of the retreat. The verdant images of bucolic rivers and medieval villages give way to a highly constructed interior arrangement that destabilizes viewer positioning on how to interpret the film as either realism or allegory. For example, the lyrical shots of nature are soon displaced by violence as armed soldiers capture young male and female peasants and transport them to the retreat. There exists an ominous dread as the diegetic action links to actual events at the nearby Marzabotto where resistance to the Fascist Party resulted in the execution in 1944 of hundreds of civilians from the town. The sequence produces a poetic realism in alignment with the larger canvas of Italian neorealism in attempting to harness the reality of people living under the power structures of fascism. Yet, when the captured youths enter the retreat, the formal architecture of the building and the actions of the fascists become almost aggressively exact and precise to seem unreal or even uncanny. The film takes on an "abstract lifelessness" as "dark and sombre colors (…); icy tile floors with geometrical patterns; and mathematical combinations—sixteen victims (eight female, eight male), four libertines, four middle-aged women"[16] serve to create and extenuate the formal precision and calculated sense of space and arrangement. It is an interior closed off from the world in which exists no sense of life or spontaneity and no hope or escape for the victims. The formal properties thus suggest a Brechtian distancing from the proceedings. However, the fascists' acting out of the sexual practices and perversions to the young men and women leads to their descent into a "spiral of horrors"[17] of mania, shit and blood. In these increasingly repulsive cycles,

Top and bottom: **The authentic and the symbolic in *Salò* (Masters of Cinema).**

the violence enacted on them and their suffering is only too believable and authentic. In this respect, *Salò* captures in stark focus the violence, torture and degradation where "every horrible detail is cherished and prolonged."[18]

Roland Barthes was perhaps the most prominent critic of *Salò*. He viewed its conflation of the real and the symbolic as being inadequate to deal with the immediacy of Fascism and its inherent danger and violence. According to Barthes, "Fascism *forces* us to think about it accurately, analytically, politically. The only thing that art can do … is *demonstrate* how it comes about, not *show* what it resembles."[19] However, the opposite applies to how the violence is presented to the viewer and the affective charge that is produced in its highly stylized and ritualized arrangement. The focus on the violence and degradation of the young men and women are not merely extended sequences of torture visited onto the physical (innocent) body: an obscene transgression going way beyond simple extremity. In fact, as Lisa Coulthard points out, "*Salò* is able to truly offend because its points of violation extend far beyond the corporeal violations that form its surface."[20] The obscene forms an ethical relation to the viewer; the actions of the fascists are not merely violent and extreme but also a transgressive critique of the corrupting nature of Fascism and its subjugation of self, morality, sexuality and society to its dehumanizing social order. The affective charge that the film provides engenders a viscerally engaged viewer who is also implicated ethically in the material. The notion of the active spectator is perhaps best seen in the climactic sequence where an alignment with the fascists occurs as they look through binoculars as the young men and women being tortured and killed in a courtyard below. Tongues are sliced off; eyes gouged out; nipples burned off, and men and women raped, beaten and hanged all the while as the fascists look on in a state of sexual arousal. The cries and anguish of the victims are not heard and only seen and once again the constructed nature of the *mise en scène* provides a vivid unreality. Despite the perceived distancing effects deployed in this sequence, the ending provides such an affective force of horror because it goes beyond the carnage taking place in the courtyard to merge our gaze with that of the sadism of the fascist. It coerces our gaze with theirs but also to the intricate and complex voyeuristic appeal of cinema and its representations of violence. In this regard, *Salò* "compels us to enter" into a "web of sadomasochism [that] makes the film so disturbing, perhaps unbearable."[21] As a result, the film points to the ethical dimension inherent in the construction and reception of hardcore horror. That is, the power of *Salò* is to make the viewer complicit in the atrocities by aligning their gaze with the actions of the torturers, abusers and murderers. It shows the alignment of extreme material with an active gaze and a moral response. Thus, *Salò* ultimately provides a point of entry into films like *August Underground* to address the controversy and contestation surrounding its extreme content: Does it merely spectacularize the violence or does it facilitate an "affective turn"[22] toward ethical engagement?

Cannibal Holocaust: *If This Is Real, What Else Might Be Real?*

Cannibal Holocaust similarly deploys narrative functions of the real and the unreal to provide an affective charge surrounding an emotional and ethical connection to the film. However, unlike *Salò*, which stages the violence in a distancing world of unreality to better connect with meta-cinematic issues and realities of Fascism, *Cannibal Holocaust* provides the two narrative strands of real/unreal to fracture an "epistemological ambiguity ... between documentary and fiction"[23] to make it "difficult for audiences to know where the authentic ends and the fiction begins."[24] In doing so, the film is established as a central source for contemporary horror, primarily found footage and hardcore horror as both subgenres "borrow from it in some way or contain behavioural aspects that mimic it, consciously or otherwise."[25] That is, from the formation of amateur aesthetic conventions to wide-reaching discussions over cinematic reflexivity and what constitutes realist horror, *Cannibal Holocaust* has coalesced over the years into one of the most influential and controversial examples of extreme cinema. Its legacy regarding the *August Underground* trilogy and how Vogel's films attempt to compromise the border between the real and the constructed to *Amateur Porn Star Killer* and its avid engagement with reflexive modes of watching violent material is undeniable.

The film starts with New York anthropological professor Harold Monroe attempting to locate a documentary crew that disappeared while filming indigenous cannibal tribes in the Amazon. Monroe discovers that the crew members have all been killed and brings back their discarded rolls of film to ascertain what has happened. While in New York, Monroe watches the footage before giving it to a television network. Both parties are dismayed at what they have seen which details horrific and abhorrent acts committed by the filmmakers, including numerous examples of them torturing animals, burning down villages and the murder and rape of the tribespeople. The film ends with the TV executives condemning the footage and pointedly stating that it should not be shown publicly and instead destroyed. Despite the film taking on the conventions of a "proper" film—two-thirds of the film is constructed in the style of classical Hollywood—the general reception has been noticeably hostile and critical since the 1980 release of the film. The majority of the response has centered, perhaps not surprisingly, on how the film puts forward the idea of "authentic" footage, most notably in the numerous scenes in which animals are killed and mutilated. *Cahiers du Cinéma* denounced the "abysmal construction"[26] of the film concerning how it hypocritically evokes moral indignation while supplying scenes of gratuitous violence and entertaining spectacle. Similarly, Ian Grey, writing in the *Baltimore City Paper*, furthered the thesis of a hypocritical/contradictory directorial stance in that the film was an "almost intolerably vomitus viewing experience"[27] due to how Deodato seemed to be reveling in the violence while also condemning an audience who would want to watch such a film. The combination of the real and the unreal also incurred severe social condemnation and it was withdrawn from release in Italy little more than a month after its release as courts took action over the animal killings in the film. In the UK, the film was banned and became an exemplar of the "Video Nasties" phenomenon of the 1980s. In 1981, the French magazine *Photo* published an article titled "Grand Guignol Cannibale," marking the film out as snuff in which people were murdered. Inadvertently, the magazine bestowed an infamous reputation on the film which was still being acted upon as late as 1993 when Trading Standards confiscated the film in the UK. The resulting press coverage replicated *Photo*'s headline-grabbing stance by claiming that its seizure was evidence that it was a genuine snuff film.

These legal issues and accusations signify how effective the film was in conflating the real with the constructed to produce an unsettling realist horror accompanied by a strong affective charge of horror and repulsion. The majority of responses to *Cannibal Holocaust* cited the inclusion of the categorically real animal killings and how these frequent fissures into the narrative of the film challenged any clear demarcation of boundaries between the real and mimesis. They also exacerbated the horrors on display preparing the viewer to "expect worse will follow" and in doing so "the potency of all subsequent acts of horror is exponentially increased."[28] The anticipation of experiencing a real death, even if that appeal is a "certain fantasy of 'really' seeing death"[29] produces an affective charge and emotional effect that re-inscribes the scene as horrific and as "dangerous," which relates back to the traumatic experience of engaging with the taboo of death as outlined by Kavka. Although readings of the animal cruelty as heightening the realness of the film are correct, there is a third strand, or third film, which makes a sudden yet significant incursion into the perceived "reality" of the narrative. It is the footage from a previous documentary shot by the filmmakers called "Last Road to Hell" and is often overlooked in accounts making sense of *Cannibal Holocaust*'s confusing of the real and the imaginary. This footage, while being rejected diegetically as false and manipulated, is in fact irrefutably real in its grainy, poorly shot material of atrocities committed in a civil war from an unnamed African country. "Last Road" is the "actual transgression"[30] of showing real death that the footage of the ill-fated documentary crew only pretends to be. The short film becomes a vital mechanism in showing the "unimaginable reality which *Cannibal Holocaust* (falsely) disguises itself as."[31] It is instrumental in not only how the film collapses the boundary between the real and the constructed but in how Deodato enables a horrific affective charge to permeate the film and make watching it such a potent and unsettling experience.

When Prof. Monroe returns to New York, a local TV channel interviews him and the unseen footage, now titled "The Green Inferno," is to be shown. At this point, neither the professor, the TV executives nor the audience has seen any material pertaining to the original documentary crew. What follows is a "behind-the-scenes" segment wherein the TV channel constructs the

Destabilizing the boundary between the real and the constructed (*Cannibal Holocaust*, Grindhouse Releasing).

footage ready to air. As a precursor to the anticipated footage of what happened to the filmmakers, the executives show "Last Road to Hell" as an example of their previous work. The footage starts on a viewfinder as we see an army firing squad execute a number of bound men and then switches to a full screen as numerous atrocities are seen. During this short sequence, the film cuts back to the three executives several times as they watch through the viewfinder, distraught by the authentic assemblage of real death presented to them. The documentary style of "Last Road" has an undeniable realism in its "understated tone and unsensational, undramatic depiction of fast, simple executions."[32] The footage, with its "amateur" style consisting of unfocused, blurred and poorly framed images and flickering, scratched film, clearly positions the footage as real as well as further reinforcing the conventions of cinematic-snuff and representations of real death brought into play by Alan Shackleton's gonzo, exploitation *bête noire*, *Snuff*. Yet, when "Last Road" is turned off, the audience learns that the footage is, in fact, a clever manipulation and that all the murder and violence we have seen was an elaborate contrivance initiated by the filmmakers with the help of the local army. Here Deodato skillfully, and almost subliminally, "inverts the viewer's perception"[33] and disrupts the boundary between the real and the constructed that becomes so important when the "Green Inferno" footage is eventually shown.

Immediately after "Last Road" is exposed as a "hoax," the remaining executives start to view "Green Inferno." We are introduced to the crew and presented with a diary-style video of their preparation for the trip alongside

Monroe's search for information about the mentality and psychological makeup of the team members from friends and relatives in New York. A sense of authenticity is established both from the footage of the crew preparing for their journey and in how the world of the filmmakers is extended by developing an authentic and believable social and family environment that exists away from their time in the Amazon. When the film returns to "The Green Inferno," the crew has begun their expedition and is surrounded by the environs of a rain forest. The images are overlaid by one of the executives talking about the unpolished, raw nature of the footage in that it is a "very rough cut, almost like watching rushes" and that most of the footage will be thrown out during editing. Initially, the footage is silent; when the sound starts, the dialogue is slightly out of sync. These first "Green Inferno" scenes are integral to how the film constitutes the verisimilitude of the footage, and the amateur quality exacerbates the realness and authenticity of what we are watching. After two minutes of this unrefined material, a turtle is pulled from a nearby river and horrifically killed and dismembered while the film captures, in stark detail, every repellent moment. It is both a repugnant scene and another that is "undeniably real" just as the atrocity footage of "Last Road" was. "The Green Inferno" is thus framed as ambiguous in terms of (cinematic) realism. The proximity of the real death shown in "Last Road" and the actual killing of a turtle obliterates any safe boundary between the real and the false. As Kerekes and Slater pointedly state regarding *Cannibal Holocaust*, the film muddies the waters of actual and constructed footage and thus "anaesthetises rational thought: If this is real, what else might be real?"[34]

Man Bites Dog: *Look, How Can You Accept This?*

Cannibal Holocaust provides a fundamental example which links to the formal considerations of hardcore horror. Deodato's approach developed the amateur aesthetics of Shackleton's *Snuff* coda toward a more sophisticated engagement with cinematic realism. The continued resonance of the film is how it breaks down the boundary between the real and the constructed to leave a powerful and disturbing horror experience. *Man Bites Dog* acts as another seminal historical antecedent to the formal and thematic strategies of hardcore horror and particularly the found footage aesthetic integrated into their representations of horror. In *Man Bites Dog*, the serial killer is followed around by a documentary film crew which both capitalizes on the doomed filmmakers of *Cannibal Holocaust* and anticipates the video diary format of the day-to-day life of a killer in *August Underground*. Thus, like Vogel's disturbing and horrific fusion of the banalities of everyday experience and the extreme and prolonged documentation of torture, *Man Bites Dog* portrays the violence and death as "being produced by and for the psychopathic serial killer, tending toward a pseudo-documentary style and engendering analysis of voyeurism and moral responsibility."[35] Indeed, the filmmakers sought explicitly to implicate audiences in the violent content in that it was their intention to "make the audience laugh, then have them think about what they've just laughed at. The whole point is to say to the viewer— Look, how can you accept this?"[36] Similar to Pasolini's use of allegory and the authentic to denounce Fascism alongside an indictment of the sadistic, voyeuristic gaze of cinema, so too do the *Man Bites Dog* filmmakers employ stylistic devices to implicate the viewer. Thus, the emphasis in the film concerning the viewer and their "complacency as media consumers in how violent imagery is produced and consumed"[37] is frequently articulated.

Man Bites Dog utilizes a number of jarring cuts (almost like the shock cuts engineered by the mondo filmmaker Gualtiero Jacopetti) to position the audience as complicit in the events depicted. For example, its beginning section takes a black comedy approach to the documentation of serial killer Ben and his often boorish and interminable ramblings on all manner of subjects as he casually and remorselessly kills. The tone changes at the halfway point as the filmmakers dare Ben to raid an affluent suburban home and to kill the family living inside. The sequence ends with Ben suffocating a young child while complaining that kids are "bad for business" as they are not bankable. The humor that has been foregrounded previously is downplayed through the subtheme of the corrupting and dehumanizing aspects of capitalism where Ben's victims are nothing more than potentially lucrative commodities. The tonal shifts later become more evident and abrupt; an especially effective scene has Ben and the documentary crew involved in a particularly heavy bout of drinking attendant with a raucous signing, elaborate drinking games and general bonhomie. While we follow Ben leaving the bar and stumbling down a cobbled street, we abruptly shift to a hostage scene in an apartment where Ben and the crew take turns in raping a woman. The laughter from the previous scene bleeds over to the next, providing an unquestionably disturbing affective charge as the viewer is confronted with a shocking and sickening scene of sexual violence. Here, the film has emphatically acted upon both *Salò* and *Cannibal Holocaust* in terms of "how to most effectively merge ambiguity and authenticity."[38] The reflective nature of the film and the *vérité* style of the violence at once draws the viewer in, provides an affective and immersive engagement, and engenders wider questions about why we watch violent material. All of these attributes of *Man Bites Dog* will resurface with regards to hardcore horror and whether films containing their levels of violence and extremity can navigate the terrain of affective spectacle and ethical engagement to a positive degree.

Japanese Extreme Cinema

Japanese horror in the last 20 years has emerged as "international cinema's most compelling and marketable commodity"[39] due to its innovative audio-visual properties, resonant thematic and narratological characteristics, and clear cross-cultural appeal in its motifs and traditions. By focusing only on *Ringu* (Hideo Nakata, 1998) and *Ju-on: The Grudge* (Takashi Shimizu, 2002), we can see how influential they have been on Western horror. For example, in terms of U.S. remakes, the Shimizu-directed *The Grudge* (2004) grossed over $100 million at the box office, *The Ring* (Gore Verbinski, 2002) grossed close to $250 million, there have been a number of sequels (*The Ring Two* [Hideo Nakata, 2005] and *Rings* [F. Javier Gutiérrez, 2017]) and the formal and thematic properties have influenced other horror productions. The latter have informed numerous Japanese horror remakes and U.S. productions such as Blumhouse that specializes in atmospheric and suspenseful supernatural horror.[40] Aside from the more mainstream practices of Japanese horror and the diverse and complex ways it has interacted with, influenced and been influenced by Western horror, there has also existed a historical strand privileging extreme material and which also demonstrates an intricate nature of cross-cultural flow between Japan and the West. An exemplar of the transnational movement of horror is the notorious *Guinea Pig* series which came to prominence in the West due to their reception as possible snuff films. A brief account will present how the films utilized an approach to the real and the constructed found in the extreme cinema of films like *Cannibal Holocaust* and *Salò* and how, in turn, the realist horrors of the *Guinea Pig* films influenced various production elements of hardcore horror.

Guinea Pig: Genuine Snuff?

The most famous of all anecdotes surrounding extreme cinema derives from the *Guinea Pig* films. In 1991, Charlie Sheen watched a video cassette of unknown provenance (other than it was Japanese in origin) that detailed appalling violence toward a kidnapped young woman by a Japanese man dressed in Samurai headwear. Sheen believed it was a genuine snuff movie and contacted the authorities. The ridicule Sheen has been afforded over his misguided attempt to uncover a network of snuff filmmakers centers on his supposed gullibility in treating the footage as real while it is clearly of a highly constructed nature. However, the event has to be contextualized at the time in which Sheen watched the video cassette rather than years later with hindsight and the availability of pristine copies of the film replete with English subtitles. When Sheen watched the tape, the film in question was the second entry, *Flower of Flesh and Blood* (Hideshi Hino, 1985), and was part of a gore mix-tape that was being clandestinely copied and shown throughout the East Coast of the U.S. The tape was eventually traced back to Chas Balun, the writer-publisher of *Deep Red* magazine, who had compiled the tape for a friend requesting "the most disgusting"[41] video Balun could source. Therefore, Sheen would have watched the film as part of a compilation where the removal of the credits and omission of any subtitles would have been in place. Also, the quality of the tape would have been "invariably poor and by extension more 'dangerous'"[42] due to the number of reproductions made by the time Sheen watched the footage. Viewing the film today, it is obviously not "real," and it is not possible to align the readily available, untainted DVD versions with "the shock of the grubby videotape bearing a handwritten scrawl of a label."[43] But for Sheen, and undoubtedly others, it would have been a troubling experience where the shock of the real became all too apparent.

The controversy generated by the videotapes containing *Flower of Flesh and Blood* provides the first instance to how the film series has impacted upon and influenced 21st-century hardcore horror. Fred Vogel's attempt to make a pseudo-snuff film that would convince people they were watching "the real thing" was most successfully realized with *August Underground*. The content fulfills the aesthetic of the tape Sheen would have watched with its grainy, washed-out and barely legible footage redolent of an illicit third- or fourth-generation copy. Vogel pushes the material of *August Underground* further than any other hardcore horror filmmaker, but he must have been aware of the restrictions posed by industrial, social and cultural practices of watching hardcore or extreme horror in the contemporary period: namely, that one is watching it on a video cassette or DVD that has been bought or rented and thus "legitimized." Vogel's original intention was, therefore, to release the film outside of these regulatory forms by leaving the film in public areas for unsuspecting passersby to pick up, take home and watch. Here is a direct link, and a clear line of influence, to the unauthorized distribution patterns of the *Guinea Pig* films in the early 1990s to the incendiary attempts from Vogel to replicate an illicit, unofficial and "dangerous" cultural artifact. The context in which *August Underground* was intended to be viewed would have, similar to *Flower of Flesh and Blood*, further ruptured the boundary between the representation and the real achieved by the verisimilitude of the footage.

The *Guinea Pig* films may have pushed the "portrayal of violence and gore to new extremes,"[44] but they cannot seriously be read as snuff or solely as a meditation on cinematic representations of real death. The films, particularly the two initial installments *Devil's Experiment* (Saturo Ogura, 1985) and *Flower of Flesh and Blood*, combine a realist style with distantiating effects in the manner of *Salò*, *Cannibal Holocaust* and *Man Bites Dog*. For Jay McRoy,

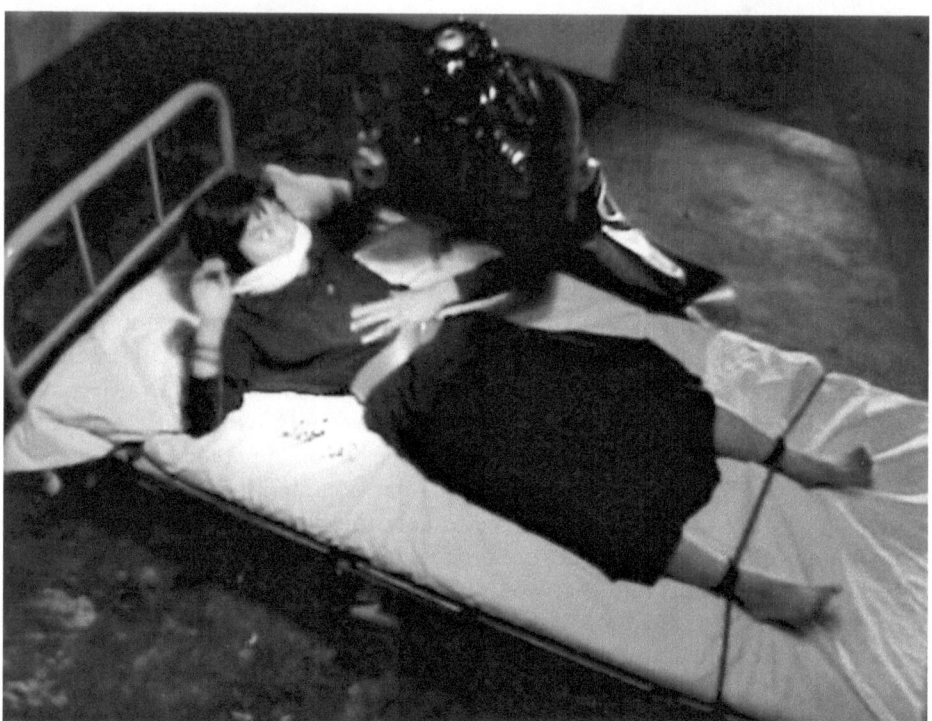

Japanese extremity in *Flower of Flesh and Blood* (Unearthed Films). Shown here are the Victim (Kirara Yûgao) and the Samurai (Hideshi Hino).

the films do test the limits of corporeal horror with graphic content surrounding the mutilation and destruction of the body, but they also address narratological and socio-political concerns. For example, the body horror on display and the male-initiated violence visited on the female body "explores profound cultural anxieties surrounding gender- and class-based transformations in Japan's socio-cultural climate"[45] post–World War II through the "economic miracle" of the 1950s-1960s-1970s and up to the last years of the successful "bubble" economy of the 1980s. McRoy says that the films "reveal a paradoxical tension within postmodern Japanese culture, namely the struggle to construct and maintain an imagined homogenous cultural identity within an increasingly transformative and 'heterogeneous present.'"[46] *Devil's Experiment* and *Flower of Flesh and Blood* are explicit in that they are reconstructions of "real" events and use an array of experimental audio and visual techniques to alienate the viewer. In doing so, they "impact radically [on] the way viewers understand the artistic creations they encounter"[47] so that an alignment across issues such as the tension between tradition and modernity, fractured national identity and a general treatise on the "complex study of [patriarchal] power"[48] can be formed. The combination of realist horror and distancing effects connects once again with previous discussions of extreme cinema and provides a more comprehensive reading of the films other than merely containing shocking and controversial imagery. Hardcore horror has positioned at its center the notion of realism and it will be important to adjudge whether it engages in realist horror in the ways *Salò, Cannibal Holocaust* and *Devil's Experiment* do, or if its focus on realism "typically showcases the spectacular nature of monstrous violence"[49] and empties out thematic content.

Alongside the *Guinea Pig* films, Japan has produced many more examples of extreme horror cinema. Body horror has been picked up and continued in the films of Satô Hisayasu, including *Lolita Vibrator Torture* (1987) and *Naked Blood* (1995). The former film continues the graphic and extreme content found in the first two installments of the *Guinea Pig* series in that the narrative concentrates on the almost ritualistic abuse and torture meted out to a variety of schoolgirls. Both films play with the theme of social disease mapped onto the terrain of the physical and social body and concomitant anxieties circulating pre- and post- the collapse of the "bubble" economy in the early 1990s. Satô's films of this period also take in influences from cyberpunk and can be seen as indicative of a larger film movement during this time, including Shinya Tsukamoto's seminal *Tetsuo* (1989) and Shozin Fukui's delirious *Rubber's Lover* (1995). Both films articulate anxieties over technology and changing gender roles in Japan during the 1990s through an apocalyptic treatment of the transformation of Japanese society in the age of late capitalism. Picking up on the end-of-days imagery posited in Japanese cyberpunk are a series of horror films looking at alienation and displacement within youth culture. In Matsumura Katsuya's *All Night Long* (1992–1996) series, Katsuya puts forward a dark, brutal and controversial examination of the changing landscape of Japan in the 1990s and the destructive consequences for the young forced into brutal social conditions. Each series entry uses extreme content, *à la* the *Guinea Pig* series, "as a component of a larger paradigmatic cycle of violence and suffering permeating contemporary Japanese culture."[50]

All Night Long's commitment to graphic imagery can also be seen in the gore-soaked, reflexive treatment of screen violence of Takeshi Miike's *Ichi the Killer* (2001) and Daisuke Yamanouchi's notorious commentary on the rampant excesses of Japan as a capitalist, commodity-driven culture, *Red Room* (1999).

Guinea Pig *Redux: Grotesque Cinema*

Japanese extremity in film follows an almost undisturbed trajectory from the *Guinea Pig* films to the present day. Examples range from the mainstream such as Sion Sono's wildly over-the-top and frenetically violent commentary on Japanese cinema, *Why Don't You Play in Hell* (2013), and the independent production *Destruction Babies* (Tetsuya Mariko, 2016), which was dubbed "the most extreme 108 minutes in the history of Japanese cinema,"[51] to more niche and underground markets exemplified by the continuing production of death films (*Death Women: Josei Shintai Shuu*, Bakushishi Yamashita, 1994) and the scat porn of V&R Planning.[52]

One important transnational example that emerges from this vast range and heterogeneous assemblage of extreme film, *Grotesque* (Kôji Shiraishi, 2009) acts as a kind of bookend to this brief section on Japanese cinema: It resembles both the formal arrangement and thematic concerns of the *Guinea Pig* series and highlights the continued interest the collection of films have for an international audience. Moreover, and with greater specificity to this study, *Grotesque's* transgressive content resonates with the regulatory and social policing of extreme film of which the films of hardcore horror have routinely tested.

Grotesque is a product of the violent heritage and contemporary interest in the cinematic violence within Japanese cinema. The producer's clear intent was for the director to "make something horribly violent, so violent that it almost can't be shown"[53] in order for the film to be of interest to audiences engaging with contemporary violent cinema from acclaimed filmmakers such as Sono, Miike, Yoshihiro Nishimura and Noburo Iguchi. The film also reverts to the aesthetic of *Devil's Experiment* and *Flower of Flesh and Blood* in its narrative of a lone killer who abducts, tortures and murders a young couple. Similarly, *Grotesque* eschews narrative and character development as it consists primarily of various degrading and intense scenes of torture, sexual violence and eventual murder within the claustrophobic confines of the killer's habitus. The film's formal and thematic strategies are important to consider with regards to hardcore horror as the lack of context provided in the film; the bleak, nihilistic denouement; the extended sequences of sexual violence, and the graphic scenes of violence are all present within the films under discussion in this book. Thus, the components inherent to the DNA of *Grotesque* connect with existing examples of extreme cinema such as *Cannibal Holocaust* and act to reinforce the working definition of hardcore horror as outlined in Chapter One. The film also points to the unpalatable and repulsive nature of hardcore horror which often demarcates *August Underground* as a "malignant" artifact. The BBFC rejected *Grotesque* and called it "markedly different to the *Saw* and *Hostel* 'torture porn' series, in that those films contain a more developed narrative and there is, therefore, more contextual justification for the strongest scenes."[54] Here the lack of context provides an affective charge to the violent acts that likely "endorses and eroticises sexual violence,"[55] particularly concerning the film's most controversial moment where the killer degradingly masturbates both victims. The film becomes unanchored to a rationale or justification for the violence coupled with limited insight into both the killer's motivation and the characters of the young couple. In turn, the negative responses to films like *August Underground* have centered upon the lack of narrative convention and the removal of barriers toward the horror often put in place through elements such as character psychologies. The films become "irresponsible" in their depictions of horror that make viewer exposure more threatening and "dangerous" in that they may be seen as promoting sadistic engagements with violence or eroticizing sexual violence. In the case of *Grotesque*, and going back to the *Guinea Pig* films, it highlights the connections Japanese extreme film has with 21st-century North American hardcore horror and how it is a necessary antecedent as well as an illuminating contemporary affiliate.

The Trauma of German History and Extreme Filmmaking

Similar to Japan, Germany has made a number of significant contributions to (extreme) horror cinema. Primarily, films such as *The Cabinet of Dr. Caligari* (Robert Wiene, 1920), *Nosferatu* (F.W. Murnau, 1922) and *Vampyr* (Carl Dreyer, 1932) provided a legacy and definition for much of the horror that followed, especially in Hollywood and studios such as Universal. The horrors of World War II and the Holocaust rendered German production of horror almost obsolete in the face of atrocities committed by the Nazis and post–World War II horror suffered increasing under-investment and issues of artistic compromise engendered by the restrictive budgets. However, during the mid- to late 1980s and with the "horror film entirely disappearing from the German mainstream by the 1970s"[56] a resurgence of the genre was beginning to take hold as filmmakers rallied against the draconian censorship laws and the traumatic socio-political events leading up to the fall of the Berlin Wall in 1989. Although sharing a number of thematic elements with the previous cinematic movements of the Young German Cinema of the 1960s and the New German Cinema of the 1970s, filmmakers such as Jörg Buttergereit, Andreas Schnaas and Olaf Ittenbach transferred the focus of the family, the past and alienated (self-) identity toward an extremely violent visual tableaux within the contours of a transgressive horror film. Buttgereit's *Nekromantik* and *Nekromantik 2* (1991) stand as the two most notorious titles from this fertile period in German horror and provide further examples of (global) extreme cinema and the production practices, reception and thematic and aesthetic arrangement evident in the 21st-century permutations of North American hardcore horror.

Nekromantik and *Nekromantik 2*, with their focus on an alienated youth and their necrophilic activities, challenge the visual taboo of death and the corpse by featuring extended and graphic sexual liaisons between the young characters and a number of decomposing bodies. The films address both the "ultimate secret"[57] of death and the abject presence of the corpse in ways which produce a "profound anxiety"[58] (not to mention repulsion and disgust) in how it disturbs the boundaries and patterns of normal life and the disavowal of the materiality of the body. Yet Buttgereit pointed out that "shocking people for the sake of shock never was, and never is, our intention.... [W]e try to go for impact by way of context."[59] Indeed, the film deals in a melancholic and poetic way with the loneliness and romantic longing of a disaffected German youth which underlines a concerted engagement with German national and self-identity post–World War II. Blake reinforces Buttgereit's position when she says that the two films contain a "thematically complex and technically sophisticated"[60] arrangement in dealing with Germany's traumatic past. For Blake, the filmmakers' task "is to bring the past into the present"[61] to enable "a new form of historically and politically engaged looking at the past as a means of healing."[62] The trauma of National Socialism is thus brought to the surface through the mechanism of extreme horror commingled with a serious treatment of historical and political contingencies. In this respect, the two films tap into and continue other exemplary models of extreme cinema, such as *Salò*, which combines the shocking and unsettling with a socio-political critique.

According to Blake, the reason the *Nekromantik* films were received so negatively is the radical and uncompromising way Buttgereit deals with the traumatic past and connects it to a Germany in the "politically divided and culturally confused present."[63] While this is certainly part of the controversy surrounding the release of the two films, it does tend to downplay the content which *is* shocking in its abject positioning of the corpse and exploration of necrophilia. For Barbara Creed, the "ultimate in abjection is the corpse"[64] due to how it breaks down the boundary between the self and the other. Julia Kristeva calls the corpse "the most sickening of wastes" and explicitly "*show*[s] *me* what I permanently thrust aside in order to live."[65] Therefore, the visual taboo of the dead body undoubtedly acts as a transgressive vision and powerful affective charge. In the *Nekromantik* films, this is exacerbated through the act of sex and provides a troubling and subversive viewing position which now codes traditional notions of attraction and arousal as repulsive. Both existing moral codes and the manipulative nature of cinema in how representations of sex (and pornography) normally function are challenged.

However, the *Nekromantik* films go a step further in also confronting audiences over "their own enjoyment of horrific imagery."[66] It is perhaps no surprise to hear commentators discuss the "physical assault" of the films and how, in particular, watching *Nekromantik* was the "equivalent of clubbing oneself about the head for 75 minutes."⁶⁷ Thus, the affective charge of the films is perhaps the most significant element carrying forward to hardcore horror and once again reiterates how the affect of extreme horror is an essential component.

The complication of viewing positions through the strong horror codes and commingling of sex and death in an aberrant fashion in the *Nekromantik* films also provided a "dangerous" entity for legislative bodies and exhibition networks. The no-budget financing of the films immediately attests to an outsider filmmaking practice and one not legitimized through the use of studios and more structured financial systems. The do-it-yourself aspect continued in their bypassing of the government procedures for submitting and realizing films. Similar to the 1980s in Britain, German film censorship was very stringent in what was an austere political climate with film legislation making it illegal to rent hardcore pornography and banning or heavily cutting many horror films. Buttgereit took the decision not to submit *Nekromantik* to the FSK (Freiwillige Selbst Kontrolle—the Voluntary Self Control) who deal with the rating of motion pictures and instead took the film out directly into theaters. He was faced with potential lawsuits for doing so and often met with hostile theater owners and violent revolutionary groups, but the film became an underground success. *Nekromantik 2*'s release post-reunification faced even tougher censorship restrictions as it became a "seized video" whereby it "could neither be owned, watched or shown legally in Germany and orders were given ... for its negatives, production-related and publicity materials to be destroyed."⁶⁸ The ensuing notoriety made Buttgereit Germany's "most wanted filmmaker"⁶⁹ fearful of police raids and confiscation of his films. *Nekromantik 2* was eventually taken to court and prosecuted for "glorifying violence."⁷⁰ In preparation for the court case, media scholar Dr. Knut Hickethier submitted a lengthy defense in which he sought to convey the artistic merits of the film. The article was chiefly responsible for overturning the original decision. What is noteworthy about the defense is how Hickethier marks the film as "fictional" and how "it is made clear to the audience from the start that here is a genre-developed world."⁷¹

Hickethier is correct to point out *Nekromantik 2*'s constructed nature; neither film can be seen as an example of realist horror which attempt to break down the boundary between the real and mimesis. In this way, they follow films such as *Salò*, *Cannibal Holocaust* and *Man Bites Dog* in how they use extreme material but connect the content to symbolic and allegorical codes to engage in political themes and critiques of the cinematic apparatus. Buttgereit's films follow in this vein, but also bring to the fore the affective charge of extreme cinema and the often unconventional production and distribution practices.

Other horror films which emerged in this period eschewed any overtly political or cinematic commentary in favor of a more resolute non-realist horror featuring excessive and extremely bloody scenes of violence. Andreas Schnaas' *Violent Shit* (1989) is a low-budget showcase of various gory tableaux tangentially connected to a masked killer called Karl the Butcher. In this respect, the film plays out like the compilation death tapes prevalent during the 1980s as each scene shows various unconnected people suffering ever increasingly imaginative and violent deaths at Karl's hands. The film positions the violence as an entertaining spectacle, and despite the extremity of some scenes, *Violent Shit* reduces the affective charge, and hence realist coda, in favor of a puerile, crude and over-the-top concoction of arterial spray, dismembered limbs and eyeball-gouging. Schnaas went on to direct several more *Violent Shit* films and along with other contemporaneous films such as Olaf Ittenbach's *The Burning Moon* (1997) reinforced the growing focus on gore rather than realist or allegorical horror in German cinema. Ittenbach's treatment of the horror genre is very similar to Schnaas as evidenced by the low-budget production, exaggerated performances and an overwhelming cascade of blood and dismembered body parts. In the climactic scene, and the most notorious in the film, a character is sent to Hell and their body subjected to horrific torture as eyeballs are gouged out, teeth drilled through and limbs ripped apart.

The body is fundamental to Schnaas' films, and Ittenbach's *The Burning Moon* (as it is in the films of Buttgereit), and of course is one of the central organizational elements in the films of hardcore horror. Yet the development of an irreverent tone, which acts as a suitable framing device for the excesses of gore, suggests early Peter Jackson films and the splatterpunk of Brian Yuzna than it does as a precursor or global relative of films like *August Underground*. More recently the critic-baiting *Human Centipede* films (Tom Six, 2009–2015) have used distorted and deformed arrangements of bodies to produce a spectacle of discomfort and offense. Although the films, especially 2011's *The Human Centipede II (Full Sequence)*, have been banned or heavily cut in certain territories, the taboo potential has been diluted via a parodic and camp treatment within popular culture and through the final film which privileges a fantastical and absurd treatment of horror.

This is not to say that German cinema has relinquished its hold on transgressive imagery established by Buttgereit. Marian Dora is a 21st-century filmmaker who can be seen as much more indicative of contemporary extreme cinema in that he has simultaneously moved back toward the extreme realm of Buttgereit while highlighting that the form and tone of hardcore horror are traceable across other national contexts. Through films such as *Cannibal* (2006), *The Angels' Melancholia* and *Carcinoma* (2014), Dora combines an extreme realist horror with a poetic and often beautiful *mise en scène.* At the heart of these films is an exploration of the "realness"[72] of the body which is usually represented under great duress and suffering. For example, in *Cannibal*, Dora adapts the true crime of the notorious "Rotenberg Cannibal" Armin Meiwes who was sentenced to eight and a half years for the mutilation, killing and eating of a willing man he met through the Internet. Dora's film does not look at the far-reaching socio-political ramifications of the case and instead focuses on the psychology of the two characters before rendering the taboo of cannibalism in explicit and horrific detail. The film begins with an extended look at disaffected and alienated male identity and thus joins up with the contours of Buttgereit's meditations on loneliness and unfulfilled sexual longing. The second part shows the almost ritualistic desacralization of the body as the Meiwes character systematically violates bodily boundaries in his preparation of a final, grand cannibalistic feast. The ending, and the extremity in which the body is treated resonates with North American horror through the traumatized body as spectacle recurrent in the *Saw* movies and "torture porn" to the realist positioning of the violated body in hardcore horror. *Cannibal* thus attempts to marry the psychological motivations of the two characters with extreme violence and the transgressive behavior of cannibalism. The squalid interiors, fetid atmosphere, graphic sex and the protracted, intense violence of *Cannibal* does provide a powerful, and at times horrific, affective charge. The authentic performances and convincing special effects work frames the intense experiential charge, yet the film presents a constructed (re)presentation of a "real" event. The majority of the running time is dedicated to an exploration of aberrant human behavior rather than exploitative and sensationalized violence. Therefore the film reduces the "shock for shock's sake" reminiscent of Buttgereit's opinion over *Nekromantik* and as a result presents its narrative more as a fictional retelling than found footage or realist horror.

Dora continues the almost beautification of the horrific in his next film *The Angels' Melancholia*. Considered by many "the most notorious, undeniably hardcore German release to date,"[73] it presents a nightmarish landscape of an almost *Salò*-Sadean quality. The narrative focuses on a group of people residing in a dilapidated rural house who engage in a continuous cycle of depraved and extreme acts covering coprophilia, urolagnia, genital mutilation, animal cruelty and sexual violence. The film continues Dora's preoccupation with body horror and the abjection residing where the "I" becomes the "Other" and where the inside becomes the outside of the body. A place where life becomes death and according to Kristeva for "a terror that dissembles" and which in turn "disturbs identity, system, order."[74] *The Angels' Melancholia* goes on to suggest that at this point of abjection a purification of a traumatized mind (and identity) through bodily self-sacrifice can occur and is connected in the film to a meticulously constructed allegorical reading of

German identity in the 21st century. Here Dora once again connects back to the *Nekromantik* films in continuing a key theme incorporated in both: "Die unbewaltigte Vergangenheit—the past that has not been adequately dealt with."[75] Various references to the German past from filmmaker Rainer Werner Fassbinder, controversial author Wolfgang Koeppen, Red Army Faction members and hostile denouncements of National Socialism populate the film and are given a horrific countenance due to the "improper" and obscene nature of the film's extremity. Finally, the film features numerous instances of animal killings and which resumes a predilection of extreme cinema discussed previously in *Cannibal Holocaust* but also contained in *Nekromantik*, which features the skinning of a rabbit. Buttergeit sees the inclusion of the rabbit-killing sequence as necessary to the emotional charge of the film so "that people are positive it is not faked—that it isn't fun any more."[76] Twenty years later and Dora provides an almost identical rationale for the inclusion of real animal killings in *The Angels' Melancholia*. Among the numerous reasons put forward the main two were a question of verisimilitude in that "the closer you come to reality, the [more] intense pictures will be" and of an apparent need for a "declaration that the film you are watching is not made for entertainment."[77]

A Serbian Film: *The Nastiest Film Ever Made?*

Both Dora and Buttgereit highlight the importance of undermining the boundary between the real and representation in their films. Furthermore, the realist horror that emerges connects to an unsettling affective engagement which engenders a displeasure in the viewing experience. The outcome is that the films, and especially Dora's, are supposed to be experienced as uncomfortable even to the point of causing outright disgust at what is being screened. Thus, the position both filmmakers adhere to with regards to authentic and extreme horror links to a number of essential criteria for hardcore horror. Namely, in forwarding a convincing authenticity to the horror and of producing an affective charge which induces terror, horror and revulsion within the viewer.

The final example to be considered along the contours of extreme global horror is arguably the most notorious of all contemporary cinema and has been condemned, banned or censored in many provinces with some film labs even destroying prints of the film. In this context, Srdjan Spasojevic's *A Serbian Film* takes on a "decidedly threatening cadence"[78] in how its "confrontational use of explicit imagery related to pornography, bloody violence and snuff"[79] facilitates a "metaphorical re-enactment of the horrors of the 1990s Balkans conflict."[80] *A Serbian Film* lives up to the hype over the nature of its extreme content as the filmmakers purposefully set out to be "deliberately transgressive."[81] Scenes from the film include the violent suffocation of a woman while forced to fellate a masked torturer, a woman decapitated by her rapist, a man killed by having an erect penis thrust into his eye and, perhaps the most extreme and shocking of the entire film, the rape of a newborn baby. The outcome was that *A Serbian Film* engendered a caustic and adverse reaction which included general audiences and film critics through to regulatory and legal organizations. Thus, *A Serbian Film* converges on the discursive modal points of transgressive material linked to filmic content, production practices, exhibition and reception. As such, the "archaeological" foundation posited by the film supplies another relevant and incisive access point into the trajectories of extreme content found within hardcore horror.

A Serbian Film tracks the decline and descent into the hellish underworld of snuff filmmaking by a retired porn actor who is tempted into making one final film by a mysterious producer. The film aggressively tests multiple boundaries with regards to cinematic content, regulatory and legal frameworks, and taste cultures with its explicit and transgressive representations of sex, violence and sexual violence. In turn, it deploys its shocking and taboo material to cast a sensory-overloaded eye on the "catastrophic nature of Serbian society in the [Slobodan] Milosevic era."[82] The configuration of sociopolitical concerns with a transgressive content to enable an allegorical treatment of the recent Serbian past has been met with ambivalence rather than being accepted as a 'legitimizing' framework for the visual atrocities thrown up by the film. One of the reasons for the general reluctance to see past the extreme content is that the more outré sequences definitely and defiantly put forward a "fictional grotesque that oversteps common sensibility."[83] Initial responses established a wholesale rejection of the film as providing any worthwhile and insightful socio-political commentary due to the nihilistic onslaught of atrocity images on display. A.O. Scott, writing in *The New York Times*, situates the extremity of the film as a device to offer up a "corrosive social criticism" but that its aim might be obfuscated due to the "sheer inventive awfulness"[84] of the material. Scott explicitly cites the inclusion of shocking imagery of necrophilia and pedophilia as the cause of redirecting audience attention toward surface content in favor of attaining any deeper reading of the film. Mark Kermode, reviewing the film as part of the Simon Mayo BBC Radio1 show, goes further than Scott and dismisses the allegorical intention of the film in that it "gets lost amidst the increasingly stupid splatter."[85] For Kermode, the film follows the "mold of Buttgereit and Deodato" with regards to the thesis of realist horror and the use of shocking imagery but is now accompanied with a "silly and incidental" treatment of its subject matter which ultimately produces a "nasty piece of exploitation trash."[86]

Shaun Kimber has talked about how controversial films which push "at the very edges of cinematic acceptability"[87] can provide useful test studies with regards to the cultural and social thresholds of contemporary horror films. *A Serbian Film*, through its taboo and transgressive material, has "genuinely tested, infringed and also reinforced a gamut of social, cultural, political and aesthetic boundaries."[88] For critics, the extreme content of the film breached the limits of acceptability and resulted in many of them denouncing the material as nasty or awful. In turn, their repudiation of the transgressive material invalidated any socio-political commentary contained in the work which they saw as completely sublimated to the transgressive spectacle. Despite the protestations from Spasojevic, who continually asserted that *A Serbian Film* was a "literal metaphor about how violated we feel as a nation, how abused we have been by our own government,"[89] the majority considered the film to be of poor quality and to feature "illegitimate" content. As the film moved from the taste cultures of critics to the regulatory and legal frameworks of film classification bodies, *A Serbian Film* again provided a clear example of how transgressive material can confront official standards and the effective policing of their borders. A number of countries including Australia, Spain and its home country Serbia banned it outright. Here, the transgression openly contravenes what is tolerable within national standards of acceptability. In this respect, the UK offers an important variation on the policing of national regulatory frameworks and the monitoring of its effect on the British public. After viewing *A Serbian Film*, the BBFC called for 49 cuts to over 11 scenes and totaling just over four minutes of excised footage. The main issue were the "scenes of sexual and sexualised violence and scenes juxtaposing images of sex and sexual violence with images of children"[90] and how they impinge on the Board's guidelines and classification policies. However, in this instance and unlike other examples such as *The Bunny Game*, *Hate Crime* and *Murder Set Pieces*, the film was not rejected; instead, the cuts were ordered. The rationale was that the cuts would limit the explicit nature of the sexually violent sequences and removed children from any compromising footage. The BBFC acknowledged the transgressive character of *A Serbian Film* and how it challenged their existing guidelines, but that "its contraventions could be brought into their existing regulatory frameworks,"[91] thus restoring and reinforcing the thresholds of acceptable material and its effective regulation.

A Serbian Film elucidates the value of examining extreme cinema in the context of transgressive material. The brief outline highlights the discursive and complex mechanisms at play where the film can impinge on boundaries of taste yet also reinforce the regulatory frameworks which govern what is and what is not acceptable regarding sex, violence and sexual violence in film. These boundaries are marked out through social, political, economic and aesthetic contexts and highlight how *A Serbian Film* provides a bridge or point of entry into an examination of hardcore horror. These films, from *Scrapbook* to *The Bunny Game*, engage similarly with national practices, film-horror conventions, regulatory and legal frameworks and taste cultures. As we move to include North American horror into the discourse of extreme film, then we will be able to adjudge how contemporaneous and historical global extremity combined with the genealogy of extremity in North America influences, reinforces, negotiates and contests the film conventions and practices of hardcore horror.

FOUR

"A malignant, seething hatework"
The Films of Hardcore Horror in the 21st Century

The categorization of extreme films post-millennium has increased in both size and scope. The range moves through the French horror–French New Extremism hybrid of *Haute Tension* (Aja, 2003) and *Martyrs*, the East Asian extremity of *Oldboy*, to the "torture porn" franchises and remakes of controversial 1970s and 1980s horror such as *I Spit on Your Grave* (Steven R. Monroe, 2010) and *Maniac* (Franck Khalfoun, 2012). Although it can be argued that the term "extreme" is only applicable to a minority of these films, it does show how a foundational base of challenging, confrontational and controversial content has emerged in the 21st century. In North America, there have been a number of films which exist in between the "mainstream extremity" and the underground and illicit locus of hardcore horror.

The most prominent is Nick Palumbo's *Murder Set Pieces*, which is organized in very similar ways to *A Serbian Film* and *August Underground* in its frequent scenes of graphic violence, sexual abuse and torture. The film is a series of standalone sequences of the violent behavior of a psychopathic neo–Nazi. The extreme nature of the murders he commits is exacerbated by the focus on non-consensual sex which emphasizes the pain, torture and degradation of the victim along with various incidences of the terrorization and killing of children. *Murder Set Pieces* was rejected by the BBFC precisely because of the "portrayal of violence, most especially when the violence is sexual or sexualised, but also when depictions portray or encourage: callousness towards victims, aggressive attitudes, or taking pleasure in pain or humiliation."[1] The film did not act as an example to reinforce the policing of boundary thresholds in the way that the extensive cuts in *A Serbian Film* allowed and was instead seen as a risk to audiences. For the BBFC, the film had the "potential to trigger sexual arousal [and which] may encourage a harmful association between violence and sexual gratification."[2]

The BBFC rejection of *Murder Set Pieces* along with its extreme content might align it alongside examples from hardcore horror in that it upholds a number of the definitional criteria. However, the film does put forward a stylized *mise en scène*, which although deploying credible special effects is not concerned with providing an authentic or "real" aesthetic. The film follows a conventional approach to narrative filmmaking and film form. In these terms, *Murder Set Pieces* replicates a number of other North American horror films, which although providing extreme content do not adhere to the definition of hardcore horror as they do not sufficiently provide a realist aesthetic, especially with regards to performance and the visual arrangement of form and style. Thus, there is a diminishing of the affective charge of the film, and a firm barrier between the real and the constructed is erected. Ryan Nicholson, Brian Paulin, Chris Woods and Bill ZeBub have all made films broaching the standards constitutive of hardcore horror. For example, in Woods' *AmeriKan HoloKaust* (2013) there are frequent scenes of extreme violence detailing castration, disembowelment, violent rape and cannibalism. The film, reportedly made for $1000, was unrated and released via the Internet as part of Icon Film Studios distribution in the U.S. However, *AmeriKan HoloKaust* and further examples of *Live Feed* (Ryan Nicholson, 2006), *Stockholm Syndrome* (Ryan Cavalline, 2008), *Fetus* (Brian Paulin, 2008) and *Breaking Her Will* (Bill Zebub, 2009) do not break down the border between the real and the simulated or produce a sustained affective charge of horror or dread. It is primarily because of an inauthentic performativity which is amateurish, juvenile and/or implausible and thus diminishes the threat and horror in favor of schlocky thrills and spectacular entertainment. Despite the fantastical and excessive nature of these films, they do attest to the movement of extreme horror through various filmic forms and how hardcore horror overlaps with synchronic U.S. and Canadian configurations of extreme cinema as much as it does with historical antecedents and global examples.

As opposed to the films briefly cited above, the films of Fred Vogel, Shane Ryan and Lucifer Valentine incorporate the main criteria set out as a definition of hardcore horror. Their films, such as *August Underground*, *Amateur Porn Star Killer* and *Slaughtered Vomit Dolls*, all privilege disturbing showcases of violence, including many instances of sexual abuse and torture. They also offer a realist aesthetic predicated on authentic special effects and convincing performances which produce a strong affective charge underscored by feelings of dread, fear and horror. The films were not submitted to classificatory bodies and did not secure a theatrical release, despite the opportunities for screenings at horror conventions and festivals. The examples of Vogel *et al.* constitute a clear view of the definitional qualities of hardcore horror. From these specific criteria emerge the contours of four distinct representational strategies: firstly, the removal of barriers to the horror on display; secondly a realist violence; thirdly the focus on sexual violence; and lastly, the use of a found footage aesthetic.

The formal properties of hardcore horror link to a larger thematic concern accentuated by the technological developments in the new millennium toward affordable, accessible and lightweight recording equipment. These "technological innovations of the digital age"[3] encapsulated via the narrative and form of hardcore horror provide a cultural articulation on how this technology impinges on socio-political contingencies of the 21st century. Events such as 9/11, atrocities committed in Abu Ghraib, eyewitness testimony from the wars in Iraq and Afghanistan, the cellphone footage of the Arab Spring, and more localized incidents of the viral death films of Isis, the Dnepropetrovsk maniacs and Luca Magnotta all attest to an utilization of an amateur, direct and intensive documentation of 21st-century atrocities. In turn, these events have provided a focus for hardcore horror to understand, work through and act out the "unsettling and disorientating present"[4] captured through the visual image. Also, alongside these traumatic and psychically damaging events is the pervasive rise of social media platforms (such as YouTube and the shock sites Bestgore and the YPC) which have hosted and disseminated the subsequent footage. Not only have these sites provided a stark exposure to the rise in surveillance culture, but also have engendered a palpable sense of fear surrounding the very recording devices being used.

The examples of horror cinema framed through the use of new digital technologies acknowledge this anxiety while simultaneously attempting to bridge the gap between the viewer and the changing visual readings of the world around them. Rather than "being rendered obsolete by the changing faces of information and media distribution,"[5] horror films can instead offer pertinent responses in their transgressive representations of reality and the real. In this respect, hardcore horror, along with other filmic strands of horror such as found footage, can "offer reflections on contemporary fears"[6] in how the nexus between real-world violence and digital technology has produced fear and anxiety circulating within various socio-cultural contexts. Indeed, hardcore horror has emerged as significant loci for a range of extreme, transgressive and marginal horror films which forward distinct aesthetic and thematic strands connected to the real and its representation. The commonality of these films might not necessarily engender a community or even a movement of a horror subgenre, but they nonetheless attest to collective fears and a common expression of disturbing, intensive, and liminal horror as a process to engage, confront and work through contemporary anxieties.

Scrapbook: *The Progenitor of 21st-Century Hardcore Horror*

Eric Stanze's *Scrapbook* represents the earliest example of North American hardcore horror in the 21st century. The film is a clear progenitor of hardcore horror in general and of Fred Vogel's *August Underground* films in particular, with its stark and explicit portrayal of a killer's violent and misogynistic psychology.

Scrapbook focuses on Leonard (Tommy Biondo), a 27-year-old, sexually repressed serial killer, and his sustained and prolonged torture and rape of a young woman named Clara (Emily Haack). Leonard's pathological feelings of abandonment, insignificance and emasculation are meticulously recorded in a diary, which offers both a baroque visual testament of the suffering of the women he abducts and kills and a sophomoric fantasizing of regaining a complete and dominant masculinity. In fact, the book acts as a reaffirmation of his selfhood and embodiment of his desired ontological being. Because of the symbolic importance of the book to Leonard, its content must be carefully managed and organized (primarily through entries by the abducted women) as any deviation from Leonard's fantasy self will leave him further exposed and vulnerable. To this end, Clara can reverse the power dynamic between victim and aggressor by forcing herself to write self-validating passages about Leonard and her (falsified) feelings of attraction to him. In doing so, Clara is able to seduce Leonard, whereby she ties him up and mutilates his body. Her final act of defiance is to take a Polaroid of Leonard's anguished, pain-wracked face to include in the book along with the pictures of all his female victims. Taking the scrapbook, Clara escapes.

Biondo brought the project to Stanze in 1998 after working on the treatment for almost five years. At this point, Stanze was emerging as a low-budget, independent horror filmmaker whose previous films, S*avage Harvest* (1994) and *Ice from the Sun* (1999), had been picked up for distribution. After the schlocky and gory Sam Raimi–influenced content of his earlier films, Stanze was "interested in doing something that pushed boundaries"[7] with *Scrapbook*, a film which he wanted to take an unflinching look at the warped mind and violent actions of a serial killer. Shot over 13 days on a budget of $4000 and primarily in one static location, the film challenges the threshold that demarcates the real and mimesis with an unflinching and uncomfortable focus on sexual violence, degradation and humiliation. It continually challenges the viewer through its deployment of extended, often single-take sequences featuring a collision of unsimulated sex and graphic violence. The authenticity of the performances of Biondo and Haack and the squalid production design further complicate any safe or regulated categories between the real and the

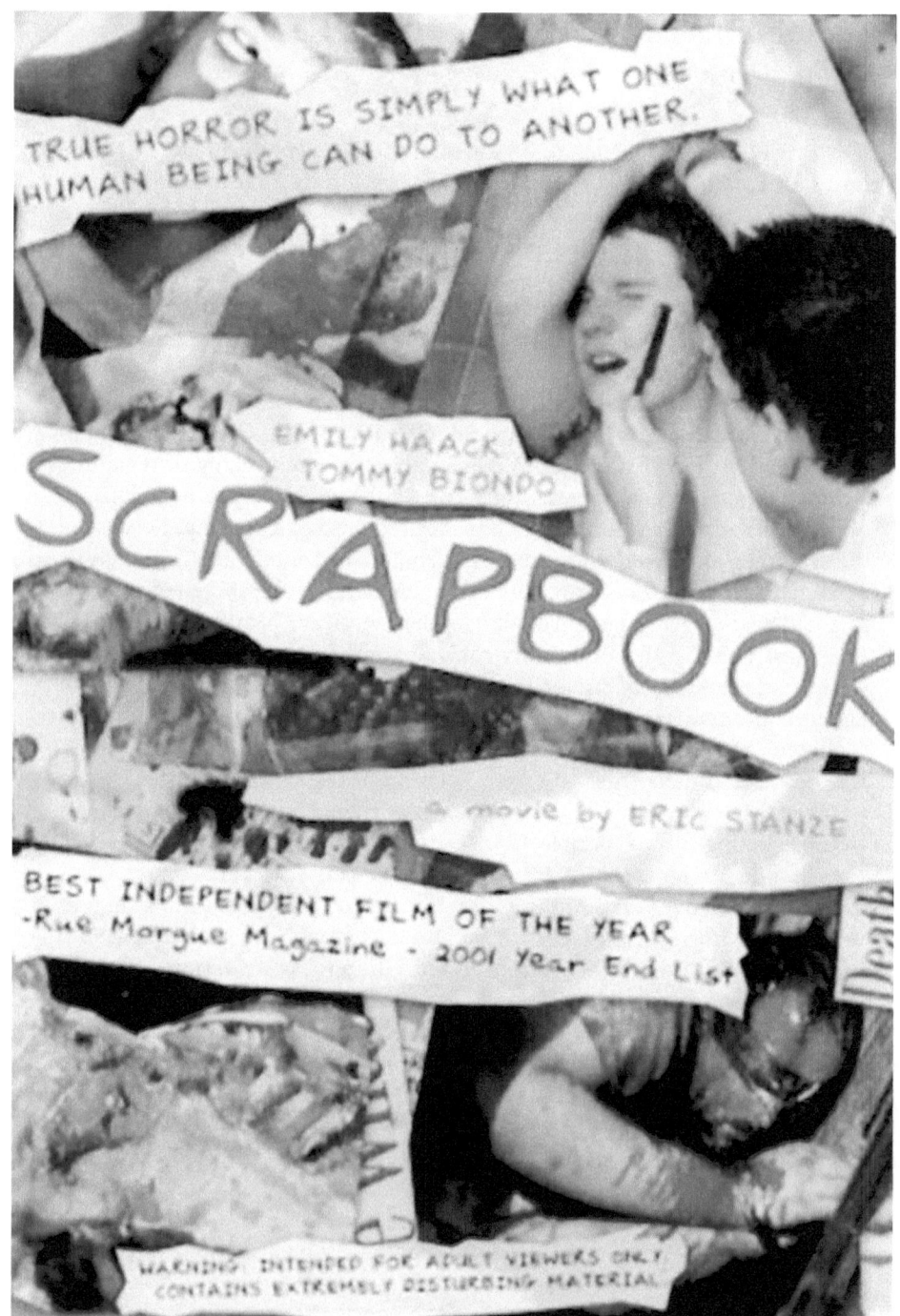

constructed. The result is that these formal properties attest to a film which provides an intimate, uncompromising and almost first-person horror which generates an immediate and horrifying affective connection. For example, the first scene between Leonard and Clara culminates in prolonged sexual violence as he chains her to a filthy, blood-soaked cot and physically abuses her before enacting a brutal rape. The scene fades to black with Leonard urinating over Clara's battered, bloody and exhausted body. The sequence lasts just under three and a half minutes and although shot via multiple camera set-ups it is still apparent that the scene has not been stopped during production and is occurring in real time. Later in the film, Leonard sexually abuses Clara in a shower while we see the footage through the video camera he has set up to capture and playback Clara's distress. In both of these scenes, the sense of authenticity is palpable, exacerbated by the sense of unabridged footage of the rape scene and by the found footage aesthetic in the shower sequence. Furthermore, the authentic production design and the suffering exhibited by Haack (which, at times, seems genuine) generates the perception of the "real" in these scenes.

As previously mentioned, the filmmakers behind *Scrapbook* were clear that they wanted to add a corrective to the glossy, sympathetic and glamorous Hollywood portrayals of the serial killer in the 1990s, encapsulated by Anthony Hopkins' performance as Hannibal Lecter in *The Silence of the Lambs*. For producer Jeremy Wallace, "nobody had really shown the serial killer, serial rapist, kidnap-crazy person the way we had shown it,"[8] and if *Scrapbook* "didn't unsettle viewers," then Stanze would concede that they "screwed up."[9] The authentically disgusting *mise en scène* and believable characterization and performance by the two lead actors primarily achieved the convincingly horrific appearance of the film. To responsibly capture the pathology of the killer, the filmmakers presented the material as being as "ugly as possible"[10] and to not "pull any punches"[11] when it came to represent the violent power dynamic between the killer and the victim. For Stanze, the success of the project as providing a counter-narrative to the sanitized and entertaining Hollywood serial killer film was possible not just through the authentic violence, but also by getting credible performances from Biondo and Haack. Stanze encouraged an almost entirely improvisational and ad-libbed performance and for the majority of the filming process withheld character information so that neither actor was aware of how the other would act or indeed how far they may go in any one particular scene. Further to this aim, Stanze also gave separate direction to the two leads which were purposefully not communicated to the other to increase the sense of spontaneity in the more dramatic and violent set-pieces. This technique provided a useful

Opposite: Scrapbook DVD artwork (courtesy of We Live Network).

mechanism for bringing a "real" quality to their performativity.[12] When talking about the film's first extended sequence of sexual violence and humiliation, Haack said, "I was really, really upset by this scene. I was really disgusted by what [Biondo] was doing. It's so cruel.... I didn't really know what to expect from him and he was extremely cruel."[13] Despite the intensity of her scenes, Haack was committed to producing a performance in line with the realist ethos of the film and fully trusted her co-filmmakers not to exploit her contribution. Haack continued, "[I] needed to make it look as realistic as possible, even if that meant getting hurt.... I didn't mind getting hurt."[14]

The total immersion of Biondo and Haack in the film does draw attention to the ethics of performance which disrupts the established and safe separation of boundaries between the actor and the character in hardcore horror. For many involved in the film, such a conflation of the factual and fictive was terrible to witness. Associate producer Todd Telvin, who also had a minor role in the film, pointed out, "[It was] very painful for us to be on the crew and watch them do their thing because [...] it felt like it was real. [...] [W]e were all squirming[,] we should not be here, this does not feel right."[15] Ultimately, the cast and crew persevered as, for them, to show the sexual violence as anything other than in "its truest, rawest form"[16] would have been to glorify the rape and the violence.

Biondo's role as production designer reinforced the authenticity of the material. Before the shoot, he spent several months living and working in the trailer that was used for the killer's domicile, carrying out what Stanze would call "method production design"[17] whereby Biondo would set up and design the house in character as Leonard. The interior was littered with pornographic magazines. Rotting food, full of maggots and flies, was purposefully left in the trailer and not removed throughout the shoot. Animal blood was daubed on the walls, including "I'm winning" in the torture room—bedroom as an "in character" design by Biondo of Leonard's fractured self-identity and lack of control. Stanze refused to allow anybody to clean up or open a window while shooting and even refused to let crew members clean or replace the cot which was covered in urine after the scene where Leonard first rapes Clara. Thus, the production design offers a severe sense of the abject through its collapse of the border between the inside and the outside of the body and forces viewers to experience horrific though emotionally affective reactions. Here, the *mise en scène* and performance produces the sense of horror and provides an authentic exploration of the violent, debased and murderous mind of a serial killer.

Editing *Scrapbook* took Stanze more than a year due to a reluctance to immediately return to the material after such an arduous and intense shooting experience.[18] When the film was finally released on VHS in 1999 in the U.S., it was through a minor distribution company called Salt City Home Video.

Four. "A malignant, seething hatework" 87

The abject "method production" in *Scrapbook* (Wicked Pixel Cinema).

It was not released theatrically; instead, according to Stanze, it "built its reputation on word of mouth and small fanzine exposure [and] screenings at film festivals [which] helped get the indie horror fan base talking about *Scrapbook* and recommending it to friends and fellow horror fans."[19] The momentum developed slowly but culminated in 2001 with Canadian horror magazine *Rue Morgue* calling it as the Best Independent Film of the Year[20] and the B-Movie Film Festival awarding it Best Director and Best Villain. Wicked Pixel Cinema, the production company formed by Stanze in 1995, promoted the film with the aim to produce independent films for the home video market. The company funds and produces a range of films and gives Stanze an ideal platform to promote and sell his own films, thus bypassing the convoluted and highly competitive process of selling films to an external distribution company. The growing interest in *Scrapbook* and the alternative marketing and distribution methods enabled the film to be picked up and released in numerous countries. Most notable was *Scrapbook*'s first overseas deal: In the UK, Cryptkeeper Films initially traded on the reputation of the film by selling it uncut and without any official certification through their website. The complex and ambiguous legislation over websites selling uncertified films benefited outfits such as Cryptkeeper but was curtailed when the BBFC withdrew the film and recommended 17 minutes of cuts for any future, approved UK release. In 2005, the film was re-released on a much wider scale in the U.S. when it was picked up by the major home video distribution company Image Entertainment.

Discussions of the film have been found on many horror forums, which further confirms the film's continued relevance and integral status to North American hardcore and independent horror films of the 21st century. Audiences often cited the impact of the film and its disturbing "never-want-to-see-again" quality. In 2004, posters on the Cult Movies Forum praised its uncompromising approach to horror and responded with comments such as "I think it's a bravely acted, well-made shocker totally committed to putting it's [sic] viewer through discomfort. A true horror film, devoid of all compromise."[21] The affective charge of the film regarding the fear, dread and horror conveyed was a recurrent theme discussed amongst fans and viewers and is evident in the first post of a 2004 thread in *The Mortuary* which began,

> A 95-minute assault on the senses that made me feel violated [...] I have not seen a movie quite this relentless in some time [...] There were a number of points where I flinched at what was being shown and at least one point where I was truly horrified that director Eric Stanze dared to commit the character's actions to celluloid [...] but the performances and direction of this film are brave, unflinching, realistic and superb.[22]

Looking back on hardcore horror, *Scrapbook*, with its meticulously developed production design, authentic performances, explicit representations of violence and sexual abuse, strong viewer response and alternative production, marketing and distribution practices, emerges as a progenitor of the subgenre. Also, it acts as an important precursor to the next significant development in 21st-century North American hardcore horror: Fred Vogel's *August Underground* films.

August Underground: Ur-Texts of Hardcore Horror

The *August Underground* trilogy provides an archetype of hardcore horror and the nexus between the social and technological configurations of the 21st century such as 9/11 and social media sites like YouTube. The films provide an intense and unexpurgated document of violence and death and follow, in home video-found footage style, the day-to-day lives of serial killers from their daily visits to junkyards and railway bridges to extremely graphic and extended scenes of torture and murder. *August Underground* was made for approximately $1500 and filmed on weekends over the summer of 2001 while Vogel worked during the week at Tom Savini's Special Make-up Effects

Program in Pittsburgh. The focus is on a lone killer called Peter (played by Vogel) and his unseen cameraman-accomplice (co-writer Allen Peters). The narrative does not provide any clear exposition or context for the violence committed by the pair and thus withholds any rationalization for their behavior.

The film starts with the killer leading the cameraman into a basement where he, and the audience, are confronted with a horrific scene of a severely tortured woman. The ensuing sequence, in which the pair ritually humiliate and abuse the kidnapped woman, lasts six minutes and is presented as one continuous, unedited take. *Scrapbook*'s notion of "method production design" seems apposite here as the room provides a hellish, abject *mise en scène*. Similar to Leonard's home, the basement's spatial arrangement is littered with pornographic ephemera, discarded and rotting food, and various effects props of excrement, dismembered limbs and substantial amounts of blood. The production design coupled with the first-person perspective immerses the viewer in the action and makes it a very affective opening. As the narrative proceeds, the viewer is presented with a seemingly random collection of "home video" exerts detailing occasions such as when the killer visits a tattoo parlor or when he attends a hardcore metal concert alongside further protracted and explicit sequences of violence and terrorization. The expectation of random and spontaneous violence is effectively constructed through the diegesis of the film and provides a strong affective charge of impending horror. For example, midway through the film the killer and his cameraman arrive at Roadside America, a popular Pennsylvania tourist attraction. The footage abruptly switches to the inside of the attraction as the two characters wander around a model village. On the diegetic soundtrack, a nearby family can be heard clearly, especially the voices of young children. The scene should play out as one of innocence and family fun, but because of what we have seen, and the level of graphicness linked to the violence, the viewer understands that *August Underground* has the potential to broach the limits of acceptable content and expects that the family and/or the children might become the killer's next victims. Instead, the scene plays out in rather a banal fashion and the abrupt or potential shock cut takes us to the subcultural space of a comic book store rather than the transgressive space of the killer's basement.

The film trades further in affective expectation in its climactic sequence which presages its violent dénouement of the murder of a prostitute with an extended ten-minute segment interminably building up to the inevitable moment when the woman is targeted by the killer.

Similarly, the notion of anticipation is raised through the reception of *August Underground* (and by extension hardcore horror) in which "viewers may anxiously approach the text with the primary expectation of being shocked and disgusted."[23] An account of the forces at play in how expectation influences reception appears in Kavka's work on the snuff film and David Church's work on "sick films." Kavka argues that anticipation can "overwhelm artistically 'preferred readings'"[24] due to alternative viewing formations based on fan-critical discourse that shapes these viewing positions. *August Underground* and its sequel *Mordum* have often appeared on lists of the "sickest," most "extreme" and "disturbing" films ever made and have thus formed a reputation as powerfully affective films. Church says that films such as these, which he terms "sick films," have "cultish reputations because their fans perceive them as culturally inaccessible, very difficult to watch, and extremely different from 'mainstream' horror, supposedly rendering them the 'exclusive' domain of horror fans with higher levels of subcultural capital than more casual horror viewers."[25] The reputation thus engenders an affective charge before viewing that chimes with Kavka's approach to the snuff film which consists of a "fearful anticipation of a future moment"[26] contained within the "affective fact"[27] that what we are about to watch will be disturbing and horrific. Fan discourse around "sick films" on horror forums taps into the "affective fact" of watching an extreme film and how such approaches can shape textual readings and experiences. Though most fans respond after viewing and directly evoke the affective impact the films have had with posts such as "[*Mordum*] really, really got to me. It's the one time I said to myself "Goddamn, they've gone too far"[28] and "I had to turn off after 35 minutes because my stomach was nauseous and I wanted to scrub my eyes with bleach,"[29] others do post in advance of watching and directly draw upon the reputation of the film. One fan, who hadn't seen the *August Underground* films, expressly engaged with the affective fact of how the viewing experience might impact on them: "i have read some reviews of the *August Underground* movies. my goodness they sound awful. i have read about some of the stuff depicted on screen … i don't see how that film isn't banned. my curiosity is up though."[30] Here the expectation of the film was sufficient to shape the poster's interpretation of the film and to develop their affective strategies in anticipation of watching the film. Indeed, hardcore horror as a whole exemplifies the importance of expectation-reputation in viewing positions and shows how a film like *August Underground* can put forward affective reading strategies that mark the film out as inaccessible and exclusive. That is, something to be "mastered" yet coterminously instilling a strong affective displeasure toward the film and its content.

The affective qualities of *August Underground* are primarily connected to the notion of realism and achieved through two of the essential categories for the definition of hardcore horror concerning authentic effects work and credible performance. Vogel furthers the concept of the realism of the footage and access to the horror in his desire to completely bypass the notion of an official release via the legitimate channels of theatrical exhibition or of release via VHS and DVD. Although Vogel was unable to ultimately "leave" the film in public places and move the film outside of the cultural spaces of legitimate and sanctioned cinematic practices, his intent did inadvertently tap into the importance of the horror community in providing alternative promotional and distribution routes. Alongside the idea of leaving copies of *August Underground* in public places such as libraries, he also mailed the film to approximately 200 people who Vogel thought might be receptive to its extreme content and who also might generate interest within the underground horror scene. In turn, it was passed on to *Rue Morgue* magazine, who received the film as an unsolicited curio of unknown provenance. According to staff writer Jovanka Vuckovic, the film arrived as a VHS cassette in a "red clam shell with no label and had this very found object quality."[31] Vuckovic's account certainly reflects Vogel's intention to break down the divide between the real and the artificial as well as that of presenting the object as unauthorized and illicit, though now to a potential viewer who is more receptive to underground horror conventions. According to Vuckovic, when the editors screened the film, most left during the first 15 minutes and that she was the only person left watching at the end.[32] Despite the initial reaction to the film by staff members as being an illegitimate horror more in alignment with "gorenography,"[33] the magazine did publish an article in their January-February 2003 issue. It generated a great deal of interest as readers were alerted to what *Rue Morgue* described as "the most disturbing film ever made,"[34] which perhaps served as the originating moment the film began to take on a reputation as being an unprecedented and viscerally affective horror film. The reaction to the article and the number of people who contacted Vogel afterward provides a clear example of the importance of the horror community and how it can be utilized to generate alternative marketing and distribution practices to those found in more commercial and mainstream horror. *Rue Morgue* along with other horror magazines such as *Ultraviolent* and Internet sites like Xploited Cinema and Cinema Wasteland championed the film. Thus, with *August Underground*, most people first experienced it through the written word via articles and reviews and saw the film a considerable time later, often through contacting Vogel himself or via individuals who were among the recipients of the first 200 copies. The official DVD of *August Underground* was released in 2005. Following in 2007: a limited Snuff edition, containing more extras and signed by the crew.

Proceeding from the growing grass roots attention surrounding *August Underground*, Vogel set up Toetag Pictures with fellow special effects artist Jeremi Cruise in 2002 and the company became instrumental in promoting and distributing the *August Underground* trilogy, particularly *Mordum* and *Penance*. In these next two installments, the filmmakers move the films closer to conventional narrative strategies. That is not to say that the violence is tempered in any way. In fact, *Mordum* provides an excessive and delirious documentation of the murderous activities and sexual deviancy of the killers that far exceeds the levels of explicit content in *August Underground*, and which prompted *Rue Morgue*'s oft-quoted tagline that the film was "a malignant, seething hatework."[35] Instead, Vogel introduces a more constructed plot development in his focus on the relationship between the killers. In *Mordum*, Vogel continues as the debased instigator-patriarch Peter but is now joined by his girlfriend Crusty (Christie Whiles) and her brother Maggot (Michael Todd Schneider). This family-like dynamic is under threat from the start as Peter catches Crusty having sex with her brother and rather impotently screams from behind the closed door, "Why do you fuck him?" This incestuous relationship results in a climactic confrontation when it is implied that Peter kills Maggot to restore himself as the sole object of desire for Crusty. Jones has pointed out that this marks *Mordum* "as a love story, however unconventional," and that their sexual relationship and pleasure attained while torturing and killing people is a manifestation of the displacement of their "own damaged selves."[36] Thus, along with the random inserts of graphic and "real"-looking violence and sexual abuse, the film also tracks the declining relationship between the three killers. Primarily, the dysfunctional environment surrounds the close, albeit incestuous, relationship of Crusty and Maggot and underscores the lack of agency and control embodied by Peter.

Penance further exposes the deteriorating relationships and mental health of the killers through its plot construction. The film focuses much more on the everyday activities of Peter and Crusty (Maggot does not feature and is only mentioned at the end when the relationship between the two has irrevocably broken down) and includes extended footage of banal and empty sequences of the two of them as tourists visiting a lion in a zoo or walking alongside a railway viaduct. The two killers have become trapped in a cycle of increasing acts of depravity where this can no longer provide any thrill or excitement as it did in the first two installments. The amount of time the film dedicates to mundane activities carried out by the couple, which is unfulfilling and alienating, reflects back on their lack of connection to themselves and their murderous actions. The film ends with Crusty removing herself from the killing, and Peter's incessant abuse of her, and attempting suicide. Here, Vogel cleverly moves *Mordum* and *Penance* away from the faux-snuff tableaux of *August Underground* due to the success and infamy generated by the film since its initial exposure in 2002. The position of *August Underground* as a "found object" and as a film which Vogel hoped would "fool people"[37] into thinking it was genuine snuff was not possible with *Mordum* and *Penance* due to the exposure the film and Vogel now experienced within the horror community. Therefore, Vogel retains the first person found footage aesthetic and extended sequences of violence and sexual abuse but develops the motiveless actions of the killers in the first installment "to place stress on the consequences of violence"[38] by the end of the trilogy. In fact, the realism of the violence and subsequent affective reactions to watching such material was articulated in many fan responses to the trilogy whereby responses ranged from "why am I sat here watching this [*August Underground*]"[39] to "*Mordum* is a cinematic masterpiece. The grittiness, the filth and the oh so fucked up gore is what I need when watching a faux snuff film" and "it's fucking appalling. Without exaggeration, I felt sick on several occasions."[40]

Vogel's *August Underground* trilogy does share a number of similarities with Stanze's *Scrapbook* from the realist aesthetic to the corrective of the Hollywood serial killer film and the starting-up of a production company to promote and release the films. Both films are early examples of the found footage phenomena which, although commencing in the modern period with *The Blair Witch Project* (1999), peaked in output and popularity between 2006 and 2008. They are also early proponents of hardcore horror, unmistakably trade on their reputations as "sick" films, and exemplify the categories essential in their definition.

However, the *August Underground* films provide a more pertinent examination of digital recording technologies and their capture of traumatic events. The use of the camcorder in *August Underground* builds from previous explorations of the potentially threatening presence and use of analog video technologies found in *Videodrome* and *Henry*. The reemergence in *August Underground* of a more primitive visual recording device conflated with how they were being used to capture images of unspeakable violence through instances such as the decapitation videos of Americans Daniel Pearl in 2002 and Nick Berg in 2004. Although Vogel was not directly addressing the sociocultural anxiety and trauma that emerged after the videos, his tapping into the democratizing nature of filmmaking in the early 2000s by utilizing the low-fi and amateur aesthetics of the home video/camcorder inadvertently replicated their degraded, technically inept yet graphic content and form. The nature of the amateur footage and its unrestricted access to "reality" in *August Underground* become less a tool of directorial empowerment and more a technological advance that is to be feared in terms of what it might actually capture and broadcast back to us.

The Amateur Porn Star Killer *Trilogy:*
True Crime as True Horror

The fear over recording technologies is picked up and developed through Shane Ryan's *Amateur Porn Star Killer* trilogy, which can be seen to "[speak] to cultural anxieties about the ubiquity of camera and surveillance technologies and amateur videography"[41] and its dissemination through social media platforms. Ryan initially made *Amateur Porn Star Killer* due to a combination of a "bad personal setting surrounding the film"[42] and a number of previously aborted feature-length projects. Thus, Ryan approached the idea of a quick and straightforward film project and decided on a single-take shoot with a first-person point of view and crew of just two actors/camera operators would be the easiest and most logical way to complete a feature-length film. The resulting film focuses on a young white killer Brandon (played by Ryan) who picks up a 13-year-old girl Stacey (played by 19-year-old Michiko Jimenez), takes her to a motel and proceeds to manipulate her into sexual congress before raping and strangling her. The film was shot over three hours primarily in a motel room, edited over a week and reportedly cost $35 to make: $25 for the motel room and $10 for video tapes! The film is a mix of the sensational and the provocative, showing sexual violence in a way in which Brandon uses subtle manipulation rather than overt violence.

Amateur Porn Star Killer 2 continues in much the same vein as it takes place primarily in one setting and again focuses on Brandon as he picks up a young woman (Kai Lanette) before taking her home where he eventually kills her. The power dynamic between the two is more appropriate and balanced in this film and the sex begins as consensual, if rough and at times violent, before turning aggressively brutal and murderous. The formal properties of the film are very stylish and Ryan uses a number of technical innovations to distort and manipulate the footage. Although there is real, unsimulated sex and the interaction is at times genuinely violent, the look and feel of the film aligns itself with more avant-garde film techniques and the hyper-stylized narratives of the Cinema of Transgression movement. The stylistic properties are toned down for *Amateur Porn Star Killer 3: The Final Chapter* which takes place mostly inside a Sports Utility Vehicle (SUV). Here Brandon's manipulative and sadistic game playing is the focus as he torments, humiliates, rapes and kills Nikki, a former adult movie performer (played by adult performer Regan Reece). The film ends where the trilogy began with Brandon talking with and offering a lift to a 13-year-old girl who is looking for somebody to buy alcohol for her.

Ryan's aim was not to make an underground horror film but to make a "true horror"[43] about a genuine subject that would get audiences to "question things, actually put thought into things they don't want to look at."[44] In this respect, Ryan's approach connects with comments Marian Dora made regarding his films and that they were not to be viewed as entertainment. Here, Ryan's contention to show unsettling and potentially unpleasant material taps into the recurrent facet of extreme cinema which promotes a strong affective quality connected to "heightened moments of unpleasure."[45] Ryan immediately frames *Amateur Porn Star Killer* with a quote from Paul Schrader about snuff movies which contains the line: "I think it's conceivable these films exist, but whether they do or not is less important than the public's belief that they do; their willingness to believe in an evil fantasy." The quote situates the film (and the other installments) within the cultural mythology of snuff and allows Ryan to explore the dichotomy of repulsion and attraction which is invariably tied up in spectatorship of extreme and controversial films. Fictional snuff, from its early cinematic manifestations in the exploitation film *Snuff* and more mainstream variations found in Schrader's own *Hardcore* to the recent permutations *Snuff 102* (Mariano Peralta, 2007) and *The Cohasset Snuff Movie* (Edward Payson, 2012), infuses the discussions on hardcore horror. Primarily through the axis of how the films can utilize the aesthetics of snuff to "mediate and exploit discourses of death imagery, accentuating the epistemological breakdown of the real and the fictional"[46] and viewing positions which oscillate between fear and fascination. Both of these elements—form and reception—merge into the central facet of realism inherent within hardcore horror examples, such as *Scrapbook* and *August Underground*, so that Ryan's trilogy can bring "all manner of sociocultural, socioeconomic and sociosexual structures [into] sharp relief."[47] In this respect, the *Amateur Porn Star Killer* films act as useful harbingers of the fear-fascination opposition disseminated through contemporary society via digital technology and its representation of "real" death.

For example, Ryan's contention was to present the film as a document of actual violence and murder, but one which has now been picked up by a production company and manipulated to make it more palatable and entertaining to audiences. Such a position which addresses the triumvirate of filmmaker/studio—footage—audience is incisive and prophetic in an age where we have seen atrocity footage of real death framed through the lens of technical sophistry. In 2012, Luca Magnotta's infamous snuff film *1 Lunatic 1 Ice Pick* did not show a protracted on-screen killing of Lin Jun, a 33-year-old Chinese student, but instead showed a tightly edited assemblage of post-mortem details with on-screen titles and a musical soundtrack. This "Grand Guignol showreel" acted as a sort of "grotesque performance art evidently intended to be interactive and engage the audience from the outset."[48] More recently the development of Isis propaganda videos has developed from crude and technically inept recordings of the beheadings of Westerners to promotional films "exhibiting slick production values and often bamboozling the viewer with a succession of post-production camera tricks" so that the "jihadist recruitment video has gone the way of Hollywood."[49] Here Ryan, perhaps inadvertently, enters his own take on the dichotomy of real and simulated death on screen and in doing so explores the complicated viewing strategies bound up in snuff films as well as further problematizing the possibility of achieving an authentic and realist representation of on-screen or cinematic death.

Although Ryan deliberately manipulated the footage to give the viewer the impression it had been doctored by a distributor, he was also acutely aware of the limitations, in terms of promotion and distribution, of making a low-fi, micro-budget "found footage" film presenting an uncomfortable and prolonged sequence of rape and murder. Ryan has often talked about his lack of a background in horror and his general lack of interest in the genre as a fan or filmmaker.[50] However, financial directives for the film meant that he embraced horror as a means to get his "art house talky drama"[51] noticed when he said, "I realized that if you have no money to make a film, or are an indie-underground filmmaker, the only real place for support is the horror community. You have about 100 times as many places willing to cover your film, it's insane."[52]

Continuing to stress the importance of the horror community in getting the film released and seen, Ryan went on: "[B]asically [I] tried to disguise my art house films as horror and erotic, to gain attention and support, while trying to tell stories about characters and events I thought were interesting. I'm very much into true crime, but for the mystery, the psychology, etc., not the blood, at all."[53] In this respect, he decided to adapt the title to provide the film with a more dramatic and alluring connotation and to firmly place it within the horror genre, despite the lack of more conventional aspects of horror contained within the film. Although the *Amateur Porn Star Killer* trilogy left a divisive mark on horror fans, it did slowly generate a cult following with people who considered Ryan "ahead of his time"[54] in how, through the films, he "took all of voyeuristic nuances and approach to filmmaking that Michael Powell did in *Peeping Tom* (1960) and he brought it forward and stripped it bare."[55] MTV was quick to point to how this pared-down treatment of violence and murder provided an effective commentary: "In a world of reality TV and home video on the Net, *Amateur Porn Star Killer* is sobering, believable and more timely than ever."[56] Thus, for many, Ryan presented a confrontational and challenging film, not only about effective horror that's relatable but about providing an ethical charge that "points the finger at the audience."[57] Particularly, in regards to why they are willingly watching a film which from its very title suggests a sensationalized narrative of violence, sex and murder.

Amateur Porn Star Killer debuted at the Action on Film International Film Festival at Long Beach, California, in 2006 and received a limited theatrical showing the following year in the art-house Sunset 5 Laemmle Theatre in Los Angeles. From this, the film was picked up by Cinema Epoch, a U.S.–based distribution company specializing in "internationally acclaimed art house films, contemporary American films and edgy cult & midnight works."⁵⁸ Cinema Epoch continued to work with Ryan and released the next two installments as well as producing *Amateur Porn Star Killer 2*, in both a movie and pared-down "snuff" version, in 2008 after limited theatrical screening in Los Angeles a couple of months before. A 3-D edition of the trilogy was released in 2012 and was followed by *Amateur Porn Star Killer: The Complete Collection*, which also contained interviews, various commentaries and the documentary *A Boy, a Girl, a Camera* released in 2014. What these various screenings, DVDs and editions highlight, along with the more overt stylistic developments and techniques, is that they "underline that the films are contrived, edited, commercial products."⁵⁹ In addressing how films are presented and how they are viewed, the trilogy provides a useful foundation of how hardcore horror can provide a germane way to engage with ways of seeing concerning "camcorders, murder and the media"⁶⁰ in the 21st century.

The "Vomit Gore" Films: A Death Knell for Hardcore Horror...

The final major strand of hardcore horror in the 21st century (to date) has been the "vomit gore" films of Lucifer Valentine: *Slaughtered Vomit Dolls, ReGOREgitated Sacrifice, Slow Torture Puke Chamber* and *Vomit Gore 4: Black Mass of the Nazi Sex Wizard*. Valentine's films move away from an overt commentary on real death and media effects of violence, which underpin Vogel and Ryan's approach to hardcore horror. Instead, they forward an intense and intimate psychological examination of its main character, Angela Aberdeen (Ameara La Vey, though played by many actresses over the course of the four films) as she attempts to escape the physical and sexual abuse she has suffered since her early teenage years. Her life is seen as a progression of exploitation and ill treatment at the hands of men, initially through the sexual abuse of her father and a priest with whom she is relocated. As an adult, Angela moves from being a stripper, an adult movie actress and finally a bulimic prostitute with a severe drug and alcohol addiction. The extreme trauma and suffering of Angela over this prolonged period result in a mental breakdown and eventual suicide via drowning in a bathtub. Although *Slaughtered Vomit Dolls* primarily maps out the narrative progression of Angela, her life is played out over the four films and often by different actresses in distinct time frames. Thus, in their disregard for narrative cohesion, the films suggest an overlapping multidimensional reality-consciousness and a synchronicity of congruent events which speaks to a more general "Angela" and the "horrific manifestation and physical materialization of extreme darkness and loss"⁶¹ that characterizes their lives. In the second film, *ReGOREgitated Sacrifice*, we follow Angela immediately after her suicide as she is led down into the Kingdom of Hell by the Black Angels of Hell (played by the Canadian horror filmmakers, the Soska Sisters). The Black Angels act as protectors of Angela and ritualistically attack, kill and destroy the representative archetypes in Angela's life such as the "Stripper" and the "Teen Porn Star." (The male oppressors always appear off screen and are never punished.) The film ends with Angela entering the Kingdom of Hell and submitting to the dominant presence and command of the Devil. *Slow Torture Puke Chamber* sees Angela return to the surface and infect another Angela character (now played by Hope Likens) to also lead her down into the nightmarish realm of Hell. Here, the third installment suggests a never-ending cycle of suffering and abuse that provides a dark, brutal and bleak treatment of the physical and psychological impact of extreme trauma. The fourth entry *Black Mass of the Nazi Sex Wizard*, released three years after *Slow Torture Puke Chamber*, acts as a sort of prequel to the original trilogy as it again explores the life of Angela Aberdeen and the idea of the simultaneous nature of the films and the everywoman character of Angela. Overall, the vomit gore films provide a highly symbolic, controversial, extremely graphic and realistic composition of hardcore horror.

The brief outline of the films suggests an unconventional and alternative approach to horror, from their very emotive and incendiary titles to the themes of sexual abuse, hardcore pornography and Satanism. When attention focuses on the content and themes of the films as examples of "vomit gore," there emerges a clear distillation of alternative filmmaking practices, extreme violence and realist horror which position the films as a sort of end-point or *coup de grâce* of hardcore horror. It is therefore unsurprising that the question "What is 'vomit gore'?" is one that is continually asked Lucifer Valentine in interviews and is a recurrent point of discussion in film commentaries and behind-the-scenes features. It is perhaps the central aspect of his artistic and creative endeavor and integral to how these films are viewed within 21st-century hardcore horror.

For Valentine, the term is the coming together of two separate constitutive parts—vomit and gore—to achieve a type of transcendence from personal trauma and tragedy. Valentine mentions the primal response to his films and that the term vomit "has to do with the actual physical repulsion one can feel when watching an extremely terrifying movie"[62] and that the sight of people gagging and vomiting can often induce similar acts and responses. The severity of the reaction to vomit and vomiting, and certainly with regards to his films, is to affect the viewer both psychologically and physically. Of course, there is a long history of using vomit or the fear of vomiting as a promotional gimmick or device to increase the immersive and affective quality of horror. One of the first instances of using "barf bags" was Herschell Gordon Lewis' seminal gore film, and key antecedent to hardcore horror, *Blood Feast*, where Lewis and producer David Friedman seemed to dare audiences not to get physically ill as a result of the images on screen. Since then, a number of horror films have utilized sick bags to exploit their extreme nature and the responses they may invoke: *The Exorcist* (William Friedkin, 1973), *The Beyond* (Lucio Fulci, 1981) and a recent example at the 2015 Fantasia Film Festival for the bug-human metamorphoses horror *Bite* (Chad Archibald, 2015). Therefore, Valentine taps into this recurring promotional item by literally putting a significant amount of actual vomiting into his films, thus transferring the act of vomiting to the screen itself with the intention of then "projecting" it back to the audiences.

Another primary factor is Valentine's emetophilia. Although not necessarily planned to form such a significant part of the films, it came about due to the "time and place"[63] of shooting *Slaughtered Vomit Dolls* and his intense sadomasochistic relationship with Ameara La Vey. Thus, vomit gore became for Valentine a "venue and a premise for making movies that are of an extreme, raw, uncensored (obviously!) expression of myself; as honest and primal as I can be in my ... expression of creativity or just art. That's what vomit gore is, a literal purging of just raw emotion."[64] This emotion, which was often traumatic and destructive, needed to be expelled and directed toward the creative process of filmmaking. The working through of trauma was the case for Valentine and certainly for the actors in the films, such as La Vey and Hope Likens. Thus, Valentine was adamant that the process of vomiting, while sexually arousing for him, could also serve as a creative function to confront and work through past trauma. He has stated, "Whatever is inside of you that needs to come out, just like let it come out, just don't judge it, don't judge your sadness, don't judge the trauma, the tragedies of your life, just instantly rip it out of you and look at it and revel in the disgustingness of it all."[65]

The confrontational attitude to pain and suffering and the process of vomiting as a way to purge these feelings link to the "gore" part of the term which also focuses on extreme forms and representations. For Valentine, "the gore part is the extreme destruction and obliteration of the human form"[66] through a variety of procedures such as disembowelment, decapitation, sexual abuse and necro-sadism. Valentine continues, "I lean toward extreme gore ... just to show, like metaphorically, we are destroying the human form because it is not necessarily about having a human form."[67] That is, in the case of the vomit gore films, the extreme violence serves the purpose of highlighting the self-destructive tendencies, such as alcohol and drug abuse, bulimia and self-harm that exerts a debilitating weight on the characters (and actors). So, in obliterating the "human condition that puts you in a state of trauma, grief, sorrow, darkness,"[68] Valentine's artistic brief was to provide an uplifting outcome. That is, a "way of literally glorifying and celebrating the ritual, the insane, bloody, vomit-soaked ritual of destroying yourself, because when you do that, you can overcome and transcend your so-called sad story of your life. You can literally go beyond it."[69]

The concept of vomit gore also enabled Valentine, a Satanist, to explore and "purposely exaggerate themes of violence and human suffering in order to surpass the normal human threshold of perception of these things to transcend them and create something new beyond that."[70] Therefore, the term or genre of vomit gore facilitates the representation of a grotesque, violent and transgressive visual spectacle combined with a personal and spiritual redemption through engaging head-on with trauma and suffering. It is a "revelatory and illuminating" process, but one which is "ongoing and unending"[71] for Valentine in terms of its engagement with feelings of "tragic, sickening emotions and traumatized, fragmented psychological states."[72]

Valentine's idiosyncratic and deeply personal approach to making the films is further underlined by how he selects the projects he works on and his working relationship with the actors, especially Ameara La Vey and Hope Likens. According to Valentine, "When I come to making movies, I just let the chips fall where they may."[73] He added, "The movies that I end up making kind of just come to me in the form of a person and a circumstance in life that I am meant to encounter and experience."[74] In the case of *Slaughtered Vomit Dolls*, it was the advent of La Vey into his life that structured the film and indeed the rest of the films within the vomit gore cycle. Their relationship was very intense and intimate and defined through their agreement to form a dominant-submissive partnership where Valentine was allowed to film La Vey at any time. The creative affiliation between the two of them over the following months certainly underlines Valentine's statement "I normally take aspects of my actors' real lives and origins and integrate my stories around theirs."[75] It is, therefore, no surprise that La Vey combines her traumatic past coupled with an abusive and exploitative present of pornography and strip clubs to provide the real-life basis for the story of Angela Aberdeen. Similarly, for *Slow Torture Puke Chamber*, Hope Likens contacted Valentine via MySpace and through continued correspondence and a growing friendship, Valentine asked her to perform in the film. Likens' personal circumstances, especially as somebody who suffered from bulimia, shaped the visual and thematic content and thus dictated the narrative flow of the film. In fact, the presence of female actors, both through their performance and embrace of the role(s) as well as also using their background to structure narrative elements and authenticate the thematic strands predicate all four films. La Vey is instrumental again in *ReGOREgitated Sacrifice* as are Jen and Sylvia Soska as the Black Angels of Hell. In *Black Mass of the Nazi Sex Wizard*, it was Valentine's close relationship with the masochistic performers Sister S and Heather Cage which structured the narrative development and vomit gore sequences. In all these cases, the films are created by the female actors-characters and Valentine's lengthy and revealing process of filming them 24/7. Valentine has talked about how this is a "prolonged portrait"[76] of people like La Vey and Likens and how the practice of filming them almost invariably led to the formation of each project.

The filmmaking process for Valentine is not predicated by commercial imperatives and/or exposure necessarily into the horror community or independent film circulation. Valentine talks about his work more as personal creative projects. "I have never had any major movie—ambitions and dreams, I do not like it either. For me, filmmaking is about to [sic] document my life and the super-cool, secret friends I meet along the way."[77] Yet the vomit gore films have been released and have gradually built up a small but dedicated fan base.

Unlike other examples in hardcore horror which have depended on festival screenings and conventions for promotional opportunities, the vomit gore films have never been shown at a horror festival, and Valentine has never appeared at a horror convention to talk about and promote them. Festivals rejected the films due to their extreme content and the distressing affective qualities the sexual violence, vomiting and sadomasochistic performativity may cause. Valentine bemoaned horror festivals' reluctance to take on the films by pointing out the irony in evaluating them as "'vile and disgusting,' 'physically revolting,' 'inappropriate for our audience'" or, Valentine's favorite, as "'too extreme.'"[78] Promotion of the films was equally difficult to secure and often happened at grass roots levels such as via horror forum boards. A high-profile example of the resistance to picking up and promoting Valentine's work was *Fangoria* magazine, which refused to feature advertisements for *Slaughtered Vomit Dolls*. Valentine recounted that this was due to the DVD case featuring a hand-drawn picture which proved too disturbing for the editorial staff: They informed him, "[T]here is nothing entertaining about a picture of a girl with blood gushing out of her vagina."[79] Despite the adverse reaction to the films as unpalatable, even for the horror crowd, the films did find niche outlets into the horror community. Valentine formed Kingdom of Hell Productions with producer and friend No One Body, and they were able to distribute copies of *Slaughtered Vomit Dolls* through Canada and the U.S. However, it was not until late 2006, when Unearthed Films picked up distribution rights to the film, that it reached a wider audience. The respected and well-established web-based outlet of Unearthed Films meant that Valentine's vomit gore movies could be sold and marketed to both domestic and international audiences. Unearthed Films was formed in 2002 to release extreme horror and cult films. Its CEO Stephen Biro, director of *American Guinea Pig: A Bouquet of Guts and Gore*, has significantly aided Valentine's entry into the film market due to his standing within the underground horror community. Biro's early horror adventures as a VHS bootlegger and owner of the notorious Tampa-based Video Mayhem store in the 1990s has meant that Unearthed Films has become a trusted place to obtain extreme and hardcore horror. In turn, his enthusiastic representation and promotion of the vomit gore films have provided a great deal of positive exposure. More recently, Valentine has signed a distribution deal with German-based Black Lava Entertainment which again specializes in underground and extreme horror and have released *Black Mass of the Nazi Sex Wizard*. The acquisition of the latest vomit gore installment has provided Black Lava with one of their most successful titles as the limited edition hard box version sold out minutes after being posted on the website.[80]

The vomit gore films have proved extremely problematic concerning how they have been received, especially within the forum boards of the horror community. Here, the reaction has vacillated between extreme resentment and uneasy spectatorial identification. For example, on *Rue Morgue* magazine's horror forum, the response has been severe and dismissive with poster The Gore-met commenting that Valentine is a juvenile filmmaker possessing limited talent: "I like Barf. I invented vomit gore. Other than that, dude has nothing to say."[81] Valentine has also been a frequent poster in horror forums and his presence on the *Rue Morgue* boards was singled out and criticized as shameless self-promotion and trolling, which significantly impacted on and contributed to the early and continued negative responses meted out to him and his films.[82] Other forums, such as the Internet Movie Database (IMDb), have also taken the films to task with Cremasterfan responding to *Slaughtered Vomit Dolls* by saying, "The film is rubbish because it has no plot, no real characterization (so the 'gore' has no affect), no decent dialogue. I will stop here, I can't be bothered to go on."[83] Valentine's vomit gore films are an unacceptable presence within the horror community as people seem unsure or unwilling to consider the visual and thematic content due to the troubling dynamic of the sexualized sadomasochistic violence and the paraphilia of vomit. It becomes easier, and perhaps safer, to dismiss and reject the films as not advancing serious entries into the horror canon; not adhering to the codes and conventions typically found in "quality" horror. A sense of danger and the unknown permeates all aspects of the vomit gore films from their extreme and unsettling content to the mysterious aura surrounding Valentine and his intense dominant-submissive relationship with Ameara La Vey. As such, there has been a fair amount of reticence from viewers (and often fans) in probing deeply into the films. Perhaps they are put off or unnerved by the claim Valentine has made that they have an occultist energy as he wanted to make "viewers actually feel [a] demonic presence/energy"[84] while watching! More likely is the pornographic focus on vomit as a specific paraphilia and that the fans who do not share Valentine's fetish (the vast majority) are unlikely to derive value from films which privilege a fetish such as emetophilia. Valentine's contention that the vomit gore films possess a diabolical quality can be displaced on to the niche appreciation of transgressive fetishism, but they do provide an unprecedented level of horror which is unflinching in its approach. The films provide a fascinating and integral perspective on the alternative filmmaking practices and aesthetic and thematic representational strategies of hardcore horror.

The Bunny Game, Hate Crime *and* American Guinea Pig: *Further Exemplars of Hardcore Horror*

Outside of the trilogies of Vogel and Ryan and the vomit gore series of Valentine, there exist a number of individual films which also forward extreme material *and* address a realist aesthetic in concerted and effective ways. A key example is Adam Rehmeier's *The Bunny Game*, a film "not for the casual viewer"[85] in its ferocious and horrific representation of a destitute sex worker who is kidnaped by a truck driver and held over five days while she is repeatedly tortured and sexually abused. It serves as a useful companion piece to Valentine's vomit gore films in the way it came about through the close creative relationship between Rehmeier and lead actress Rodleen Getsic. The extensive collaboration between the two for the film and the inclusion of violent and traumatic events from Getsic's past meant that the film promulgates a determination to providing a realistic and convincing account of cinematic horror.

The creative process that was so important to *The Bunny Game*'s sense of horror and commitment to realism initially started in the late 1990s, but the screening of the final film did not occur until 2010. The protracted production schedule included an aborted attempt to film *The Bunny Game* in 2006 after actor Gregg Gilmore backed out citing concerns that he may go too far with his character in his treatment of Getsic. Rehmeier confirms that Gilmore, in "delving into darker and darker territory during his preparatory phase," was "convinced that he might actually hurt Rodleen."[86] Despite this setback, the film was finally completed in 2008 on a budget of $13,000 with non-professional actor Jeff Renfro now playing the part. The filmmakers wanted *The Bunny Game* to be "hardcore and didn't want to hold back when it came to dealing with violence,"[87] meaning that much of its content happened for real and was not a special effect or a technical sleight of hand. The film had its "world premiere" on the University of Southern California campus in 2010 and then toured within the horror community for the next two years, playing in over 20 alternative and underground horror festivals including Lausanne Underground, PollyGrind in Las Vegas and the Arizona Underground Festival. Fan reception was mixed and reiterated the limitations specific to hardcore horror about form and content. Audience members spoke of the difficulty of watching such disturbing content despite the often powerful performances and technical achievements. Although many categorized the film as a "harrowing tale"[88] of an intense nature which qualified as an "important part of modern horror,"[89] it was often mitigated with concerned responses about the ethical direction of the movie; how "[t]he film becomes frightening not because of manufactured scares, but out of a sense of wondering how far filmmaker and actors are going to push themselves."[90] As a result of this spectatorial position and the discussions taking place around the controversial use of violence to which Getsic was subjected, the film generated considerable interest and continuing visibility and popularity on the festival circuit. In 2011, distribution company Trinity X picked up the film for an initial release in the UK only for them to be forced to drop it after the BBFC rejected it for certification. The BBFC's rationale underlined the perceived threat posed by the combination of sexual violence and realism that has surrounded other examples of hardcore horror: "The principal focus of the work is the unremitting sexual and physical abuse of a helpless woman, as well as the sadistic and sexual pleasure the man derive [sic] from this [which in turn] may encourage some viewers to enjoy and share in the man's callousness and the pleasure he takes in the woman's pain and humiliation."[91] Not surprisingly, the ban provided further publicity and notoriety and in 2012 the film was finally released via DVD and Blu-ray in the U.S. by Autonomy Pictures. *The Bunny Game* has since received distribution in a number of European countries such as Germany and Sweden, though it remains banned in the UK.

The problems associated with distributing *The Bunny Game* align with a disturbing and uncompromising vision whereby Rehmeier and Getsic attempted to generate a potent and immersive film to present the audience with a horrific audio-visual experience. The intuitive process of capturing the action in one single take and performing as much as possible as real meant that Renfro and Getsic added significantly to its visceral nature. Rehmeier intimates that it was a lack of technical resources responsible for the ossification of the authentic in the film when he says, "We didn't have effects, everything was real,"[92] but it also points toward a documentary impulse: "[In] an increasingly artificial and visual world, nothing must appear to be unreal, meaning that nothing must be left unseen."[93] *The Bunny Game*'s fictional realm is rendered convincing and credible due to the numerous examples of real violence which punctuate the narrative. The most controversial and infamous of these is the sequence where Renfro brands Getsic's back in a single, continuous take which pre-empts any ambiguity as to whether the scene was staged. Further scenes of gagging and asphyxiation are present along with an intense physical performativity that engenders some genuinely disturbing footage. Indeed, there is a sense that we should not be watching the material and, in doing so, have to question why we are.

However, this seems to be the intention of Rehmeier and Getsic as the film, for them, is a clarion call to what they see as the passive spectatorship linked to antiseptic and anodyne horror. They both hoped the film "sort of crosses a line with the audience and breaks the wall of the comfort zone."[94] Thus, in representing violence as brutal, authentic and with very real consequences, Rehmeier intended that audiences would question "their motivation for continuing to watch"[95] and not, as the BBFC suggested, appellate the viewer instead with the sadistic glee evidenced by the truck driver in his treatment of the woman. Rehmeier's position is not necessarily new or original, and the idea of collapsing the real-representation boundary has a long lineage in extreme cinema to which Rehmeier directly exploits. Thus, the discrepancy between the aim of the filmmakers and the response of classificatory bodies such as the BBFC does return hardcore horror to questions of the ethical dimension of realist horror. In turn, it refers back to Stanze's treatment of Emily Haack in *Scrapbook* and Lucifer Valentine and Ameara Le Vey in the vomit gore films. Here the ethical dimension is inseparably linked with spectatorship and affect and whether the transgressive nature of *The Bunny Game* (and hardcore horror in general) provides either an "empty gestural stance"[96] of gratuitous and exploitative rape and murder or an understanding of viewer complicity in the narratives of extreme violence and hardcore horror.

Linked to *The Bunny Game* and its engagement with the ethical perspectives of content, the viewing of extreme material and spectator effect is James Cullen Bressack's *Hate Crime*. Utilizing found footage aesthetics, it centers on a home invasion in which a group of neo–Nazi thugs break into the home of a Jewish family during the birthday celebration of their youngest child. The film then focuses, in explicit detail, on the group's torment, torture and the murder of each family member. It ends with the disclosure that the eldest daughter was in fact found alive and testified against the perpetrators. This positive resolution, of sorts, is embedded in on-screen titles which provide information relating to the rise of hate crimes in the U.S. and especially of anti–Semitism. In turn, this reinforces the filmmakers' argument in detailing such an abhorrent event and attempts to legitimize the extreme violence and brutality on display. Many critics corroborated to the affective power of the film, with Anton Bitel, representative of the majority of reviewers, pointing out that *Hate Crime* "is a film of constant, explicit threat and horrific consequence, leaving viewers themselves feeling assaulted by the constant barrage of thuggery, and convinced that they have seen far more than is ever actually shown on screen."[97] Bitel's acknowledgment that the extreme nature of the material may prevent any other viewing position or affective response links to the dichotomy of sensationalism vs. subversion within hardcore horror. That is, do these films, in their recourse to violent, extreme and realistic horror, merely shock audiences into a single interpretation (a spectacularization of horror) or do they challenge "existing values, institutions, mores and taboos"[98] such as the ethical dimensions of violence and its use in the media? Bressack's addendum to the film (that it is a moral response to and critique of anti–Semitism) can therefore seem disingenuous when viewed alongside the effectiveness of the violence and the particular viewing position it engenders in most viewers. Similar to *The Bunny Game* and *Murder Set Pieces*, *Hate Crime* contravened the policies and classificatory guidelines of the BBFC who rejected the film. The BBFC did not see any validation of the extreme content of the film due to its treatment of the social reality of hate crimes and instead saw the transgressive material as not conforming to its guidelines in that the film may "risk potential harm," and be "unacceptable to broad public opinion" due to "its unremitting manner" concerning how it "focuses on physical and sexual abuse, aggravated by racist invective."[99] The film does mark out the actions of the group as abhorrent and sadistic and does not present the violence and sexual abuse gratuitously and sensationally, or certainly in a way which encourages identification with the assailants. However, the aesthetic and technological areas of found footage and the hand-held digital camera amplify the intensity of the action, meaning that for many the message of anti-religious attacks will be subservient to the affective shock of the film as a disturbing home invasion horror. Once again, hardcore horror provides a discordant platform from which to address and examine the complex uses and outcomes of cinematic realism and how transgressive material, in its probing of the threshold of acceptable representational strategies within fictional films, can interact with a broad range of social and legislative practices.

Another major example of hardcore horror is 2014's *American Guinea Pig: Bouquet of Guts and Gore*. The film is a U.S. remake or continuation of the infamous Japanese *Guinea Pig* series, especially the second installment *Flowers of Flesh and Blood*. It plays upon the snuff mythology generated by the original films and increases the extremity in its desecration, mutilation and complete material destruction of two young female victims. What is interesting about *Bouquet of Guts and Gore*, the first entry in a proposed series,[100] is its nostalgic mode of looking back to one of the ur-texts of snuff and how it has been culturally disseminated and mythologized, especially within the contours of North America. In a subgenre categorized by innovatively using new digital and recording technologies to forward realist treatments of horror, the film does perhaps represent an end point or retrograde movement away from contemporary frameworks. It is predominantly connected to how the film posits a lack of engagement with socio-historical contingencies connected with real death represented in screen media and in using recording technologies to examine our relationship to cinematic reality and realism. In this respect, it adheres to Fredric Jameson's famous dictum that we "will no longer be able to invent new styles and worlds"[101] due to the fermentation of postmodernism within our social and cultural condition. Jameson cites the dependence on pastiche as an incisive cultural expression of this "failure of the new"[102] in that it presents an empty form "in which stylistic innovation is no longer possible."[103] Instead, pastiche represents "the imitation of a particular or unique style, the wearing of a stylistic mask, speech in a dead language."[104]

Bouquet of Guts and Gore's revived American take on the Japanese originals take on the countenance of the "mannerisms and stylistic twitches"[105] of this other style in an attempt to produce a more authentic and realistic version. Undoubtedly the process is disturbing and horrifying, not least because the female victims lie prone and passive throughout. However, the film does not use distancing effects or deliberately alienating aesthetics to evoke viewing positions that are at once sadistically enjoying the violent spectacle while simultaneously confronting anxieties surrounding corporeal, social and national cohesion in the U.S. during the 21st century. In fact, the aesthetic takes on the form of found footage, increasing the verisimilitude of the footage and making the process both immediate and immersive. As *Bouquet of Guts and Gore* implies and, in turn, suggests of hardcore horror in general, the real concern is realism—both in the presentation of the footage to the viewer and in the authenticity of performance and the representation of violence—than it is about any sustained reflexive articulation of the dehumanizing effect of violence and/or thematic concerns of self and national identity. Ultimately, *Bouquet of Guts and Gore*'s determined allegiance to the original, but one hollowed out of any critical component, results in a copy rendered as pure pastiche. Indeed, emerging post–9/11, post–YouTube, and in a landscape where recording technologies have "altered what we take for reality,"[106] the film seems oddly anachronistic; a homage to the heady days of illicit and unsanctioned snuff tapes circulating in society and being mistaken for the real thing.

Despite the regression back to the cultural mythology of snuff and the 1980s Japanese originals, the approach to the production, promotion and exhibition of *Bouquet of Guts and Gore* does align itself with the criteria of hardcore horror. It was funded via the crowdfunding website Indiegogo and offered incentives or thank-you gifts to donors depending on how much they pledged (for *Bouquet of Guts and Gore,* pledges ranged from $25 to $2500).

Most of the incentives were signed posters and various DVD limited editions, but if $2500 was pledged, the investor could receive the full bust of one of the victims used in the climactic gore scene! While such a process helps pre-sales of the film and potentially reduces piracy of the movie when released, it also brings the fan closer to the production and marketing of the film. Taking ownership of the film by fan-investors again reinforces the importance of the horror community in finding alternative routes to produce and release hardcore horror. *Bouquet of Guts and Gore*'s Indiegogo campaign was also extensively linked to social media sites such as Facebook and Twitter and achieved $35,455 in investment, considerably more than their rather modest $2000 target. A clear demonstration of the opportunities of alternative production practices within the horror community. Unearthed Films distributed the film in the U.S. and also released *Hate Crime* and the first three vomit gore films. The company (formed by Stephen Biro in 2002) previously acquired the American rights to the Japanese *Guinea Pig* films; Biro is now the creative force behind the U.S. continuation of this series. Similar to Eric Stanze and Fred Vogel, he has used his position as head of a distribution company to make, promote and release a film in which he has had direct involvement. This allows Biro a foundation to release the film in an unrated version and to be able to promote the film from the website and, as we have seen, though the Indiegogo project and social media. Biro, via Unearthed Films, can bypass CARA and still be guaranteed a decent-sized platform to promote the film outside of more commercial and mainstream outlets. *American Guinea Pig: Bouquet of Guts and Gore* may represent a violent and hardcore throwback to the Japanese pseudo-snuff of the 1980s, but it also utilizes cutting edge and innovative methods for its production, promotion and exhibition.

In *Found Footage Horror*, Alexandra Heller-Nicholas talks about the "generational territorialism"[107] with regards to reception surrounding the re-emergence of found footage horror in the 21st century. The marginal status of hardcore horror in academic discourse links to a difficulty (or unwillingness) in assigning the amateurish, low-fi and extremely violent examples to more established forms of quality horror, but we can see also a generally dismissive attitude from the horror community. What the following sections have argued is that although hardcore horror may not be seen widely as "proper" horror or even as an example of a "proper" film, it does provide a great deal of confluence with outstanding examples of extreme cinema. The overlaps surround aspects such as affect, reception and unconventional marketing and distribution patterns and show the importance of mapping out historical and national contours with regards to the study of extreme film. The emphasis on contextualization also clearly highlights the break hardcore horror advances with antecedent and concomitant global examples. Hardcore horror can provide cultural value to discussions of the horror genre, its genre makers and genre users. Particularly regarding realism, which cuts through all the examples from *Scrapbook* to *Bouquet of Guts and Gore*, hardcore horror can develop and add to both the notions of cinematic realism and its formation in horror texts. Therefore, the next two chapters deal with this most important of subjects for hardcore horror and bring films such as *August Underground*, *Amateur Porn Star Killer* and the vomit gore series within the remit of larger academic debates about cinematic realism. While such coverage may "legitimize" the transgressive qualities of hardcore horror in a way in which critical discussion and space should perhaps be resisted, the inclusion and subsequent analysis will provide a much-needed outlet for new relationships and investigations to form with the marginal, "improper" films which constitute the hardcore horror subgenre.

Five

The Realist Aesthetic of Hardcore Horror[1]

Christopher Williams' brave attempt to map out the historical contours of cinematic realism opens with the sentence: "Discussion of realism, in film as in other art forms, tends to be tortuous or circular."[2] At the turn of the millennium, 20 years after the publication of Williams' book, Julia Hallam and Margaret Marshment reiterate the complex, convoluted and contested scope of realism by saying that it is "a contentious arena of debate across a broad field of scholarship embracing philosophy, aesthetics and the social sciences in an ongoing dialogue about the role of all forms of representation—from fine art to photojournalism, autobiography to scientific reports—in the construction and understanding of the social world."[3]

In the 21st century where communication technologies and portable recording devices have "annihilated the distance that separates the viewer from the event,"[4] the boundaries between the real and the representational are complicated and altered to the extent that we ponder if "reality is no longer what it used to be."[5] Debates circulating around realism in cinema are not, and have never been, "singular or univocal,"[6] nor have they been static, immutable or culturally and historically homogenous. However, despite the complexity of realism in cinema as a multifaceted and protean configuration, its examination is crucial as it offers the opportunity to take us to the very heart of film mechanics and an understanding of its historical development. In this respect, cinema's encapsulation of "historical, technological, aesthetic and sociological factors"[7] lends itself to a dynamic and stimulating discussion of realism as notions of the real factor in each aspect. The real, therefore, is never far from discussions of cinema.

The organizing principles of cinema, from elements such as narrative form, cinematography, editing, *mise en scène* and sound in orchestrating its audio-visual elements, all link to artistic choices made by the filmmaker. A main, integral factor of the aesthetic organization is the ability to capture the world in terms of "how it really happened" or "how it really was." Such a conception has been the mainstay of Western aesthetics since the time of Aristotle's *Poetics* and runs through various strands of historical-cultural expression, ossifying with the invention of photography in the 19th century and its "almost 'scientific' accuracy in reproducing the visible circumstances of life."[8] Cinema emerges from this argument and has added to the realist and naturalist form of the single frame photograph in its "panoply of techniques for melding the sequences together."[9]

From the imposition of narrative and spectacle, underpinned by a commercial imperative, early examples of cinematic realism often centered on unbelievable and spectacular tableaux rendered credible through the use of realistic techniques. The Lumiere brother's famous, oft-cited single-take film *L'Arrivee d'un train en gare de la Ciolat* aka *The Arrival of a Train at La Ciotat Station* (1895) and Thomas Edison's *Joan of Arc* (1895) and *Electrocuting an Elephant* both thrilled and terrified onlookers in their development of the single, still images of photography into a series of consecutive shots presented to give the impression of continuous motion. The films placed the audience into a realistic and direct experience captured by the "world-as-it-happened" nature of these events. The early forays into these new authentic visual experiences by filmmakers such as Edison have provided a number of significant realistic moments that accentuate the multifarious and contested arena of film realism. For example, Soviet filmmakers of the 1920s, such as Sergei Eisenstein and Dziga Vertov, deployed the feature of montage to develop a style of editing to highlight the differences between shots to produce new structures of meaning. Realism here became a political tool linked to the socio-historical contingencies of Russia post–1917 and the October revolution. Italian neo-realism in the 1940s, through its main practitioner Roberto Rossellini, further developed the exacting "mirror" of realism into more poetic and political forms. For Williams, the material reality of Italy post–World War II "permits the artist to discover realistic 'means of expression,'"[10] captured through the lives of ordinary people cast against the socio-political landscape of Fascism and the emerging lens of left-leaning, liberal humanism. Other key developments are present in British cinema, from the British documentary movement to British New Wave; 1980s new American cinema characterized by individuals such as Jim Jarmusch and movements such as Queer Cinema and New Black Cinema. Indeed, classical Hollywood also serves as a lightning rod for cinematic realism and can be traced through the use of long takes and deep focus in studio films by Orson Welles and William Wyler to New Hollywood re-workings through the anti-establishment narratives of *Bonnie and Clyde* (Arthur Penn, 1967) and *MASH* (Robert Altman, 1970). Most recently, examples of cinematic realism have ranged from the meticulous restaging of World War II and its pre-millennium resurgence with films such as *Saving Private Ryan* (Steven Spielberg, 1997) and *The Thin Red Line* (Terrence Malick, 1998) to the fantastical narratives and world settings of the 21st-century universes of Marvel and DC.

Concomitant with the various national developments of cinematic realism has been an insightful and ongoing theoretical discourse about the problems inherent with realism and its application to cinema. Initial positions became entrenched within the realism vs. anti-realism dichotomy, with Siegfried Kracauer and André Bazin proponents of a realist cinema and Rudolf Arnheim and V.F. Perkins who respectively adopted anti-realistic and connective approaches.[11] Added to this is Colin MacCabe's use of a psychoanalytic framework to introduce notions of political ideology and spectatorial positioning in classical realist cinema. For MacCabe there is no possibility of getting at an absolute "truth" or knowing the world "as it really is" because of a "dominant specularity"[12] produced by the narrative of the film that "resists questioning"[13] due to its unambiguous meaning and ideological construction. In this respect, "[r]ealism is no longer a question of an exterior reality nor of the relation of the reader to the text: It is simply one of the ways which [audience members] interact amidst specific social and political circumstances."[14] Bordwell, Staiger and Thompson's imperious text *The Classical Hollywood Cinema* provides a comprehensive engagement with American narrative film, its production processes and how this gave rise to a defined film style. Here, the authors track an aesthetic of realism enmeshed within dominant and popular narrative structure to provide a useful bridge linking the discursive approaches of cinematic realism together.

Another intriguing and insightful strand of academic discourse on realism is in how cinema represents the past. Cinematic history addresses a number of the theoretical strands mentioned above, mainly in its modernist-postmodernist split which is reminiscent of the realism vs. anti-realism divide. Although talking about capturing the past, postist approaches provide illuminating ways to approach the area of realism in cinema and particularly within hardcore horror. Historians Dominic LeCapra, Keith Jenkins and Hayden White all see history as distinct from the past in that history is "always apprehended and appropriated textually through the sedimented layers of previous interpretations and through the reading habits and categories developed by previous-current methodological practices."[15] Here, Jenkins' statement has direct relevance to cinematic realism in that it is historically contingent, beholden to former industry and technological practices and developments, and is given "life" through representation of the formal aesthetics of cinema, in terms of essential properties or narrative design, so that accounts of cinematic realism are always already represented. Therefore, cinematic realism, like cinematic representations of the past, is a kind of text rather than the thing itself. An example of this will be picked up by *August*

Underground and how the film becomes *cinematically* realist rather than a representation of the real "as it was" or "as it happened."

A key Hollywood example would be the claims to historical realism of the film *Saving Private Ryan*. Here audiences were most likely basing the verisimilitude of the film, and especially its 30-minute opening sequence, not on the referent of the D-Day landings but other films dealing with warfare and World War II. In this case, *Saving Private Ryan* emerges as the most realistic *film* to deal with the D-Day landings and not as a realistic document of the event itself. As such, the theoretical approaches and cinematic moments of realism represent a complicated spectatorial position and one which forgoes any easy summation of realism as "real" or of "reality" as realism or anti-realism.

The very brief outline of some of the key realistic cinema moments and associated theoretical discussion is to stress the lack of homogeneity and subsequent impossibility of looking at realism (if we should at all) as a Manichean concept between the antagonistic realms of realism and anti-realism. It is to underline how realism is socially and historically contingent and offers up a contract between the film and spectator that is predicated on complex issues such as social positioning, present-centeredness and previous knowledge and experience. It is to make clear that as we move into the 21st century and developments in portable recording technologies and the continued pervasiveness of computer-generated imagery, our understanding of realism is once again in flux. Within this bewildering series of realistic moments and theoretical concepts and contemporary challenges to what we perceive as authentic emerges hardcore horror. With its concerted attempt to obfuscate any clear divide between the real and mimesis, its utilization of low-fi camera technology, its evocation of fear, anxiety and fascination circulating from real-world predicaments, and its break with pre-existing and familiar notions of realism, hardcore horror provides another, new realistic moment.

Hardcore horror enters into the historical development of cinematic realism by addressing the nexus of technology—socio-historical context—aesthetics embedded within 21st-century discourses. In marking out the realist triumvirate at the turn of the millennium, a distinctive stylistic form of horror has emerged which embodies conceptions of the real as our world moves into a globalized digital age. The aesthetic form which most insistently signifies this nexus, therefore, is a realist horror which utilizes portable and digital technology to articulate fears and anxieties engendered by real-world horrors such as 9/11, terrorism, the wars in Iraq and Afghanistan, pandemic disease and environmental catastrophe. However, this is not a horror film which depends on special effects to render fantastic or unbelievable worlds real and credible. If new recording technologies have, to cite Joel Black, "altered what we take for reality"[16] due to the now pervasive agency of filmed records detailing everything from the quotidian to the spectacular, then this is not necessarily to say that movies "are becoming more 'realistic,' more like real life."[17]

For Black, cinema is becoming "less credible and plausible than ever, [though] certainly more graphic—more physical and explicit."[18] Graphicness for Black has significant connotations for horror and particularly for hardcore horror. Horror's use of special effects and CGI brings the imaginary and the artificial closer to the realm of the real as a convincing and believable experience. Yet, paradoxically, the closer the filmmakers come to achieving credible representations of the fantastic, the further away they get. This is underlined by the amount of technical staff credited for films using CGI and the understanding from viewers that the elaborate and effective supernatural entities in films such as *Cloverfield* and the 2011 remake of *The Thing* (Matthijs van Heijningen) are just successfully captured physical and explicit effects. Or, as Heller-Nicholas points out, events which say to viewers, "If they *did* occur, this is how they might look."[19]

The paradox of the real inherent in much of 21st-century horror released through a more mainstream and commercial platform relies broadly on presenting a realistic spectacle as one ultimately coded and received as constructed and artificial. That is, a narrative which puts forward "a set of signifying tropes of the real in a fictional context,"[20] whether it be marauding monsters over the Manhattan skyline or demons from other dimensions threatening the sanctity of the all–American family. This type of graphic realism of supernatural and fantastic imagery "speaks to our relationship to new media technologies"[21] in the way the viewer "gets" the intricate illusion. Here, the connection between the fantastical nature of the horror and the spectator is one where the real-seeming *mise en scène* is embraced but not to the extent that disbelief is entirely suspended. The aesthetics of the snuff film and found footage horror have arguably been the two most effective and consistent strands in forwarding a realist horror in the 21st century. The use of amateur tropes and immersive *mise en scène* in films such as *Diary of the Dead* (George Romero, 2007) and *The Last Exorcism* (Daniel Stamm, 2010) enables viewers to engage with the "what if?" scenario that if the scenes in the film *were* real, then this is how they would look (in this case, the respective threats of a zombie apocalypse and demonic possession).

But this interaction with the real is mitigated by the very knowledge that the films are making authentic the decidedly inauthentic: cinematic artifice as reality. Hence, a barrier is erected between the viewer and the real on display in that the film does not denote a referent that exists in the world outside of the film. The audience remains distanced from the horror, and its power is reduced in terms of its intensity and affective charge precisely because the imagery exists within the film's diegetic arrangement and construction.

Five. The Realist Aesthetic of Hardcore Horror

Although the horror presented in these films uses contemporary contexts and technology to shape its themes and formal structure, the result replicates much of classical or secure horror in that its properties do not "threaten us directly, we are protected knowing that they are in fact impossible."[22] Thus, snuff and found footage, despite their reality claims, can be seen to adhere to strict formal arrangements and thematic strategies. While the majority of examples, from those cited to the pioneer productions *Snuff, Cannibal Holocaust, The Great American Snuff Film* (Sean Treeta, 2004) and *Paranormal Activity*, may well break with the conventions of mainstream cinema in general, and horror in particular, their form has condensed into a set of familiar tropes as the 21st century has progressed. Thus, for formalists such as Viktor Shklovsky, and picked up and applied to cinematic aesthetics by scholars Bordwell and Thompson, the term of "defamiliarization" becomes paramount in creating a convincing sense of the real in film. In changing the film's narrative and stylistic form, a challenge to the cognitive processes of the viewer emerges due to the establishment of unconventional patterns. The incredible success of *The Blair Witch Project* was necessarily predicated on its combination of unfamiliar plot mechanics, effective (perhaps too effective) marketing strategies that positioned the film as real in terms of the three filmmakers who might actually be missing, possibly dead, and the innovative and original manner of the construction of found footage. The film achieved a successful defamiliarization as it ruptured the homogeneity of parodic and self-referential treatments of 1990s horror characterized by the commercial and popular successes of the *Scream* franchise and acolytes such as *I Know What You Did Last Summer* (Jim Gillespie, 1997). Thus, when *The Blair Witch Project* premiered in 1999, it provided audiences with an authentic and credible horror generated through the film's break with established and popular horror forms and styles.

August Underground takes the innovation and originality of *Blair Witch* and aligns it with a graphic violence which was elided or sanitized in much of North American horror during the 1990s. As such, it stands as the archetypal example of hardcore horror in terms of its engagement with the real and provides a key example of defamiliarization as it moves the nascent success of found footage horror into the underground. In doing so, the film uses the aesthetics of snuff and found footage horror but instead focuses on the "realistic-ness" of amateur footage taken of traumatic events and actions to disrupt any coherent boundary between the authentic and the artificial. The intention is to withdraw, as much as possible, the barrier between the viewer and the horror on display. The "amateur event' surrounds the on-screen depiction of "real" death and the violation of the body. *August Underground*'s verisimilitude of this taboo provides a critique of outstanding horror realism and positions the film regarding MacCabe's use of metalanguage: a text "privileged as the bearer of the truth … against which the truth or falsity of the other discourses [filmic texts] can be judged."[23] *August Underground*'s entire production process, formal aesthetics and promotion and exhibition attempts to move the film outside of a familiar understanding of the cinematic process to achieve, in the words of Vogel, the capacity to "fool people" into receiving the film as an actual snuff movie.

Examining how *August Underground* engages with notions of the real, the opening scene will be discussed. It is an example of how the film's formal properties and sense of verisimilitude of the *mise en scène* destabilize the boundary between the real and the constructed to an extent largely unseen in dominant mainstream horror. Then it will be possible to situate the realism of the film within its larger production practices and reception. Doing so will provide a more detailed exploration of cinematic realism and how issues such as defamiliarization and the contract between the viewer and the film exist both with the film itself and outside of the image in regards to how the film was distributed and exhibited. *August Underground*'s innovative approach to realism and understanding of the media effects of violence will serve as an entry point into alternative and marginal horror and how it can provide a discursive move away from and challenge to commercial and mainstream horror in the 21st century.

"You are going to love this..."

August Underground starts abruptly, without warning or production credits that may render it a constructed and authored piece of film.[24] The first image is the outstretched arm of an unseen and silent male figure apparently videotaping the footage as he purposefully spills the contents of a beer bottle out over the ground. It is night, and we hear an off-camera male say, "That is the waste of a fucking full beer, dude." As the camera tilts up to take in the figure that has entered the frame, we see an indistinctly realized male figure carrying a bucket walk toward the camera from what looks like a farm building. The character continues toward the camera and through another door behind the man with the video camera. Here, we can discern that the setting is rural and the interactions of the two male characters and the poorly handled camera seem to signal that the protagonists may be drunk. Nonetheless, this establishing sequence is relatively innocuous in its content and purposefully misdirects the viewer.

The next scene has the male who emerged from the house come up to the person filming and say, "Come on, I've got something to show you," as he walks into a brightly lit room (made worse by the garish high contrast of the camera) and down steps to a basement. He then turns back to say, "You are going to love this."

Five. The Realist Aesthetic of Hardcore Horror

At this point, approximately 35 seconds into the film, the viewer has little idea of the direction it is taking. When the camera turns the corner, and the full violence of the scene is revealed, there is the palpable sense of the horrific. The images on display provide a filmic zone not sanctioned or regulated by legitimate and official controls found in mainstream cinematic representations of horror. The main reason is the degraded nature of the visual arrangement, dominated by discarded rubbish and bodily waste. In this abhorrent space, seated under a mural of pornographic imagery, is a naked woman who is tied up, her tortured and mutilated body a brutal spectacle of the abject and stark depiction of hardcore horror's violation of the body. A bucket of her feces lies at her feet, and it is evident that its contents have repeatedly been smeared over her body; her wounds in particular. Other parts are covered with vomit and blood. There is also an uncomfortable and distressing sense that this could be real or, at least, something we should not be watching. Indeed, it refers back to Heller-Nicholas' dictum that if this was real, then this is what it would look like. During this sequence, which is one continuous take of roughly six minutes in duration, a matter-of-fact approach is established as the killer shows the camera operator his "murder room." We see a castrated male in a bathtub, his penis in an adjacent bloodied toilet, and we learn he is the husband-partner of the woman. The camera is continually in motion, revealing the room as a dirty, disgusting space covered with blood, excrement and vomit and littered by body parts. The violence and degradation carried out by the killers are shown explicitly to the viewer so that, according to Vogel, it can "visually play with all your senses" by enabling audiences to "put themselves in the scene."[25] The main part of the sequence is given over to the ritual humiliation of the woman, in which Peter marks her out as his "prize" and as his "favorite." The killer's friend also becomes complicit in her torture by repeatedly focusing on her naked body with his camera. The behavior and actions of the two men denote the violation and degradation of the woman as sexual objectification. The scene ends with the killer asking, "Do you want a beer?"; he gets the reply, "You bet." It is a chilling exchange, which effectively emphasizes the sociopathic nature of the men and their utter detachment from their actions.

A sense of "real" horror is achieved in this scene through two interrelated cinematic strands: First is the strand of realist horror, which Cynthia Freeland defines as a subgenre of horror that "showcases spectacle, downplays plot, and plays upon serious confusions between representations of fiction and reality."[26] In turn, we have seen how Freeland's seminal work has shaped and influenced the key criteria which define hardcore horror. *August Underground* conforms to this outline in that it takes a seemingly objective view of everyday horror, evidenced by the familiar space of the basement, the amateurish quality of the footage, the badly framed compositions, inferior image quality, convincing special effects and the authenticity of the actors' performances. In its presentation of the material, the film effectively downplays plot (we see a series of random, repetitious and seemingly unconnected sequences throughout the narrative, starting with the opening scene) in favor of an emotionally flattening, yet unsettling and disturbing spectacle of violence. In addition, the film corresponds to Freeland's argument that, in rupturing the border between mimesis and reality, the narrative often integrates into the plot realist news reports, especially of everyday monsters and catastrophic events.[27] *August Underground* makes explicit this connection by presenting the film as "live" footage and, thus, aligns it with 21st-century news, which often uses live amateur footage in their reporting of events in war zones and the aftermath of disasters. Vogel has talked at length about how important *Henry: Portrait of a Serial Killer* was in the gestation of the film.[28] At the time of its release, *Henry* was marketed as an authentic account of the serial killer due to its social realist tendencies and faux documentary style. For Vogel, *Henry* addressed the enthralling mainstream portrayals of serial killers by offering a counter position, especially in the notorious home invasion sequence which the killers capture in real time on a cheap portable camcorder. The resultant poorly shot footage detailing the torture and murder of a middle-class family is thus framed with a "proximity to the real world."[29] Indeed, Vogel singled out the home invasion scene as its most realist segment:

> I was tired of all the serial killer movies that didn't show you what's really going on.... *Henry: Portrait of a Serial Killer*'s "home invasion" scene always freaked me out. So, just imagining a feature of that went through my mind, *but*, five times more real. Really show the viewer what these people are like, not like how Hollywood shows us.[30]

In *August Underground*'s opening sequence, we are indeed offered an elongated version of *Henry*'s home invasion scene and, just as the audience watched along with Henry and his accomplice Otis as they (re)viewed the footage on TV, so we watch through the killer's eyes in the basement. Also similar to Henry and Otis, the *August Underground* killers seem to be making the video for their own pleasure and to experience the "realness" of the event over and over again.

The second strand of realism manifests in *August Underground*'s adherence to conventions found in the mondo documentary. *Faces of Death* became one of the most popular and influential "death" compilations in the late 1970s and early 1980s in North America. The film (and later examples such as *Death Scenes*) provided "a fierce critique of the traditional horror film"[31] in their graphic, intensive and "unmediated" representations of death and the defiant violation of the physical body. Their very nature as ruptures from "'sanctioned' horror film narrative[s]" represented, according to Brottman, the "'hidden' version of the mainstream horror film."[32] As with realist horror, these films pushed representations of death in ways that established horror could not. That is, despite the technical sophistication of contemporary special effects which can render death in ever more credible ways, mainstream horror films "can never reveal the violation of the physical body in the same way that mondo can show 'actual' human death."[33]

August Underground, in exemplifying these cinematic strands, breaks with established conceptions surrounding the horror film, especially the threshold relating to representation and the authentic, and with its focus on the physicality of the violated body. With regard to the latter, considerable time is devoted to an almost forensic examination of the trauma many bodies go through at the killers' hands. As with the horror mondo films, the *August Underground* narrative explicitly shows the body in various states of "fragmentation, dismemberment and collapse."[34] Both these strands move away from legitimate and official representations of horror cinema and their circulation via conventional distribution routes (the auditorium, the video cassette, DVD). In fact, the last aspect of *August Underground*'s pursuit of the real connects to the regulations of classification boards and conventional distribution networks that mainstream horror has to adhere to in order to be seen by an audience. The film was not submitted to CARA due to the extreme and prolonged nature of its violence. Neither was it released as an unrated film, which would have at least guaranteed a legal release despite a heavily restricted outlet for promotional activity and exhibition. In fact, Vogel intended to leave unmarked copies of *August Underground* in public places such as airports and libraries to move the film out of any officially sanctioned realm and into the category of an illicit "found object" to be picked up and consumed by curious passersby. By deploying this distribution process, the film emerges as a realist text outside the cultural space of legitimate and sanctioned cinematic practices. That is, the film takes on the form of a series of recorded images passed off as a "found object" and, in doing so, actually obscures the boundary between representation and the real. Vogel was unable to release the film in this way, and his insistence on moving it outside of industrial, social and cultural practices highlights how realism is not only connected to visual representations but a defamiliarization concerning how the material is presented to and received by the viewer (or curious passerby).

"You are going to love this..." Redux

Vogel's attempts to produce a snuff movie were ultimately limited in that he was never able to distribute *August Underground* in the way he originally intended. Had he been able to, it would have provided a fascinating insight into the paradox of representing death in horror films and the complex relationship between mimesis and realism. Vogel's mischievous and transgressive act would have undoubtedly produced a film where viewers could not disavow the footage as fictional due to the verisimilitude of the *mise en scène* and the manner in which they had procured the tape. It would have produced a profoundly unsettling and troubling experience, exacerbating the difficulty of differentiating between real and simulated violence. It is likely that some viewers would have informed the police and that an investigation would have ensued and as such is reminiscent of Charlie Sheen's misadventures with *Flower of Flesh and Blood*! Indeed, Vogel was happy to be arrested and spend a night or two in jail if it meant the film was able to be distributed in this seditious manner. However, Vogel's lawyer talked him out of the marketing plan due to the proximity to 9/11 and the subsequent possibility of being incarcerated for a lot longer than a couple of days. What this event effectively shows is that, while Vogel was able to traverse the codes and regulations of cinematic representation and distribution methods, he was unable (or unwilling) to contravene societal structures and dominant taste cultures that were circulating at the time. As Vogel admitted, "My marketing plan for *August Underground* had to change to letting the world know that it was an actual movie and not a real snuff film."[35]

In 2006, Toetag Pictures distributed *August Underground* on DVD. Prior to the release, it had been circulated "unofficially" through Vogel's friends and acquaintances and via independently distributed bootlegs. Viewer responses ranged from "[I've] definitely not seen anything like *August Underground*" to "It wasn't even a movie…. I don't know what the hell I was getting myself into."[36] Yet the official release of the film was not received as an authentic and real documentation of murder and death because Vogel's presence in the film as both on-screen "killer" and distributor marked the film out as a construction. Indeed, the sense of mimesis of the film was heightened by its official release via the accepted and legitimate form of the DVD. The film itself had changed, with a warning letting people know that it "contains adult language, graphic violence, and nudity. Viewer discretion is advised." End credits appeared, clearly detailing the actors and technical staff involved in making the film. Therefore, the status of the film shifted from Vogel's initial intention of creating a "real snuff movie" towards realist horror. The forbidden, illicit, potentially illegal status of the film was scaled back, turning its content into something that has to be endured and aligning it more with the hardcore horror films to follow. Hence, the film moved away from countering the paradox of showing real death and murder in horror films to an oppositional stance, situating itself as "real" only in opposition to other cinematic texts. In this respect, the film links to discourse over historical fealty in cinematic representations of the past, where *August Underground* is measured as realistic *against* other horror films and not of the act itself.

"[August Underground] is real. Well, as real as I could make it."[37]

In *Mordum* and *Penance*, Vogel does not necessarily abandon the project of making realist horror, but does develop the films toward more familiar storytelling techniques. By his doing so, they move away from the "real-ness" of the first film to more conventional narrativity. The performances of the actors become less naturalistic and obviously governed by script designs, character development and directorial cues.

This is not to say that *Mordum* and *Penance* do not provide realist horror that disconnects from sanctioned representations of violence and death found in independent or Hollywood productions. While the scenes of violence and death are now clearly received as imitative due to the growing exposure of Vogel and the notoriety of *August Underground*, there is still the sense that we should not be watching them due to the reprehensible nature of the acts. They are so far removed from mainstream horror that their frequent occurrence in the narrative still offers a troubling and uneasy viewing position.[38] For example, in *Mordum*'s climactic scene, the brother is seen having intercourse with the partially decomposed corpse of a child in a bathtub as his sister Crusty films the surrounding room. It is a place so overridden with a pestilence that maggots are swarming over all the surfaces. This repellent environment is exacerbated by Vogel's off-camera screaming, which contributes to the sense that delirium and madness are taking hold of both the characters and the actors playing them. The film ends in an out-of-control orgiastic display of violence in which Vogel cuts the throat of a tied-up woman and forces Crusty's brother to drink the blood. The physical and verbal violence directed toward Crusty and her brother from Vogel-Peter and the combination of impressive special effects work mark the scene as intensive and authentic. We may receive the film as a constructed reality but it nevertheless induces an affectation of fear and horror as something we should not be watching. The real-ness of the snuff coda may have been supplanted by more conventional film devices but the imagery and its stark contrast to most other horror texts still produce a "dangerous" and disturbing film.

The *August Underground* films fail to break down the paradox of representing "real" death on screen and thus forward a sense of the "real" ultimately connected to artificial elements and previous visual examples. However, this is not necessarily due to constraints in the making of the film. In fact, Vogel was successful in this respect but was unable to distribute *August Underground* in the way he envisioned due to the prospect of serious criminal charges. Thus, *August Underground* attempts to develop the realist horror outlined by Freeland into a real-reel snuff film but, thwarted by societal regulations, ends up providing a corrective to horror realism exhibited in mainstream cinema instead. Here, Vogel flattens out the glamor, plot designs, performances and high-gloss spectacle inherent in films such as *The Silence of the Lambs*, which audiences during the 1990s saw as a yardstick in how the cinematic serial killer should be presented. Instead, Vogel's characters are "ordinary" people, the violence unpredictable, ugly, brutal and thoroughly degrading, and the plot subordinate to the spectacle of killing. Vogel's wish to "show you what's really going on"[39] seems a key approach in how he sought to defamiliarize *August Underground* from the prominent and dominant examples of 1990s horror in North America and establish an innovative approach to horror realism.

However, Vogel encountered numerous difficulties in producing a horror film in which the material could be received, and even accepted, as "real." Primarily, the restrictions on Vogel's commitment to realism were due to his reliance on dominant horror to situate *August Underground* along the axis of other marginal practices such as snuff-fictions, mondo movies and the standalone example of *Henry*. The film also emerged at a time where significant developments in accessible and portable visual technology coupled with the prevalence of amateur testimony radically altered notions of the real in terms of its capture and dissemination. With regards to the cultural, social and technological contingencies impressing on *August Underground*'s production and exhibition, it is no surprise that Vogel's responsibility to realist horror could not entirely escape the influence of external processes. In a time where there has been a noticeable confection between the proliferation of (mass-) mediated violent imagery, its capture by non-official sources via digital recording devices, and the importation of subsequent formal and thematic properties into 21st-century horror, notions of realism have coalesced into a defined form dependent on socio-cultural contingencies. That is, the real and the fictional have become ever more blurred and ever more contested, complex and controversial. Perhaps in this landscape, *August Underground* was, indeed, as real as Vogel "could make it."[40]

The "True Horror" of Amateur Porn Star Killer

Shane Ryan's *Amateur Porn Star Killer* films similarly engage with the aesthetics of snuff and of forwarding a realist horror. Over the course of the three films, Ryan purposefully manipulates the aesthetics of fictional snuff. Rather than just documenting death with a "sense of real world authenticity through a primitive gaze,"[41] the trilogy points toward a more complex engagement with how the mythology of snuff is experienced and disseminated by 21st century screen media. Central to this mythology are the reality-based mechanics of snuff and how their use and manipulation via amateur recordings of atrocity to propagandistic extremism and news reportage has had "far-reaching consequences for the ways in which we might understand images of violence and murder."[42] It has been well-documented that Ryan's background and approach to the *Amateur Porn Star Killer* films did not originate via a love for horror or even knowledge of the genre.[43] However, the genealogy of *Amateur Porn Star Killer* originated with the mainstream horror film *8MM* (Joel Schumacher, 1999) which takes as its plot the investigation of a snuff film in which a young girl may or may not have been murdered on-camera. Just as Vogel became interested in widening out the aesthetic design and affective power of *Henry*'s home invasion sequence, so too did Ryan want to focus on the snuff film in *8MM* in terms of expanding it to make a film about the victim, "from toward beginning to end, how she handled the situation."[44] As Ryan's approach to filmmaking is to focus on human behavior and the often disruptive and violent dynamic it possesses, it is logical that he became interested in the human interaction and violent context inherent within the contours of the fictional snuff subgenre. Therefore, Ryan took the snuff concept and developed it as a true crime drama, with the particular focus on a realist treatment of the relationship between the assailant and the victim. However, due to the *in extremis* nature of the film's budget, it was necessary to adapt the original concept toward horror stylistics to appeal to the underground horror community. The outcome is a mix of drama and horror and of the real and the constructed, which takes from both the ultra-realism of *August Underground* and the cultural mythology of snuff.

Amateur Porn Star Killer advances a genuinely unnerving and entirely credible formulation of a sexual predator's manipulation of a 13-year-old girl into sexual congress. The film ends with the girl's shocking murder and perhaps reflects Ryan's awareness of including more overt horrific moments for future promotional activities. The realism in the film is primarily due to location and performance rather than the intensive gore special effects of Vogel's *August Underground* films. In fact, the physical violence of the murder happens partially off-screen and in a hyper-stylized manner of slow-motion combined with a discordant musical track. The focus for Ryan is the interaction between the two characters, Brandon and Stacey, and the psychological processes involved. The film starts with an intertitle stating that the film is "inspired by true events" before cutting to a confrontational scene of a naked man attacking a woman. The camera is placed directly in front of them, and although we can generally discern what is happening, we cannot see their faces and we don't know *why* it's happening. It is a disorientating sequence and one which aligns itself clearly to the snuff aesthetic of amateur footage, victimization, patriarchal authority and sexually violent imagery. A quote from Paul Schrader addressing the mythical nature of the snuff film follows this brief insert:

> Movies are a flexible medium. It's easy to simulate death on film, which is partly why people think snuff films exist. They've seen simulated versions and believe they are genuine. I think it's conceivable these films exist, but whether they do or not is less important than the public's belief that they do; their willingness to believe in an evil fantasy. That's what's interesting here.

Afterwards the footage returns to the killer in the motel room. The insert of the Schrader quotation is important to the representation of the real in *Amateur Porn Star Killer* in terms of how it shifts viewer perspective from receiving the film as an authentic and realist horror to situating it as part of the larger discourse around the snuff mythos and its presence in the 21st century. It will be necessary to return to Schrader's quote and how the film comments on real death and its dissemination via media forms, but first an understanding of the realist elements of the film needs to be reached.

The narrative of Brandon and Stacey begins with footage from the interior of Brandon's car while it is in motion. The camera positioning is haphazard as if a secondary concern and the visual quality is purposefully degraded so that the frame constantly flickers and black, vertical scratches repetitively appear. The opening sequence where Brandon meets Stacey and takes her to a motel is the longest in the film (18 minutes in a single take). The unedited footage provides an intimate and immersive account of what is initially an awkward encounter full of stilted conversation, long periods of silence and banal small talk. The sense of realism is established via the amateur quality of the footage and the naturalistic familiarity of the motel room but is fulfilled via the convincing performances of the two actors, especially Michiko Jimenez as Stacey, who plays the scene in a believably naive and vulnerable manner. Any sense of an overt threat during these early interchanges is minimal though that is not to suggest that the film is setting up a prelude to a benign drama examining the romantic aspirations of the two characters as they seemingly engage in a one-night stand. The camera does sexually objectify Stacey at times, and due to the authority invested in Brandon as operator of the camera and wielder of the gaze, the scene plays out with a forceful power dynamic that puts Stacey in an unequal and borderline oppressive situation. At the end of the sequence, Stacey takes the camera from Brandon and turns it on him. It is a shocking development as it is the first time that we fully see Brandon's face after 25 minutes of the film has elapsed. Prior to this reversal in subjectivity, the viewer had been aligned with Brandon/the camera's faceless gaze as he/it exerted control over Stacey via a scopophilic motivation whereby her body is gradually objectified and presented to the camera/Brandon/viewer as a source of gratification. From this moment, the tone of the film changes toward a more menacing atmosphere as Brandon manipulates Stacey, both verbally and physically, into performing fellatio and ultimately sexual intercourse where he suffocates and beats her to death.

Amateur Porn Star Killer reflects on a number of cinematic movements in its low-fi style and sense of voyeuristic realism. The inarticulate and improvised quality of Brandon and Stacey's early conversations plays out like the romantic situations in mumblecore where characters are often unable to express how they feel about each other and, instead of consummating relationships, end up in a never-ending process of circuitous verbal exchanges.

Brandon (Shane Ryan) is finally revealed (*Amateur Porn Star Killer*, Mongolian Barbeque).

Mumblecore's "micro-budgeted minimalist aesthetic"[45] combined with a concerted focus on characters as drivers of the narrative is also evident in Ryan's film, which takes its time to explore the psychological dimension of the characters through a minimalist approach. The slow pace of the film and its deployment of a "real-time" aesthetic links it to certain New French Extremism examples such as Catherine Breillat's *Fat Girl*, Gasper Noe's *Irreversible* and Bruno Dumont's *Twentynine Palms*. In Breillat's film, there is a lengthy sequence, about 25 minutes, showing the seduction of 15-year-old Elena as her 12-year-old sister Anaïs looks on in increasing discomfort. The realist aesthetic, which is flat and dispassionate, de-eroticizes the sex and disengages the audience from reading the scene as an example of male virility and sexual prowess. In doing so, Breillat foregrounds this "excruciating portrayal of adolescent sex" so that it can be "accompanied by a merciless critique of male romantic discourse and machismo."[46]

The gaze in this sequence is also instructive as it switches from being directly on Anaïs' face as she becomes more distressed by the events unfolding before her or from her perspective as she helplessly watches the "seduction and ultimate humiliation of her beautiful sister."[47] The use of character perspective is to provide an ethical charge to the event and to move it away from being a voyeuristic spectacle for the viewer. Instead, they become implicated in the seduction and acutely aware that they are intruding on a scene which they should not be watching and that should never be coded as erotic or acceptable as a manifestation of male potency. Ultimately, in exposing the male gaze and its suggestions of ownership and control by re-orientating to the gaze of 12-year-old Anaïs, "Breillat explores with great lucidity the traps (for women) of conventional heterosexuality"[48] and how they tend to be exalted on the cinema screen.

Breillat's acknowledgment of the male gaze in *Fat Girl* references the relationship between the cinematic gaze and the viewer as formed from Jacques Lacan's notion of the "mirror stage" and Laura Mulvey's pioneering work on the masculine and sadistic gaze of classical narrative in Hollywood.[49] In turn, this connects to the use of a first-person narrative in the slasher film and how such a perspective aligns the viewer with the sadistic gaze of the killer. For example, in the opening scene of the slasher progenitor *Black Christmas*, the audience takes the view of the killer as he prowls around the perimeter of a sorority house. The 2009 reboot of the *Friday the 13th* franchise dispenses with the voyeuristic gaze of the killer Jason as he stalks his victims, but still withholds identification by having his face covered until the final shot. Notably, when the hockey mask is finally removed, and Jason dumped into Crystal Lake, it is the mask we follow to the bottom of the lake and not Jason. When Jason inevitably returns for one final scare, the mask is firmly back in place. The representation of the killer in these examples is usually withheld from the viewer to generate tension and enable a horrific affective charge without resort to extreme violence. However, withholding the identity of the killer from the viewer by obfuscation or absence serves another purpose in that the killer is "depersonalised in a literal sense, with his body and the more intricate workings of his consciousness hidden from the spectator."[50] The viewer does not identify with the killer since nothing is known about him but rather "with the killer's look."[51] Here, access is provided to the murderous activities of the killer but rarely for their motivation and psychology or involvement in the killings. Instead, the viewer "is freed from sharing the emotional or moral implications of this act"[52] by the very way the narrative is organized. Hardcore horror aligns the viewer to that of the action and is intensified by the first-person perspective of the camera operator which is so integral to found footage horror. Thus, our gaze is linked to that of the camera which directly connects to how we receive the characters and their experiences.

In the found footage pseudo-documentary *The Poughkeepsie Tapes* (John Erick Dowdle, 2007), the police find videotapes at a suspected serial killer's home. When these tapes are played back, we see the killer target and kill his victims from a first-person perspective. The killer's identity is never discovered, leaving a powerful affective charge of dread and horror. If we return to hardcore horror and *Amateur Porn Star Killer*, then we get a restricted view of Brandon. (In *August Underground* we never see the camera operator.) The viewer is not granted access to the interiority of his character despite Brandon being an active agent of narrative development in his continual verbal and physical interactions with the victims. Here, the alignment of the viewer with the look or gaze of the killer withholds identification with the *character* of the killer and instead focuses on the emotional impact and spectacle of violent action.

Five. The Realist Aesthetic of Hardcore Horror   127

Amateur Porn Star Killer presents a realist and convincing account in its focus on the manipulation and coercion of a young girl by a sexual predator which ends in her murder. The use of found footage aesthetics strengthens the credibility of the narrative and ultimately provides an unsettling and disturbing viewer experience. However, in doing so, the film taps into and builds upon a number of cinematic movements in its representation of the real. The formal properties connect to existing discourses of American independent cinema and European art cinema while the first-person perspective and the withholding of information about the killer locates the film within the contours of horror conventions relating to the slasher and the gaze of the camera-character embodied within found footage horror. While this does not suggest that the realist horror of *Amateur Porn Star Killer* should be rejected or is severely compromised by its configuration of disparate cinematic movements and forms, it does, once again, indicate that realism is contingent on other cinematic strands and representations. Ryan's quickly assembled "do or die" attempt at making a full-length film situates itself against other cinematic representations and especially recent films such as *Scrapbook* and *August Underground* which propose a more realist and authentic representation of the serial killer. In the case of *Amateur Porn Star Killer* then, the realism can be contemplated as a matter of form where digital recording devices have enabled greater access to an authentic and credible *mise en scène*. With the very use of digital technology, it also points to the notion that realism is as much about national and historical specifics than simply just the formal mechanics of film. It is with the use of digital technology in the film and its connection to the cultural mythology of snuff that *Amateur Porn Star Killer* ends up moving away from an authentic representation of cinematic realism toward presenting an insightful treatment surrounding the advent of film documenting real death and its propagation in 21st-century society. Intertwined within Ryan's realist approach to "true horror" are a number of artificial and deliberately manipulated features which undermine the overall thesis of producing a "real" record of a traumatic event. Ryan's intention was certainly not to get people like Vogel to believe his film was a "found object," filmed by the killer and discarded for somebody to find. Instead, Ryan modified the film to suggest that it had been "found" by a distribution company that had touched it up to make a more palatable and dramatic version. Rather than moving the film further into the realm of the fictional, Ryan's purposeful tampering with the finished film paradoxically moves the film closer to the real. As the realist aesthetic of snuff develops toward a more entertaining spectacle of violence as images of real death became more preponderant in the media during the 21st century, *Amateur Porn Star Killer* ends up providing a prophetic examination.

To return to the Schrader quotation, *Amateur Porn Star Killer* utilizes the excerpt to stress the cultural legacy of the snuff film and the interface between the viewer and the "idea" of snuff. In the quote, Schrader positions snuff as a filmic event that lends itself to audience responses of it as being genuine. It is the belief by the viewer that these films exist that is important and not that there may be a referent in the world outside of the constructed and fabricated. For Schrader, the cultural capital and mythology that has emerged alongside the phenomena of the snuff film is the point of focus. Therefore, the insertion of the caption featuring the quote immediately brings attention to the film as a construct and the notion of snuff as a cultural imaginary; an "evil fantasy" that audiences are only too willing to believe. Indeed, the affective charge and horrifying nature of fictional snuff are "not because the footage looks realistic, but because its apparent authenticity is a reminder of how real human cruelty is."[53] What is interesting about Schrader's quote is the idea that the viewer would not necessarily receive genuine footage of real death as authentic because of its incongruence with simulated death. Such a stance contradicts the defamiliarization required for footage to take on the patina of realism and reinforces Joel Black's thesis of the "*graphicness*" of contemporary movies which produce a realist effect to make "events *seem real*."[54] If genuine snuff emerged, or more likely atrocity footage, then it would be compared to prevailing standards of visual realism circulating in sociocultural representations. Cinematic and televisual modes have, by and large, constructed dominant conceptions of the "real" and would seem to provide an emphatic disjuncture with amateur and "unofficial" examples circulating on the Internet. However, as we have seen post-millennium, from the footage of real death originating with the unprofessional and frequently botched decapitation videos of Daniel Pearl and Nick Berg to the more accomplished and stylistic death videos of Luca Magnotta and Isis, examples of filmed real-death or ostensibly snuff films have moved from a stark reality which seeks to simulate an "unmediated" representation toward a more heightened experience. Indeed, we have seen an increased mediation in how unsimulated depictions of violence and death have been (re)presented, which has positioned them more in line with their cinematic and televisual counterparts. The outcome is a further level of complexity onto notions of realism in the 21st century, and it is precisely this conflation of the fictional and the real, and how it pertains to snuff and/or actual death, that *Amateur Porn Star Killer* addresses through its continued manipulation of the realist frame.

Not long after the Schrader quotation, the film uses a projected insert in the bottom left-hand corner of the frame featuring another young woman named Loren, who is being "auditioned" by Brandon as she gradually undresses while providing information about herself. The image explicitly links Brandon to serial killings and the sexual nature of his modus operandi. These inserts appear at various points in the film, and in particular cases, multiple projections are used to connect Loren to Stacey regarding their victimization by Brandon. The technique highlights that the pathology of Brandon and his murderous activities are not localized or in fact restricted to the events documented in this particular film. Connected to these visual inserts of further victims are individual fragments of dialogue that appear on the screen with titles such as "What's your name?" and "How old are you?" despite the audio being clear in these scenes. The use of presenting dialogue through titles flashed up on screen is used throughout the film and underscores (and alerts viewers to) the most dramatic exchanges between characters. Later, when Stacey is reluctantly undressing for Brandon, she admits how old she is, and we get a title on the screen saying "I'm actually 13." The use of titles, therefore, is to increase dramatic tension and to develop a sense of dread as the disturbing direction of the film becomes evident. After the murder and while Brandon is removing Stacey's body, the caption "Brandon made the Top 10 Most Wanted list in 11 different States by the age of 20" appears. The presentation of the information is to impress on the viewer Brandon's exalted status as a nationwide fugitive despite his relatively young age. It seems odd displayed here considering that the reality of Brandon's crimes has been presented in a horrific and unpalatable way and goes some way to exploit the tension between fear and attraction in watching shocking, extreme and controversial images. Indeed, the title and its proud undertones suggest that the intention is to spectacularize Brandon's murders and elevate him toward the public fascination and obsession with well-known and notorious serial killers such as Ted Bundy and Jeffrey Dahmer. During the end sequence where these final captions appear, others mention how Brandon swapped VHS rentals with his recordings so that unsuspecting renters would access his "films" instead. Such a detail complicates the providence of the recordings as either from a third party distribution company or Brandon as well as further linking the film to the cultural mythology of snuff by evoking the video cassette and the moral panic surrounding violent and unregulated content.[55] The coda of the film serves as a connecting bridge to Vogel's *August Underground* and how the acceptance of the texts as real must necessarily also include how they are circulated and received by the viewer.

What we have seen through the realist displays in *August Underground* and *Amateur Porn Star Killer* is the social, cultural and historically contingent nature of cinematic realism. *August Underground* breaks with convention and particularly with a pre-existing "cultural knowledge of story structures"[56] to provide an unprecedented representation of the cinematic serial killer. The footage presented is certainly defamiliarized through the level of violence and its explicit display, but the film also utilizes the growing ubiquity of the video camera and, although inadvertently, stresses its developing connection with the "real" and atrocity footage as the 21st century proceeded. Instilling an almost "complete and final knowledge of events"[57] within viewers, *August Underground* convinced many early viewers that it might be authentic and remains one of the more realist and convincing horror films ever made. The social context in viewing *August Underground* was also essential to conceptions of the real. Watching on VHS and later DVD imbues the artifact with a sense of the artificial and as a commercial product. If Vogel successfully released the film as intended, it would have provided a pertinent case study with which to test the dependence of format and location regarding how successfully a text is received as real.

Ryan attempts a similar approach in manipulating the fictional snuff of *Amateur Porn Star Killer* as if released through an independent third party. It may seem to undermine the real in the film as the viewer is clear that what they are watching is a construction but a sense of ambiguity nonetheless runs through the film due to how "real" material has often been embellished to provide a more spectacular and entertaining product. From reality TV programs such as *Cops* (20th Century Fox Television, 1989–present) and *The Real World* (Bunim-Murray Productions & MTV, 1992–present), which utilized highly contrived narratives, to the stylized techniques of "ideologically motivated snuff videos"[58] of Islamic extremists and terrorist networks, representations of the real have often been co-opted by mediated effects. Indeed, "nowhere has the blurring of fiction and reality occasioned more confusion and controversy than in the media's depiction of violence."[59] *Amateur Porn Star Killer* comments on the context for the "real" in the 21st century and suggests that if genuine snuff were to emerge, it would not be shown in its unexpurgated form, but would instead be (re)packaged as entertainment or ideology. Reality further recedes from our grasp as Ryan seems to suggest that even the real would be questioned and eyed with suspicion if not mediated through various stylistic or ideological filters.

Six

"These movies have brought me many problems"
Performance and the Traumatized Self Within Hardcore Horror

Providing an examination of the representation of the real in films such as *August Underground* and *Amateur Porn Star Killer* reiterates the centrality of an authentic and credible narrative in 21st-century horror. The commitment to providing a realist horror aligns with the narrative direction of found footage and pseudo-snuff films, yet the "unofficial" status of hardcore horror can facilitate further explorations into cinematic realism. *August Underground*'s acknowledgment of the importance of social precepts concerning how images are obtained and Shane Ryan's purposeful manipulation of the real toward more sensational entertainment has provided a larger cultural field on realist horror to be mapped out. Thus, the synergies between hardcore horror and other cultural forms regarding how images of violence, atrocity and death are produced, circulated and consumed provide a valuable addition to the discursive practices of horror in the 21st century and the structuring element of the real.

Another aspect to hardcore horror's adherence to realist codes has to do with performance. The believability of the actors is paramount to the notion of receiving the film as authentic as well as being an essential criterion in formulating a strong emotional investment in the films. The shift in hardcore horror away from the orthodox styles of performance contained in more commercial and mainstream horror cinema restates the importance of defamiliarization in how realism is received and provides a bridge between the two chapters. However, performance can also provide another formal layer of realist horror and provide meaningful ways to look at its intrinsic intersection with the body and its relationship with the Self. That is, as hardcore horror allows for a greater emphasis on a credible performativity than more mainstream productions would require, it opens up further entry points into realism in horror by looking at the conflation and overlap of "real" human action and the imaginary realm of filmic performance. Thus, an examination of performance can facilitate a more interdisciplinary approach to film realism, which incorporates theater and performance studies to provide an insightful path to adjudge how hardcore horror's extreme material can be mitigated by addressing issues such as social identity and the working through of trauma. Ultimately, a focus on the unorthodox, excessive and disturbing processes of performance which populate the visual domain of hardcore horror provides another integral component to how we think about and work through applications of the real within contemporary movements of the horror genre.

Performance as Dangerous Praxis

The use of digital technology and portable recording devices in the rendering of realist horror, from *Scrapbook* to *American Guinea Pig: Bouquet of Guts and Gore*, has offered a way in which different types of content, meanings, formal properties, affective charge and audience interaction can be realized within contemporary horror. It is perhaps no surprise that hardcore horror has also impacted on how filmmakers approach the horror genre not only concerning new aesthetic modes but also in unique and unprecedented modes of performance. As the films provide a "dangerous," challenging and confrontational experience for the viewer, so too do the particularities of performing in these films. In a number of cases, actors have pulled out of the roles and/or dissociated themselves from the films. The most high-profile example is Cristie Whiles, who starred in *Mordum* and *Penance* and was a founding member of Toetag Pictures where she held the position of International Sales and Marketing director from 2002 to 2009. At the end of *Penance*, Whiles' character Crusty, under continual verbal abuse from Vogel's killer, refuses to engage with his actions and directions. Crusty-Cristie's breakdown and her apparent remorse shown to the victim contrasts with the intensity of her performance in *Mordum*. Although Crusty's character development connects to the theme of the destructive nature of violence and its eventual suffocating presence for the killers, it also acts as a comment on the growing porosity of character and actor, with Whiles unhappy that Toetag had returned so quickly to the realist realm of snuff with *Penance*. Therefore, when Crusty-Cristie breaks down at the end of *Penance*, sobbing into the body of a female victim tied up against a wall and saying over and over again, "Oh God, I want to leave!" and "I'm so sorry, I'm so sorry," it can be read as both the character and the actor refusing to participate and looking for a way

Six. "These movies have brought me many problems" 133

out. Post-*Penance* interviews highlighted how performing such a violent and deranged character had manifest as trauma and stress outside of the film. Whiles often talked about moving on from the pseudo-snuff of the *August Underground* films, especially because of the disruption they had caused in her daily life:

> It was very cold, and stressful.... I lost my job while making the movie.... These movies have brought me many of problems [*sic*]. I've gotten creepy emails. I hear about men getting sexual arousal from abusing women and children. My intentions were to make people aware of the pain abuse causes without sugarcoating a detail.[1]

Two years after *Penance*, and when publicity was completed on Toetag's first commercial horror *The Redsin Tower* (Fred Vogel, 2006), Whiles left the company and now works in textiles where she runs her own business, Twelve Oxen Design.

Another testament to the affective power of the *August Underground* trilogy and the fragile nature of the border between actor and character relates to Allen Peters' withdrawal from the original film. Peters was the co-writer and played the role of the unseen camera operator who details the succession of victims tortured and murdered by Vogel's killer. Vogel's performance throughout the first installment effectively blurs the boundary between "acting and not acting"[2] and undoubtedly the anguish and suffering he causes a number of actors involved in the film, including his brother and cousin, is genuine due to the intensity and directness of Vogel's on-screen persona. Indeed, it was Vogel's pursuit of the real and its manifestation in both credible and believable performances that instigated Peters' departure from the film. After the completion of *August Underground* and when bootlegged tapes were clandestinely distributed within the horror underground, the film began to attract certain notoriety over whether the footage was unsimulated and involved actual hurt and suffering to those involved. The convincing nature and outcome of Vogel's endeavor to produce a pseudo-snuff film and subsequent reaction to the film as an irresponsible and unethical production prompted lawyers to issue affidavits to the actors and filmmakers to ascertain the consensual nature of the process and that nobody was seriously hurt or traumatized by the experience.[3] At this point, Peters did not want anything further to do with the film, fearing that the reception and growing controversy *August Underground* was generating would impact on his life outside of the film and on his family and young child. As Vogel says, "I think he felt he had a lot more to lose if the world came crashing down on us. We both knew we were going to get in trouble for the content of the movie, but he didn't want to go for the long run, and I respected and understood him walking away."[4] Since leaving *August Underground*, Peters has neither returned to the film nor contacted Vogel or Toetag. Despite continued attention from fans interested to hear his perspective on the production of the film, it seems, to quote Vogel, as if Peters "fell off the planet."[5]

A similar incident happened during *The Bunny Game* where a central actor left the film due to concerns over the direction the character was taking in terms of the violent and brutal characteristics of the performance. Gregg Gilmore had worked with Rehmeier on a previous project and was contacted while Rehmeier and Rodleen Getsic were developing *The Bunny Game* in 2006 as a potential lead character. Gilmore was to take on the role of Hog, played eventually by Jeff Renfro. Several weeks before production started, Gilmore began to voice concerns over the violent nature of his character and the troubling conflation of the real and the performative:

> [A]s it got closer to doing it, I realized that it was going to be so dark that I couldn't go there.... I mean, I just didn't want to phone in some performance or act. It was going to be real. And the kind of stuff that was required of me would be, could be potentially permanent. Permanent damage could have been done.... It might sound absurd. I thought I could kill [Getsic].[6]

Rehmeier underlined Gilmore's anxiety by further expounding on his reticence to immerse fully into the vitriolic overtones of the Hog's character by saying, "Gregg became very apprehensive about acting in the film. He had been delving into darker and darker territory during his preparatory phase and was convinced that he might actually hurt Rodleen."[7] Here the potential breakdown of the real and the performance presents a dangerous and threatening limit to a safe and orderly identity. For Gilmore, the possibility of a fractured self, by taking on the transgressive body of Hog, had the potential to destabilize a proper sociality and identity resulting in the genuine belief that actual violence could be enacted, which may seriously harm Getsic. Gilmore's refusal to participate further with the film had significant implications for the production schedule and caused an extended hiatus. Rehmeier and Getsic did eventually return to the film though it was not completed until 2010, four years after Gilmore withdrew.

The Intersection of Hardcore Horror and Performance Studies

From the brief examples addressed above, it can be seen that the performativity associated with hardcore horror can be dangerous, threatening and occasionally too close to the real for actors to take up a particular role or to carry on in an existing one. Although we find arduous and challenging performances in mainstream and commercial cinema from actors who have to undergo extensive makeup and prosthetic work, lose significant weight for a particular role or brave harsh and uncompromising conditions, they exist within the framework of a studio, a large and interactive production crew and the notion of performance as play, as acting. Hardcore horror goes further in providing a performativity that is often unscripted, unpredictable and spontaneous. It exists in the moment, and the very nature of pushing the boundaries of the real in horror means that it can, and does, develop into a dangerous and harmful territory. It is no surprise that the actors talk about their performance in ways which attest to the intense experience and the traumatizing overlap of the character and the actor. Shane Ryan has often spoken of the difficulty of performing as Brandon in the *Amateur Porn Star Killer* films and how he regularly felt "so sick playing this character"[8] that he had to take extended breaks from the production. Fred Vogel addresses the danger of performing a character with so much rage and violence when he talks about the killer as "a voice that comes out of me and scares me. We all have that monster within us."[9] The performance connected to hardcore horror edges toward the limits of representation for the actors and positions the body and self as central to the articulation of character. In this respect, hardcore horror's authentic performativity and emphasis on the body and identity aligns it with the discipline of performance studies and particularly the movement of performance art.

Performance is "an essentially contested concept"[10] due to its multivaried use in a wide range of disciplines from the arts to social sciences. In fact, the lack of coherence and stable definition is entwined into the term and concept of performance so that disagreement is encouraged to develop a "sharper articulation of all positions and therefore a fuller understanding of the conceptual richness of performance."[11] The complex, porous nature of performance allows it to be adapted to a range of practices so that new theoretical spaces can be opened up. It is in this environment that advocates the adoption of performance to a "new" conceptual space contained with the performative dynamic of hardcore horror. One particular strand of performance studies is the notion that conflates the separateness of "self" and behavior-performance on the stage to the idea of "playing a role" in social situations and interactions. Here, "all human activity could potentially be considered as performance, or at least all activity carried out with a consciousness of itself."[12] Performance is "placed in mental comparison with a potential, an ideal, or a remembered original model of that action"[13] and links to the concept of doubleness. However, the comparison is usually put in place by an external viewer in that "performance is always performance for someone, some audience that recognizes and validates it as performance even when, as is occasionally the case, that audience is the self."[14]

The emphasis on the integrity of the performance and its ability to convince has similar formations to that of cinematic realism and how it is contingent on existing and recognized social, cultural and technological factors.

Cinema audiences judge the realistic-ness of a particular film against what is currently established, just as theatergoers may judge the credibility of an actor playing Hamlet on previous incarnations. When the form is in opposition to prevailing ideals and attitudes, then it can cause a defamiliarization in the reception that can lead to new ways, in this case, to engage and think about realism or performance. A brief survey of examples emphasizing the broad spectrum defamiliarization can encompass would include Vogel's pseudo-snuff realism, "method acting" in 1950s Hollywood, and the gender switches in Sarah Frankcom's 2014 adaptation of *Hamlet*.[15]

The lack of distinction between performance and action in everyday life coupled with the phenomenon that performance is carried out for someone who bases it on existing standards provides a relevant conceptual framework with which to address realism in hardcore horror and the border porosity between the real and the constructed. Performance in the films, from *Scrapbook* to *Black Mass of a Nazi Sex Wizard*, positions the expressive body as central. The body is often seen as either violent or violated and offers a subjectivity that is fractured and continually in the process of transformation. In this respect, performance in hardcore horror aligns with the sociocultural concerns and expressive and extreme content of the performance art movement. Performance art emerged between the 1960s and 1980s as a practice concerned with the "operations of the body"[16] and the construction of (self-) identity. Performance art has taken myriad forms underlined by its interdisciplinary outlook, wide-ranging influences and prevailing artistic practices such as cabaret, carnivals and the circus.[17] A lot of these performances, especially those of the 1960s and 1970s by the Viennese Actionism movement and artists such as Chris Burden and Marina Abramović, attempted to go beyond accepted and established representational boundaries whereby they pushed the body to extremes so that it was often subject "to considerable risk or pain."[18] The site of the body for performance artists becomes a "central object over and through which relations of power and resistance are played out."[19] Thus, performance art particularly connects with explorations of personal identity as the performance of the body is attached to the artist as subject and articulations of a renewed and invigorated social and self-identity. In performance art, the "personal is the political"[20] as it seeks to challenge dominant, desirable and accepted forms of identity expressed through a capitalist and patriarchal order. In hardcore horror, the body is central and is often pushed to the limits or taken to extremes where it is broken down and destroyed. The visual power of the scenes of body violation and/or excessive violent acts are often marked as exploitative, repulsive or unethical.

Using performance studies (and particularly performance art) can, however, provide an extra-discursive layer to approach realist horror. Rather than being solely spectacular, the performance expressed in hardcore horror can also provide an irruption into the representational construction of the narrative and a destabilization of meaning in its real acts, gestures and movements. Therefore, a focus on performance can take us past the purely representational and into the affective qualities and experiential nature of the film, especially with regards to the traumatized self and challenges to acceptable and desirable notions of the body.

"The pain you see is real"[21]*: The Affective-Performativity of Ameara La Vey*

The most prominent example of performance in hardcore horror and its connection to the violated body is that of Ameara La Vey as Angela Aberdeen in the first three installments of the vomit gore films. Her performance utilizes the physicality of the body and its gestures, functions and movements as privileged by performance artists. The heightened performance of La Vey's often excessive and subversive body sets a challenge to the strict and regulated forms of identity enforced and policed under the power exchanges of a capitalist and patriarchal society. La Vey implements such a rupture within the narrative development of the vomit gore films through repetitive acts experienced as disgusting and "abnormal" and which produces an emotional charge of repulsion, fear and horror. The fissures and ruptures of her continued acts of vomiting and sadomasochistic activity destabilize the narrative, meaning production, and the conceptual category of realism to approximate the Deleuzian framework of affective-performativity put forward by Elena del Río in her book *Deleuze and the Cinemas of Performance: Powers of Affection*. For del Río, focusing the attention on the affective qualities of the performance can take us past the rigid system of representation and offer up new ways to think about cinema as an experience. It is precisely the nature of the vomit gore films as an extreme and intense spectacle that an affective experience arises. By looking primarily at the performance of La Vey, it will be possible to move beyond the representational that marks the films out as violent, shocking and repulsive. In doing so, the status of vomit gore as "illegitimate" due to the affective shocks that punctuate the narrative, can be reassessed by viewing the films regarding their experiential quality. Drawing on del Río's work on affective-performativity as a "sensational *force* that disrupts, redirects and indeed affects narrative *form*"[22] and combining it with how in performance art the artist creates their work via "their own bodies, their own autobiographies, their own specific experiences in a culture or in the world,"[23] it will be possible to see if hardcore horror does indeed facilitate new realms of thought or if it returns us to the foundation of representation and the spectacle.

Slaughtered Vomit Dolls begins with grainy and washed-out camcorder

Angela Aberdeen (Ameara La Vey) demonstrating gender performance in *Slaughtered Vomit Dolls* (Unearthed Films).

footage of five-year-old Angela-Ameara performing for an unseen audience. Angela directly addresses the camera and says that she is to sing a "song for the whole world to see" and that "[i]t's the first time I've ever been on TV before." The footage is presented as a moment in Angela's life that is to be read as innocent and full of opportunity. It seems clear to act as a juxtaposition to present-day Angela who is seen in a traumatized and disheveled state. However, these two sequences, which on the surface seem to present a dichotomy so that the viewer realizes the extent of the trauma and suffering Angela has encountered, are in fact more closely connected than the shock provided by the discordant figures of young and adult Angela would suggest. Toward the end of the first sequence with adult Angela, we see her on all fours moving backward from the camera while an unseen male voice asks, "Would you do anything for me?" Angela nods her head and replies, "Anything you say. I'd die for you. I'd kill for you." In this short extract, it is evident through Angela's affectation and bodily movement that she is performing for the off-camera male, just as she was putting on a show for an unseen audience as a five-year-old.

Six. "These movies have brought me many problems" 139

The film commences with Angela's highly mediated image, presented on a TV screen and again through its insertion in the film frame. Later in the sequence, we again see Angela caught on camera, this time performing for the unseen male who is filming her in an intimate and intrusive manner. *Slaughtered Vomit Dolls* shows both performances as disempowering in how they take away the individual agency of Angela. The small frame of the TV screen that opens the film seems to constrain Angela's performance and as the film proceeds the footage takes on a sinister and disturbing countenance as the material is manipulated and distorted, ending with Angela singing "Somewhere Over the Rainbow" while the footage is played backward and in slow motion. Furthermore, the voyeuristic camera of the unseen male provides a claustrophobic feel as Angela is "captured" within bedrooms, toilets and hotel rooms. Angela presents a pliant, passive and submissive figure exacerbated by the dominant positioning of the camera-man that either looks down onto a compliant Angela or intrudes into her private and vulnerable moments as when she is asleep.

Performance in these two representations of Angela is reminiscent of what Richard Schechner has termed restored behavior in that it is a behavior "consciously separated from the person doing it."[24] From Angela's performance on the home video and through the archetypes of "stripper," "beauty queen" and "teen porn star" that we encounter later in the film and series, Angela has been performing a restored behavior all her life. A performativity that Judith Butler might point to as being constituted by gender so that what emerges is a "ritualized production, a ritual reiterated under and through constraint, under and through the force of prohibition and taboo, with the threat of ostracism and even death controlling and compelling the shape of the production."[25] The performance of Angela that opens the vomit gore films can be seen to offer glimpses of an estrangement from identity and as a retreat from the real and authentic to that of representation. The gestures, movements and acts performed by adult Angela align to a fabricated expression that belies any "interior essence" as it is "an effect and function of a decidedly public and social discourse."[26] Angela's performativity reinforces the restored nature of her performance of gender as an act that always already exists and which is now going through another rehearsal. Rather than connecting with any sense of self, she guides her performance by gender ideals governed in contemporary Western societies that enact "a normative heterosexuality that is a major tool for enforcing a patriarchal, phallocentric social order."[27]

Butler's work on gender performativity is strongly "indebted to the representational paradigm"[28] and works well to highlight how the archetypes of "stripper" and "beauty queen" are semiotic signs which control and define who Angela is and how she sees herself in the film. Thus, the performance of Angela as "stripper" or as the young girl putting on a show grounds a representational performance that is seen as imitative or stultifying in how it offers a repetitive sameness in line with culturally and socially predetermined ideals. The representational aspect of Angela's performance exemplified in the opening montage and continued via the confining labels of "stripper" and "beauty queen" posit a mimetic interface between the film and the viewer. But this material, while potentially regressive in its portrayal of female identity and agency, can also provide a critique of power structures tied up in oppressive patriarchal discourses. The spectacle of the vomit gore films, from their protracted and extremely violent set-pieces to the depiction of traumatized and abused women, can be destabilized by the affective-performativity of distasteful and "abnormal" acts carried out by Angela. Del Río suggests that affective-performativity can provide a narrative force or rupture that "upsets the balance of power between performer and world, performer and audience,"[29] to form a new realm of thinking. A focus on the creative and ontogenetic aspect of performance can engender new subjectivities to form along the conjunction of viewer and film. These new contacts are often a transformative process of deterritorialization and reconfiguration which can move past the representational strategies inherent in much of the construction of cinematic (female) identity. In the vomit gore films, encounters with the affective-performativity of Angela can, therefore, reassess her victim status and begin to track ways in which her performance challenges the power dynamics involved in the construction of female identity.

The affective-performative gestures and movements of Angela-Ameara reside in displays of repugnant and "abnormal" acts categorized by a deforming of the "clean and proper" body in which urine, menstrual blood and vomiting are presented to "provoke a shock to thought."[30] That is, the excessive and deviant body which Angela's performance often extends from is unlike anything offered up in more mainstream productions, even those broken and mangled bodies that populate the narratives of "torture porn." Therefore, the vomit gore films can provide a wider range of somatic experiences that challenge the contract between performer and performance and performance and the audience. In *Slaughtered Vomit Dolls*, the opportunity presented Angela to use her body as a performative space to resist female subjugation and to recoup a female-centered perspective on identity is significantly limited. The film takes on affective horror as its exploration of Angela's physical and psychological state and features numerous violent tableaux to exemplify her traumatized state. The archetypes are introduced in the narrative (such as "stripper," "princess" and "whore") and precede the prolonged and extensive violence and torture subjected to the "vomit doll" playing these manifestations in Angela's subconscious. The sequences are visually matched to a sleeping or distressed Angela and are events which she can only relive rather than work through. In fact, the first performative signature of the film (and

Six. "These movies have brought me many problems" 141

The affective-performativity of Angela Aberdeen (Ameara La Vey) (*Slaughtered Vomit Dolls*, Unearthed Films).

series) through the act of vomiting is carried out by one of the vomit dolls in Angela's subconscious as she vomits onto her eyeballs which have recently been gouged from their sockets. The violent tableau provides a heavy symbolism in a film which deals with Angela's estranged identity and in not being able to perceive her true or real self. The scene as dreamscape also suggests that the site of resistance resides within the deep recesses of Angela's ontological being rather than on the surface and in her behavioral actions. Thus, the viewer is given the impression of a passive woman who can exert little or no pressure on her life and its downward spiral. Nonetheless, it does hint at an affective-performativity within the character of Angela that may be able to reach the surface of her experience and effect change in her surroundings. In doing so, the representational paradigm can be disturbed, and audiences' view of acceptable and desirable female identity and its representation in the filmic realm challenged.

Later, in *Slaughtered Vomit Dolls*, Angela is once again addressing the unseen cameraman and recounting stories of being a stripper. The sequence ends with Angela entering a hotel room as a sex worker, complete with garish makeup that is to signify the female performers in Max Hardcore films.[31]

Between these two bookends of Angela's constructed identity and how it is "part and parcel of the cultural attempt to codify and contain women with safe and predictable limits"[32] is Angela's first example of affective-performativity as she sticks her fingers down her throat and vomits into a toilet. The abject nature of the image and the shock of the real in Angela-Ameara's act of vomiting subverts the notion of female performativity away from preexisting categories and clichéd emotional responses. The act is defiantly real and is shocking in its affective charge. It disturbs the way we have been viewing Angela up to this point and suggests that the archetypal categories used to confine and label her are artificial and limiting. Angela's act of vomiting is an incongruent affect to the other two performances we see in this segment: an excessive gesture of a deviant body that challenges her oppression through an act of expression. Angela's affective-performativity of vomiting appears at various points in the narrative from this point on and are positioned primarily in a critical riposte to images of her performing.

One key moment occurs after a detailed sequence where Angela performs at a strip club. The performance denies an erotic or fetishistic charge due to the noticeable bruises on Angela-Ameara's body caused by the contact her body makes with the wooden stage and by the seedy and run-down interior of the club. The disabling form of the striptease performance is undermined by a shocking affective act which is both explicit and sustained. Angela's vomiting that interrupts this sequence provides an expressive space in what started out as an oppressive act. The affective-performativity refuses the narrative goal that marks Angela out as an erotic object to be looked at or as a commodity to be exchanged by rupturing any safe and normative viewing position. Angela's oppression, commodification and exploitation do not present just a passive and subordinated identity but also a space for expression and transformation to take place. That is, Angela's mind is the "target of control and domination by the linguistic sign[s]"[33] of "stripper" or "teen porn star" but her body and its affective-performativity act as a site of resistance. Here, Angela's endless cycle of abuse and helplessness resists and fights against the "tendency to render injured parties unknowable outside of their torture in hardcore horror"[34] as Jones attests, and instead becomes a "sensational *force*" to once again cite del Río in how it can impact on narrative direction and content. The affective-performativity of Angela as *Slaughtered Vomit Dolls* proceeds inserts a fracture into the narrative that shocks audiences and disorganizes any "safe" way of receiving the films or that of female identity. The gesture of vomiting may appropriate (and even reinforce) patriarchal formations of the female subject but also fights that appropriation through an affective performance that undermines or offers a flight from totalizing or definitive representational categories.

In *ReGOREgitated Sacrifice*, Angela enters the Kingdom of Hell following her pact with Satan and subsequent suicide. The Black Angels of Hell guide Angela through this realm and act as protectors in how they confront and destroy the archetypes that have come to define and control Angela's life. The Angels initially seduce the figures manifest as "Teen Porn Star," "Stripper" and beauty queen "Miss Lake Washington" before ritually killing them in an intensive and detailed manner. The affective-performativity of Angela in the first film enabled a targeting and challenging of the representational categories which were constrictive and bound up in male exercises of power and control. In *ReGOREgitated Sacrifice*, those mechanisms of Angela's subjugation are destroyed and purged from her subconscious. The identities imposed onto Angela are thus broken down and removed, enabling her to forge a new female-centered identity of self-representation. The oppressive and limiting force of the archetypes is exposed, and in their place Angela offers a transgressive and "abnormal" female performativity. Identity is recognized as not fixed, not given, and not settled and Angela-Ameara's performance of transgressive gestures and actions proposes a transformative self that is in the process of becoming. However, although the prospect of a political engagement with gender performativity and its enforcement within a patriarchal, phallocentric social order has been set up so far, it reaches a cul-de-sac when moving forward into a post–Angela identity that is empowering and autonomous. The ritualistic killings of the archetypes in *ReGOREgitated Sacrifice* lead Angela ever closer to the demonic force of Satan. When its (male) presence is exposed, her behavior and performance revert to previous incarnations of the "whore" and "porn star." Angela once again becomes an erotic object for the scopophilic pleasure of the man–Satan. She is choked and roughly handled in a way that clearly mirrors early footage in the film of Angela as a porn star and of being abused and attacked by her male clientele when working as a prostitute. Furthermore, Angela assumes a submissive position and proceeds to undress the man–Satan to perform fellatio. The scene and film climax literally, with the man–Satan ejaculating blood over Angela's prone and naked body.

The regression back to oppressive feminine ideals and female identity is carried on through the third installment, *Slow Torture Puke Chamber*. Angela has been sent back to the surface to "infect" another Angela (played by Hope Likens) and bring her back down into the Kingdom of Hell. The identity which Angela-Ameara assumes in this film is that of a prostitute, an identity marked out in the first film as damaging and dehumanizing but one now seen by Angela as empowering as it corrupts and controls Angela-Hope. Thus, the promise of new ways of thinking through the tyranny of representational forms and practices fades as the film, and Angela, seem destined to act out and repeat the same stultifying performances over and over. In this respect, the vomit gore films finally coalesce and move back toward Jones'

An ultimate lack of female agency shown by Angela Aberdeen (Ameara La Vey) (*ReGOREgitated Sacrifice*, Unearthed Films).

formulation that the artist *does* remain absent from the proceedings. Angela is trapped in a never-ending cycle of suffering and abuse and after the first film is only ever presented as already dead. The lack of female agency to emerge over the four films, and especially with regards to Angela-Ameara, raises a troubling issue with regards to Valentine's intense, sadomasochistic "off-screen" relationship with Ameara and the question of taking advantage of a vulnerable and traumatized woman with prior and current incidents of abuse. The extent to which this is a collaborative artistic relationship or an exploitative venture is an issue which filters through hardcore horror and the relationship between the (male) director and the (female) actor. It is worth pointing out in terms of the extent it impacts on the representational practices and how it forges another link to hardcore pornography and the discourse surrounding the unequal gender dynamic inherent in many of its productions. However, the power of affective-performativity which runs through these films should not be wholly jettisoned because Valentine is unable or unwilling to provide a more positive dénouement and/or liberating form of female identity. The affective acts of vomiting, urination, the sadomasochistic activity can, and do, emerge from the basis of normative representational strategies and normalizing thought to provide a dangerous and powerful horror experience. A transgression of the safe, protected and regulated forms of horror occur through Valentine's use of "abnormal" acts which are marked and received as real. The affective-performativity of Ameara La Vey is ultimately reconstructed with the representational, but this nonetheless enables a combination to emerge that produces an uncompromising horror that melds the real and the mimetic in disturbing and unpalatable ways. The real gestures and acts of the performances merge to the representational activities of the violent special effects work to form an unprecedented realist horror. The tactile nature of the affective-performativity and Valentine's focus on the surface of the image provide an immersive quality which heightens the affective charge and sense of the real.

The focus on the traumatized self in the vomit gore films and its exploration via performance and the violated body poses a challenge to existing perceptual experiences of horror. Valentine shoots all of the scenes in the vomit gore films in confined interior spaces and via a hand-held camera which frames the action in a disorientating and decentered manner with continual close-up shots of the performers and the action. While this is obviously to underline Angela's lack of contact with the world and estrangement from her "self," it moves more toward providing an alternative visual and spatial field of action. Del Río has discussed the aesthetic qualities of Claire Denis' films, *Nénette and Boni* (1997) in particular, "as the invitation the film extends to the viewers to exchange their clichéd-oriented visual drive for a multi-sensory experience that gives them access to new thoughts, affects, and sensations."[35] Valentine's use of a subversive audio-visual landscape is to provide a singular experience which immerses the viewer in an affective and realist horror. The affective-performativity of actors such as Ameara La Vey and Hope Likens and the "abnormal" gestures of vomiting and urination disable any secure viewing positions and provoke intense and uncomfortable reactions. The affective charge of the vomit gore films, therefore, resides in the combination of the real (affective acts) and the representational (special effects, the use of female archetypes) to suggest new ways to assemble horror and new ways in which to emotionally engage with it. Ultimately, Valentine does not postulate a way forward for Angela, and how she might reconfigure a new, independent and female-centered identity, despite early indications of a challenge to social and cultural constructions of identity. The films fall short of successfully revealing the representational construction of female identity in (horror) cinema or destabilizing and fracturing meaning attached to female performance and social agency. Valentine seems more concerned with examining the darkness of the human experience and how this can be represented and aligned with extreme horror. Not necessarily to provide a potent example of how one may work through severe trauma but to use the affective-performativity and its uncompromising representation of aberrant and deviant bodily acts to destabilize the narrative form and shock audiences away from organizing the films in any "safe" way. That is, Valentine successfully contains the affective-performativity in the series of films along the contour of extreme representations to forge a new type of experiential horror and one that is primarily meant to stand in *contrast* to mainstream and commercial variants.

"Why did you do it, Rodleen?"[36]: *Working Through Trauma in* The Bunny Game

The Bunny Game acts as an appropriate companion piece to Valentine's vomit gore films through its creative partnership of Rehmeier and Getsic, which mirrors the long-term and intimate relational dynamic between Valentine and La Vey. *The Bunny Game*'s aesthetic and thematic properties further cements the two examples of hardcore horror together, as Rehmeier develops a kinesthetic audio-visual landscape filled with claustrophobic interiors and affective acts, gestures and movements in how it deals with issues of female disempowerment, abuse and transformation. Central to Rehmeier's uncompromising horror experience is the authenticity of Getsic's performance. Getsic used her own experiences, especially her traumatic experience of being abducted as a teenager, to bring a credible and believable performance as a destitute sex worker who is kidnapped and tortured by a truck driver. The film provides a creative space for Getsic to use her body as the central object to disrupt normative experiential relationships to horror and to use the tenets of performance art to provide a realist display that proposes to be both transformative and cathartic. In doing so, she uses an affective-performativity to break away from normative codes and expectations built into the conventions of the horror genre. However, and perhaps forging the last link to the vomit gore films, the film presents significant limitations in its attempt to disengage female identity from the social and cultural plane in which it is formed and constructed. Although the film was planned as a feminist tract in its "cautionary tale about drug abuse and taking rides with strangers,"[37] according to director Rehmeier, the objectification of Getsic's character and the prolonged sequences of female on-screen torture posits the notion of whether a feminist position can be taken up. Thus, *The Bunny Game* presents serious questions over whether "the affirmative character of its own affective qualities"[38] is left intact by the conclusion of the film and that it can undo totalizing categories of identity through the instigation of new ways to think about and experience horror.

The Bunny Game's opening sequence provides the film, and perhaps all of hardcore horror, with its most challenging, shocking and affective introduction. There's a low, ominous drone on the soundtrack as the name of the production company, Death Mountain Productions, appears on the screen before a shock-cut to a close-up of an unidentified woman suffocating with a plastic bag drawn tight over her head. The woman's inhibited cries and labored breathing dominate the audio-visual range as she desperately attempts to break free. The screen fades to black, and the title of the film appears. The next scene features Getsic performing fellatio on an unseen and unknown male. The discordant sound and flat *mise en scène* de-eroticizes the sex act and positions Getsic's performance as central in communicating a sense of discomfort and unease as the scene proceeds. It is again shot in close-up and in one take via a static camera. The attachment to the surface nature of the image exemplifies the sensations of bodily contact and how unwilling and uncomfortable Getsic-Bunny is in participating. The scene ends with the man gagging Getsic-Bunny on his penis to the extent that she pulls away in order to breathe. Both scenes are unanchored by any contextual connection to the narrative. Indeed, the film does not return to the asphyxiated woman until much later, where it transpires that she was another victim of the truck driver. Because these two performative acts are abstracted as standalone segments, their affective potential is significant in forcing a different, or new, viewing position and engagement with the horror. Certainly, the unsimulated nature of the two acts disrupts any safe and conventional response as the use of real and affective-performativity destabilizes a normative viewing position and challenges viewer expectation while sustaining an affective charge that is horrifying and repulsive. The film's pre-kidnapping narrative is dominated by an assemblage of similar scenes which testify to Getsic-Bunny's destitute status and exploitation and abuse as a sex worker. Here the representation of Bunny is only in relation to the men who pay to have sex with her. Any attempts at self-representation are absent, and as a result we see Bunny in a state of considerable distress and suffering.

As Luce Irigaray has discussed with regards to the exclusion of women from both the cultural and the socio-economic systems of patriarchal society, her work has relevance to *The Bunny Game*'s opening sequences regarding the withholding of self-identity from Bunny during these early exchanges. The social role of prostitute imposed on Bunny denies her any autonomy and pleasure as the process of commodification forces on her an identity only regarding its value to men. For Irigaray, "the circulation of women among men is what establishes the operations of society, at least of patriarchal society"[39] so that female identity is seen in sexualized–exchange value terms which are "evocative of characteristics of the status of a commodity."[40] Thus, the restrictive and oppressive categories Bunny is coerced into are reminiscent of how we are introduced to Angela Aberdeen in the vomit gore films and how, in turn, an affective-performativity can move toward the possibility of an "impermanence of identity" and the "openness to reinvention"[41] such acts engender. As the film proceeds and Bunny is abducted by the truck driver, the narrative form displays numerous violent acts and a correlative amount of affective-performativity. The material is punctuated by distressing and uncomfortable acts of violence acted out on Getsic-Bunny's body including choking, bondage and humiliating physical abuse. During this time, Getsic-Bunny is often tied up and in some sequences, such as when Hog molests her with a knife, unconscious. The notion of a resistive and transformative performativity which can "engage the affects and escape a totalizing or definitive appropriation"[42] is limited due to Getsic receiving a majority of the violence meted out by Hog in a passive manner. As the film draws to a close, Hog arranges for Bunny to be picked up by an unknown man; the final, extended shot follows the man as he drives his van away with Bunny in the back. In the vomit gore films we track Angela as she returns to the oppressive category of a prostitute, which undermined any radical potential her affective acts and gestures may have engendered. In *The Bunny Game*, Getsic-Bunny's passivity strengthens her position as a victim where her abduction is seen as a direct result of her marginal status and vulnerability as a prostitute. The film does not challenge those capitalist and patriarchal forces in place that are responsible for Bunny's decline. In fact, they remain in place throughout and, although marked as violent and debased, are nonetheless in complete control concerning their subjugation of women.

Getsic's identification as a performance artist enables a means to explore the limitations of the film in providing a transformative space for female identity and in challenging oppressive societal arrangements. It has been previously noted that performance art centers on the body and since the late 1960s has been viewed as the "material and medium within the space of art, with many artists using their body as a medium to expose their vulnerability and pain."[43] The Viennese Actionism movement serves as an obvious precursor to the affective-performativity of hardcore horror with their films-happenings in which there was a similar emphasis on abject bodily functions and physical violence. For example, Otto Muehl's *Piss Aktion* (1969) featured Muehl urinating into the mouth of fellow artist Gunter Brus while on stage as a transgressive act of affective-performativity. Kunst und Revolution (Art and Revolution) (1968) involved the illegal takeover of a university lecture hall to perform a variety of taboo acts such as whipping, self-mutilation, masturbation and defecation. These *aktions* were to provide an incendiary rupture in the fabric of acceptable social performance and thus directly challenge the construction and maintaining of social norms. An important part of early 1970s performance art continued the Viennese Actionism focus of pushing

Six. "These movies have brought me many problems" 149

Bunny (Rodleen Getsic) as passive victim (*The Bunny Game*, Autonomy Pictures).

the artist's body to extremes to address a variety of concerns, from the ethics of violence in the Vietnam era to structures of power and gender identity. Chris Burden's *Shoot* (1971) culminated with a friend shooting him in the arm; his other performances included "electrocution, hanging, fire and a variety of sharp objects piercing his flesh."[44] Burden's engagement with the authentic was clear throughout these performances and in his comments, "getting shot is for real ... there's no element of pretense or make-believe in it."[45] Another performance artist of the 1970s, Marina Abramović, is perhaps most well-known today through the documentary *The Artist Is Present* (Matthew Akers and Jeff Dupre, 2012) and contemporary exhibitions at prestigious galleries such as the Museum of Modern Art. Her early work positioned a "traumatized body" so that both the art and the audience could engage in new ways of meaning making and ethical reflection. In her 1975 work *Lips of Thomas*, a very confrontational and powerful piece, she appeared naked and over the course of two hours consumed a kilo of honey and a liter of red wine. When this process had finished, she broke the wine glass in her hand and proceeded to carve a five-pointed star on her stomach. Throughout this final act, her face remained impassive so that the "audience [would] focus on her body, her wounds, and her apparent suffering."[46] Despite the shocking climactic act that would be commensurate with much of the affective-performativity on display in hardcore horror, the act of self-inflicted violence links to a political engagement with the traumatic past of Abramović's upbringing in socialist Yugoslavia. Performance artists Martha Wilson (*Breast*

Forms Permutated, 1973; *Staging the Self,* 2009) and Carolee Schneemann (*Interior Scroll,* 1975; *Vulva's Morphia,* 1995) have also used the site of the body to "operate politically both within and beyond the domestic sphere"[47] that sought to confine and control aspects such as female sexuality, control over one's body and more general issues surrounding gender equality. Although the performances could be violent, transgressive and shocking, it was always connected to larger political, socio-cultural and ethical concerns.

What the above examples demonstrate, albeit briefly, is that the overriding focus of performance art was the site of the violated or vulnerable body as a way to directly comment on dominant power structures enabled in a capitalist, patriarchal society or to ethically engage with traumatic events. Getsic based her performance on her own experience of being abducted and prepared intensively for the role in a way she hoped would provide a cathartic release to the experience and a way to work through her trauma. Getsic used the vulnerable and traumatized body in order to engage with the ethics of violence directed toward women, which was underlined by an affective-performativity to shock viewers into new ways of (ethical) thought and transformation of the perceptual experience of horror. To this end, she has talked about how a key element of the film was "empowerment transcending the exploitation of female"[48] and that it served as a "spiritual experience"[49] for her. However, Getsic's performance and the narrative development of the film seem to be at odds with this particular view. This may have been Rehmeier and Getsic's preferred meaning but one that has been read in opposition by many viewers and organizations such as the BBFC, which banned the film due to the way it "may encourage some viewers to enjoy and share in the man's callousness and the pleasure he takes in the woman's pain and humiliation."[50] In the film, Getsic does appear as the absent artist. Getsic is either chained up or in such a traumatized state that she cannot escape or repeal the violent actions of Hog. Bunny is merely traded to another man at the end of the film; we are led to believe she will be killed and disposed of or her torture and abuse will continue. The incidents of suffocation, branding with a hot iron and repetitive acts of physical abuse are merely received and endured by Getsic. The potential of affective acts transmutes into spectacular representations of intensive and brutal horror rather than as irruptions into the constrictive and oppressive categories of female identity and the ethical engagement with trauma.

The breach between actor and character exemplified in Bunny-Getsic but carried through to Hog-Renfro is a direct outcome of the destabilizing and potentially transformative agency of affective-performativity. Yet the border porosity between the real and mimesis is to generate an audio-visual environment of a radically different *affect* and *sensation* than which is typically associated with and experienced toward horror cinema. In terms of producing a socio-political context of sex trafficking which the film can be read against and connected strands of patriarchal treatment of women and their bodies, it is less successful and harder to substantiate. Jenny Barrett has discussed how *The Bunny Game* can be seen as "real-not-real"[51] due to its hybrid amalgamation of documentary and expressionist modes of representation. For Barrett, a dialectic is "exposed in the film between two self-conscious 'looks' or stylistic paradigms" which call attention to the film as spectacle and which "draw attention to the presence of the male director."[52] Both styles ultimately "encourage an exploitative gaze at the objectified female."[53] If we are to apply Barrett's reading of *The Bunny Game* to the affective acts that the film engages in, then we again move back to a representational paradigm. Here, the modalities of performance contribute to the diegesis as a spectacular experience rather than to radically break away from the "normative codes and expectations of narrative and ideology"[54] bound up in patriarchal, phallocentric society.

Conclusion

The analysis of performance in *The Bunny Game* and the vomit gore films can adduce that the real is ultimately brought back into the realm of the representational. As Vogel's attempts to manufacture a "real" snuff movie were thwarted by external factors and societal considerations and Ryan's representation of the real was obfuscated through the use of spectacle and entertainment, so too do the authentic performances of La Vey and Getsic retreat from the real the closer they get. The theoretical discipline of performance studies and the Deleuzian concept of affective-performativity can move beyond the spectacle of the violent image and the repulsive and horrifying status of the films by looking closely at performance in terms of providing a realist horror and potentially a socio-political dimension. In this respect, analyzing performance does provide new ways to look at the horror on display and, as shall be addressed later, why audiences react so strongly to the narrative content of films like *Slaughtered Vomit Dolls*. In fact, the performance in the films, certainly the affective-performativity, cannot necessarily be isolated from that which exists outside of the cinema. For example, the affective gestures and acts of vomiting and urination take on their power through a relationship with an audience. Existing preconceptions of these acts from an individual to a societal level define how they are received when they appear in the films. Similarly, in *The Bunny Game*, the acts of "real torture" do not serve as a feminist treatment of male violence and exploitation of the marginal underclass. Indeed, the film operates as a form of entertainment where audiences see the sadistic violence visited on Bunny-Getsic as a type of enjoyment, especially in terms of how the female body is often objectified and sexualized in mainstream cinema. The shocking appearance and quality of these acts may well defamiliarize the horror on display, which in turn provides an often unprecedented horror film, but only on the level of experience and sensation. The performance contained in hardcore horror does provide an integral aspect to how the films are received and viewed as real (even if it only ever approximates the real) and do provide opportunities to break down normative viewing positions which may "affect and transform our perceptual experience."[55] Yet the durability and persistence of the representational ultimately work against the potential to disrupt normalizing thought and in providing new affective experiences for the viewer. It is certainly not achieved or resolved through performance in hardcore horror, but at least it offers the opportunity to bring the modality of affect and representation together to reveal their complex, contested and controversial relationship.

SEVEN

Hardcore Horror Production
An Interview with Amateur Porn Star Killer *Director Shane Ryan*

This chapter focuses on the production practices of hardcore horror and the intersection of industrial, technological and cultural pathways in the marketing, distribution and, ultimately, in the form and content of the horrors that shape this cycle of North American cinema. The chapter includes an in-depth interview with director Shane Ryan, who cogently addresses the alternative and marginal film practices he has engaged with and utilized in the making of the *Amateur Porn Star Killer* series. His films authenticate the rise in new media technologies, the availability of cheap, portable recording devices, the impact of the Internet in shaping narrative direction and content, and how these factors have engendered a rise in low–no-budget films that have come to characterize the marketplace in the 21st century. Thematically his films share clear connections to the explorations of the real found in Vogel and Valentine's work and particularly the intention to establish a porous border between the representational and the authentic.

Ryan has also experienced similar difficulties to other hardcore horror filmmakers in the production of the *Amateur Porn Star Killer* films due to the fact that "with hundreds of shot-on-digital feature films released each year, not to mention the many thousands destined never to see the light of day, it is becoming increasingly difficult to distinguish one product from another."[1] In the saturated landscape of independent, low-budget filmmaking, Ryan has provided a strategy which has seen him successfully bring the films to market. Primarily, this has capitalized on the initial notoriety the films generated due to their minuscule budgets, representations of unsimulated sex, thematic strategies of sexual violence and rape, and commentary on how real death has been disseminated and experienced in a post–9/11 Internet age. Therefore, Ryan is well positioned to comment on the alternative production practices and thematic strategies that filmmakers of hardcore horror have explored and exploited to get their marginal and transgressive films marketed and distributed.

Ryan discusses a range of topics that run through the filmmaking processes of hardcore horror and that have been evident in the approaches of Fred Vogel and Lucifer Valentine. He discusses his early career in low-budget filmmaking, the production of extreme horror, and the underlying industrial issues concomitant with marginal, underground filmmaking. It is a candid evaluation of the production processes involved in hardcore horror and thus presents an illuminating account of the alternative practices, and the corollary of hard-fought successes and myriad frustrations, of working within the field of underground horror.

An Interview with Shane Ryan

> I would like to express my gratitude and give special thanks to Shane Ryan for agreeing to do the interview and for providing such in-depth and valuable responses. The interview was carried out via email correspondence. It is presented as written in the main part to retain the expressive nature of Ryan's responses.

The term "true horror" has been applied to the Amateur Porn Star Killer *films in the same way as true crime. It fits very well with the* APSK *films. Talk about what this term means to you and why it is important to how you approach your material and form your ideas.*

I was never really a fan of horror films growing up, and although I'm still not, I think I've gained some appreciation for them. But it angered me for a long time that these films were considered horror. If you expect them to be, then you will be disappointed. They're not gore films, they're not ghost or slasher movies. I didn't know what to consider them for a long time. I thought that they fit into that mumblecore crowd, as they were, as mumblecore described themselves, movies made about and by 20-something-year-olds, shot digitally, no budget, no script, minimal location, slice-of-life stories.... So, I started calling them true horror. It was a way to describe them without feeling like I was calling myself, or my films, "horror films." They were indeed true horror. They weren't "true crime," they weren't "true stories" (although my latest film, *My Name Is "A" by Anonymous* [2012], borrows from a true case), but all of my films, not just *APSK*, are indeed horror stories that are true to life. If you were going through in your life what these characters are, it would be horrific.

Somebody had actually referenced *My Name Is "A"* as true horror. I can't recall if they actually termed it "true horror" or something similar, but I believe that is when I started calling my films "true horror films." Or "artsploitation" was another word they used for *My Name is "A,"* which I believe is accurate as well. My films are art films, not horror films, not straight-up exploitation films, but they have exploitative moments in them (the graphic sex, the in-your-face abuse of a character) although usually it's the titles or ideas (the promotional side) which are exploitation-sounding, but the movies are hard to accept ... because they are too artsy for the horror or exploitation crowd, too exploitative and horrific for the art house crowd, too true for horror fans to enjoy them, too horrific for fans of dramatic cinema to engage in. There's really no place for them sometimes, so calling them true artsploitation horror, or something like that, makes sense to me. Or maybe I just say that so I feel, and hope, there's an understanding audience for them.

The complex relationship to realism between the filmmaker and audience is clearly highlighted in that you mention that APSK 2: Snuff Version *was partially done because some complained that the first film was too "artsy." Are there specific examples of people who took this stance or was it more general feedback?*

Both. Many places point out the "artsy" approach with the effects and music in it. But two very specific examples come from that first Long Beach screening [*APSK* debut screening at the Action on Film International Film Festival at Long Beach, California, in 2006]. Two of the few people who came had full-on freak-outs about it. The first was my cousin, who called me on the way home to just go off on me about the effect. The guy is totally technically driven, like, obsessively. Cannot comprehend emotion if it gets in the way of technical continuity. Never talks about the way a person acts in a film or the character or story, just the lighting, the CGI, etc. He tore me to shreds on how a video camera couldn't possibly have that effect and continued to lecture me on it like I was a fucking moron. I explained to him (and everyone else who brought this up) that I knew that, obviously, as I shot it, and edited the effect into it, so again, obviously, I purposely made it that way. I explained that it was meant to evoke a feeling and an emotion but he couldn't comprehend it and continued to bash the idea...

I stand by my decision to make it the way that I did, though, as I'm a very emotional person. I am driven by mood more than anything else. But I figured for a special feature (and also a selling point) and to get people excited, why not have a "snuff" version for part two, which took less than three days to edit as opposed to the "movie" version, which took about ten intense editing weeks. This way, too, I could make the "movie" version as artsy as I wanted, way beyond what the first one was, but not have any fucking complaints as those complainers would now have their snuff version. And if people were to see or come across just the snuff version on the Internet, for all the fuckheads who rip off filmmakers, they might actually believe it and help spread even more word of mouth.

You talk on the APSK2 commentary about thinking whether you are "partially the Brandon character" in how you approach the films and the female co-stars! You also mention having to take a break during APSK as inhabiting this character was traumatic. Therefore I am interested in your relationship with Brandon, and a bit like Bowie and his personas of the Thin White Duke and Ziggy, they become indistinguishable from the "real" David Bowie. I am not suggesting that it was quite as severe in this case (!) but am interested in your relationship with Brandon and how this again developed over the trilogy.

In some ways, I love the approach as it's more like stage acting, really getting to live it for an hour straight, and it can be really fun for an actor (as they're getting to really, really act—or rather, actually become the part—far beyond acting, perhaps terrifying). But when it's this type of character, and you're also the director, and you're also in charge of how you handle the actress, the nudity and the sex, it becomes overbearing. You start second-guessing things. "Am I doing this as Brandon? It's not like it was written in the script, or someone else's script. Am I really turned on 'cause I do have an erection, so am I a rapist? Well, you're fondling a girl's ass, so I guess it's normal, right? Yeah, but she's supposed to be underage, repulsed by me, etc." It really messes with your head. I was so done after *APSK3*, I never wanted to put myself through that again. When I talk about Brandon, or whenever I'm describing doing a scene as Brandon, I refer to "He'll then do this, he'll then do that, he'll say this, etc." I don't even say "I" when referring to what I will do as this character, it's almost like I'm trying everything I possibly can to distance myself from him. I think Brandon is everything that I despise in a human being, and I hope I do not share any similarities with. Many people in my family have been raped, and their rapists were also other people in my family. So, I have both the blood of a rape victim and the blood of a rapist in me, and quite possibly they're fighting with each other. My body feels both, but my mind knows that it's wrong. So maybe I've been trying to make sense out of why somebody like Brandon exists. Or how to watch out for somebody like this. Maybe it is a pretty severe case, though when I'm watching somebody being raped on screen in a movie, I'm certainly not cheering on the rapist. I'm usually outraged, placing myself in the victim's shoes, wanting her/him to fight back and crack the fucker right in the skull.

I didn't even know I had taken a break during *APSK1*. It's when we switched tapes, when Brandon puts the camera on the bed and it cuts out for a second. Michiko reminded me some time later about the break. She wanted to keep going, to finish the film. I apparently told her I was going to vomit if we did. So I sat on the bed and watched cartoons to escape that mindset.

I guess she just quietly sat in character. I think she said it lasted about an hour before I was ready to start again. With Regan [in *APSK3*] I wasn't quite sure if the take came out okay, but I just made the call that it did. Hers was one solid tape, no break. We talked about maybe doing it again, but I was definitely done. That experience might have been even worse, possibly because I barely knew Regan (unlike Michiko) and was saying just awful, insulting stuff to her. With Kai I can't remember, Brandon didn't really get nasty 'til the second tape, and then we were done.

I just had an actress today, who I interviewed last night, turn me down for the new film because of this style of filmmaking. An actress I was dying to work with as she just starred opposite Jean-Claude Van Damme (my real dream; acting alongside Van Damme!). She told me she loved taking real punches, really living the character, and she had done plenty of graphic nude and rape scenes, but my style was still even too much for her after she slept on it, and also that fact about having no crew when I do this. So even people who love this type of performance (as the style and intensity did initially thrill her) are becoming afraid of me and these films. Maybe Brandon's hatred is really feeding off of me and starting to take over?

You've said, "I make films about depressing true-life shit. I need to understand why it happens. Even though I never will."[2] This was a really interesting quote as it is almost like the closer we get to the real (certainly death in horror) the further away it goes. It also links to your representational strategy of having the films as snuff but "modified" by the production company that "finds" them. This is a very interesting and insightful aspect of the films; the cultural mythology of snuff. If snuff existed, it is a great idea to suggest that people would present it more like a film. (In fact this is what the recent Isis propaganda films resemble.) Thus I want to ask, what was your relationship to the real and authenticity in APSK *and did this change/develop over the trilogy?*

Thinking back to how I first felt when I made that sudden decision to go make this film one random night nearly 12 years ago ... I recall now seeing *15 Minutes* [John Herzfeld] back in 2001, I believe. In the film, two killers grab a [camera] and record themselves during their violent spree through America. They hadn't originally intended to go around killing, or to film it, but this man's quest to get money owed to him and not being able to control his anger or emotions when he finds out it's been spent, and his associates need to film everything while obsessing over becoming Frank Capra, turns them into snuff filmmakers. They end up selling their taped recording of the murder of Robert DeNiro (the policeman pursuing them) for a million dollars. They first get the idea that they can sell their murder and that America would want it while watching *Jerry Springer*, or some trash show like that, and then in the film we are introduced to Kelsey Grammer's trash show character who ends up buying the murder. I absolutely love *15 Minutes*, and it, now that I think about it, was a lot like *Natural Born Killers*, as far as the media making killers superstars. But in *15 Minutes* they're actually making snuff, and they even kill a nude prostitute at one point on camera. It was a great statement on American society, television and our need for reality trash, and how these two killers actually use this disgusting weakness of ours to get away with publicly murdering a famous detective.

My brother and I watched it and were inspired to go shoot something. We couldn't film the big Hollywood movie around the POV stuff, so we simply made our own "two killers on a crime spree POV movie." That was actually my very first POV movie, my first improv movie, and my first faux-snuff movie. At the time I can't recall why, but I edited that to music and effects. I believe the reason for the effects being because my character, who's also very obsessed with himself and his camera, way more than my brother's character who seems more annoyed by the camera (pretty similar to the killers in *15 Minutes*), is supposed to be an amateur filmmaker, so my impression was that he would edit the movie together to rock music and cool filters and such, which is what we did. The character not only got his rocks off on murder, and on filming it, but also on being the manipulator on the presentation of it, and on his own image. He even states towards the end, "I want to fuck my camera," and the movie ends with him covering up the lens with his mouth as he says, "Give me a kiss." A kid completely obsessed with self-image and fame. Which is funny now that I think about it, as this was shot 15 years ago, way before the obsession of "selfies"—a term that simply makes me cringe. The supposed reason behind their killings is boredom. And the film shows the isolated wasteland town that they live in, in the middle of the desert drive to Las Vegas from Los Angeles.

Surely this was a major inspiration for *APSK*, as it was my first experiment of this type of movie. We tried to make it realistic for the most part though we purposefully added satirical moments more like *Natural Born Killers*.

APSK1 was always more inspired by *8MM* and the Richard Linklater movie *Tape* [2001] (just three people in a small, crappy motel room for the entire movie, shot on DV) but I had also seen a movie called *The Pornographer* [Doug Atchison, 1999]. This guy becomes obsessed with making porn, and somehow this girl gets killed at the end (I believe off camera) after she does her first porno and then regrets doing it. At the end you see her picture on the porn VHS tape which gets released anyway, and then the camera pulls back to show her image sitting there in the middle of hundreds of other VHS tapes. Hundreds of more victims, or hundreds of more who were looking for fame, or obsessed with the idea of being somebody, etc. This always stuck with me; what really went on behind closed doors? Which girls were really willing? Which ones wanted to be real actresses and ended up here? How many are dead?

It just felt so real. So, I felt that it could be. In that film's case, the distributor had altered the idea that this girl was so happy to be included in this film, when in fact her wanting the film taken back is actually what got her killed. And they distributed it anyway. I looked at *APSK1* in the way that if a distributor got ahold of this, and distributed it, what would they do? Any crime show you see, they alter the hell out of it. The news does, especially. I stopped watching TV in 1999 after Columbine because I saw them using real footage of the event to promote a one-hour special and they played the same music that Willem Dafoe dies to in *Platoon* [Oliver Stone, 1986] as he's running away from being shot at, and they placed that music over real video footage of the Columbine kids running out of the school as they're being shot at and their friends are being butchered. I got sick to my stomach and at that moment stopped watching TV. I didn't ever want to see something so disgusting—an ad in between shows like that—ever again. It was profiting off of the footage of real victims (not actors), children on top of that, in a "Hollywood movie" way. It didn't look like "news," it looked like fucking *Platoon* set in a school. They turned the Columbine massacre into an Oliver Stone film, ironically less than five years after Stone showed us this sickness of the media and its take on real death in *Natural Born Killers*. So, I knew that if the media or a film studio, [film]maker, etc., found a real killing like the *APSK*'s on camera, and somehow released it, that they would alter it to fit what they wanted it to be; more engaging. That was the idea. And it wasn't like I was uploading the film to the Internet and using an alias and waiting to see if people thought that it was real. I was actually releasing it, so I never thought to try and present it like "This is actually really straight from the tape found footage" since no distributor would legally be allowed to put it out. I figured everybody going in would know that it's fake. But I wanted them to get sucked into the reality as they watched it, and I wanted them to see it in a way that I thought the media would present a real murder; more like a movie, with music and credits and effects.

In the first film, you also mention about substituting films from a video store with Brandon's home videos. I was surprised by this discovery in the film as in the 1980s in the UK during the "video nasty" period, many horror "subversives" taped over cut or censored films with the original versions. I just wondered where this idea came from as it seems like a cultural link between the U.S. and UK surrounding horror and providing a more authentic horror film experience via the VHS cassette and the video store.

I feel like I did this at one point with my own films, or had thought about it (recording them onto rented VHS tapes from Blockbuster to try and get my films out to the world). I was always amused at how easy it was to just put a piece of tape over a rented VHS and make something new out of it for the following renter to discover. Funny you bring up video nasty. I wasn't even aware of that term until a few months ago. I seriously was sheltered from that world that so many people seem to think I borrowed ideas from. I recall *Fight Club* [David Fincher, 1999] also touching on the idea of splicing images into film reels (specifically of men's penises—that's the last shot I believe) and there's a scene where they're in Blockbuster erasing all of the VHS tapes.

The most memorable experience I had was around Christmas of 1998. My cousin hands me this blank VHS tape and says, "Don't watch this alone." I went to a friend's house and we watched it in the middle of the night. We got so spooked and had to stop it halfway through to go take an hour break to talk about if what we had just watched was real, grab some food down the street, then decide if we could come back and finish the movie. We did, and when the film ended, it just ended—no credits, nothing. We thought for sure we just watched somebody die on camera, become possessed, had proof that ghosts and witches and shit like that were real, etc. Freakiest shit ever. Well, not to sound like a chickenshit but months later this movie turned out to be *The Blair Witch Project*. Somehow my cousin had gotten a VHS tape of it, unlabeled and without credits, well before anybody had ever heard of the film, seven or eight months before it came out in theaters.

I'm pretty sure that's where a huge part of the idea came from. Nothing was spookier in my film viewing experiences other than being handed this blank VHS tape and putting it on to witness what I thought was a horror reality taking place right in front of me. Now, could you imagine if this happened to you and it was some 13-year-old girl actually being raped and murdered in front of you? Well, that's what I was going for.

You mention in an interview about "working-thinking outside of the box" as a low-, no-budget filmmaker on the APSK *films. Some are obvious, such as long takes, confined and restricted locations, but were there any others and how did they develop over the trilogy?*

Not knowing what it was that we were going to shoot I'd say would be a big example of thinking outside the box in regards to the first *APSK* (and to a lesser extent the second and third, though by then it was becoming more apparent what direction to take them). I had ideas for the original, like "Let's make people want to watch this for the sex and violence and then deliver on it in such a way that they feel disgusted for having wanted to watch it for those same reasons." But for the most part, we had no idea what was going to happen. Michiko Jimenez and I knew I was going to pick her up, have sex with her of some sorts, and kill her, but that was it. Most films, even low-budget ones, don't have the budget nor the time to waste "seeing if something works" with nearly zero planning involved, nor do they have the carefree attitude of just turning on the camera and "rolling with it." It also would be considered a safety hazard, an insurance issue, probably a potential sexual harassment or even assault issue, a severe lack in confidence from the actors, and the list goes on.

You can't just let the director be a one-man crew and run off with the actress to go do sexual and violent things with her. Even if a film costs, say, 5K, you need to be careful how you use that if that's all you got, and most people would dare not just wing it and risk losing their only 5K. I'm running into that problem right now; we're trying to do a spin-off of the trilogy with a "professional" actress. I've been getting free flights to screen the past films, to meet with investors and such, and tried casting while in these places for a new setting, but nobody likes to just wing it any more. Just a few hours ago, I had an actress tell me to fuck off for even offering her an audition for this after she applied for it. So, these days, I'd say my ways are so outside the box that I rarely seem to be able to find actors, let alone crew, to trust me any more. And actors used to want to be a part of nearly anything, violent sexual content or not; look at all the weirdos and crazy things John Waters got people to do on camera for no pay in the '70s. But times have changed since YouTube and the ability to become your own star, so finding actors to think outside the box with a filmmaker these days is hard in this new self-indulgent, sense-of-entitlement generation of Internet celebritism needs. Gaining somebody's trust with a film like *APSK*, whether done professionally or with friends, is the most important thing. And these days it's the most difficult and time-consuming, to be able to find those people…

As far as things changing with each *APSK* film: Michiko was an on-and-off fling, so we'd already been intimate together (in which case that meant feeling totally safe as anything sex-wise in the film was going to be fine), and she knew my working style as we'd made several films already the year prior. So it was just a matter of calling her up, asking her, and that was that, no big-gie, I had an actress. Three years went by before doing the second one, which I never would have thought I'd ever do another *APSK*, let alone ever make a sequel to anything. I hated the idea of sequels as Hollywood was flooded with them. But I had a contract to release a sequel six months from the date that the deal was made for the first, vs. making a new film idea happen and end up searching for another distributor for years, so I decided to try it again. But along came having to actually find an actress this time. I believe I put out a casting call in L.A. but didn't feel like I could approach an actual actress, or simply didn't receive any good submissions, I can't recall. So I went back to Lompoc[3] where I shot the first. I was having coffee, ran into an old friend, mentioned I needed somebody and she suggested Kai Lanette. Kai was down the street and came over. Strangely I recognized her as all of us (including Michiko) frequently visited the same coffee shop. And even weirder, I guess: Michiko had shown Kai the first *APSK* years earlier because they used to hang out. So in this case the casting became a bit different, and so did the approach. Michiko's character was withdrawn, really young, innocent. Kai, while the same age at the time of shooting *APSK2* that Michiko was during *APSK1*, appeared to be much older, stronger, experienced. So we came up with new ideas, and it made more sense to try a slightly different approach instead of having the girl be another victim who submits. Kai and I had both just gotten out of abusive relationships, her ex attacked her, my ex attacked me, so we decided to bring that into the equation as well as far as the idea that the girl liked being spanked around a bit. That let me figure out how my character, realistically, could adapt. If "Brandon" really experienced a new victim, with this much of a different reaction to his approach from a victim, how would he differ in response? And getting back as to how this all relates to thinking outside the box and adapting for each film, I can't think of another film or series, shot on the fly, with zero dollar budgets, where the actress and director get to discover their film together and play it out like reality and figure it out in real time as well.

APSK3 became much more complicated and interesting in the sleaziest of ways. It opens with [Brandon] screwing chick after chick before he settles down with the lead, who is actually a porn star. I approached almost every girl differently in Part 3. The first two girls I found off of Craigslist, which I hadn't done before with the other films (they were all friends and acquaintances). So I met with the girls, and the first one in the trunk [during *APSK3*'s opening scene], well, I was filming myself screwing her an hour after first meeting her. It was over at this farm in the middle of nowhere where she lived. It was actually a bit scary, as I thought, "I could have been anybody" (and so could she), and she was down to take me to her home with no witnesses within an hour of meeting me and let me fake-rape and kill (but actually screw) her. Granted she had read up on the films and was a fan of my work, but still (and I knew nothing of her for the most part).

The other blonde girl right after was the same bit pretty much. Only she didn't know about the films. I met her, she told me her high pay rate, I told her I had no money to pay, then asked if she still wanted to do it, and she said sure, after she pointed out her surprise that I was young and not some old creeper. (Uh, this is how girls actually get raped and killed ... by nice, normal-looking strangers who approach them through Craigslist.) I guess you could say it was quite ballsy of me to think I could pull this off, though I don't mean this in a complementary way of myself but more a shameful way. I think I thought that I could get away with anything, and I was. Frightening to think about it, but sort of like how ballsy Ted Bundy was, and how he was getting away with pretty much anything for a while. Granted, I wasn't really murdering anybody, but I was basically playing Bundy, shooting the murder as if it were real, and usually really having sex with the "victims," and their pretend corpses. Yuck.

But I wasn't even enjoying it. I was strictly there to work. As soon as I got the shot, I was wrapped. I wanted to get the film done and that was it. I had so many submissions, I actually had to turn girls away. Maybe subconsciously I felt like I was turning my career into straight-up porn, which is perhaps why I went with a porn star for the main role, I don't know (though I must add that Regan was a sweetheart and agreed to the film because she actually liked true crime–type movies). Maybe porn producers think this way, but horror filmmakers, dramatic filmmakers and art house filmmakers surely don't. This was thinking so far outside of the box in the sluttiest of ways that I've always feared I'll never be able to live *APSK3* down. At the same time, *APSK3* got into more retailers than anything I've ever done. This sleazy movie of mine got placed alongside every mainstream movie you could imagine. And we made it with ten bucks, on no script, shot in a few hours, post-production wrapped in a week. So, despite it being the bastard child of the trilogy, it was my biggest feat. Other films by the same distributor which cost north of a quarter million to make didn't receive this much attention or recognition. Thinking outside the box, no matter how much you resent yourself for it, has its perks in the porn star killer world, I guess.

The distribution for APSK *took roughly three years. Film Threat originally championed the film, but could you say more about how* APSK *got from this early praise of the film to the L.A. screenings and release of the DVD?*

After I completed the film in late 2004, I sat on it for a bit. I didn't want anybody to see it. Hell, it took a year until I finally decided to watch it myself with a friend of mine (I had only watched it in portions during editing but never from start to finish). I really didn't know what to do with it; one friend suggested trashing it. This was just not the kind of film I ever wanted to make nor thought I would make as I had been for years editing a feature that was more like a cross between *The War Zone* [Tim Roth, 1999] and *Requiem for a Dream* [Darren Aronofsky, 2000]. But I could tell that that film would never be finished so *APSK* was just a frustration, a need to have a feature of some sorts, by any means, under my belt. But then I decided to send it to a couple review sites and when one hated it and one loved it I thought, well, they were both very strong opinions, and one thing I did like more than anything, really, was evoking emotion, whether love or hate. Then came *Film Threat*, and their writer Doug Brunell kept writing about them, and praising them. This praise was coming to me while I was actually at Sundance for the first time watching films, so it was a bit surreal since *Film Threat* was also covering Sundance and here I was getting all this acclaim as *Film Threat*'s top featured stories while I'm at Sundance without a film, attending the festival merely because I'm volunteering my time at Tromadance and attending Sundance during some off time from Troma. Not that *Film Threat* was, say, *The New York Times*, but they were doing very well then and it was the beginning of seeing my films reviewed. After the *Film Threat* reviews, *APSK* started getting a lot more attention, and everything snowballed. I believed I could easily get the film distributed; hell, I practically lived at a distribution company (Image Entertainment[4]). My dad was senior editor there, so he got me in to see acquisitions. Unfortunately, though, the acquisitions guy there at the time just looked at the title and handed it off to Hot Topic (a major chain Gothic-cult-hip store for teens) thinking that they would be good for *APSK*. That would have been incredible but I didn't think plausible at all. He literally did this in the first meeting before he even watched a minute of the film. Turns out he didn't watch a lot of films he acquired and actually got fired not too long later. In the meantime, Hot Topic of course rejected the film so I was on to finding a distributor myself.

I contacted about every distributor that I could find. I even got the attention of a few large indie distributors. At one point, one of the producers of the film *Edmond* [Stuart Gordon, 2005], with William H Macy, contacted me to tell me how much he liked the film and would love to distribute it but just didn't know how on Earth he could distribute a film like *APSK*. While it was discouraging to think that that was the problem (people want to distribute it but don't know how), it was enough to keep me going and he gave me great words of encouragement and ideas of places to contact and kept corresponding with me to see how it was going. But nothing happened after that with anybody else (even places like MTI Video and Maverick shot me down[5]) and I finally about gave up.

I think when I finally gave up, that's when Greg contacted me. During this time, I was also getting rejected by all of the festivals that I entered. The only one that hurt was SXSW. They had premiered *Kissing on the Mouth* [2005], Joe Swanberg's first film, and Joe had actually contacted me at that time (early 2005) telling me he had heard of my film and wanted to see it since both of our films were getting a lot of response for their graphic sex acts and do-it-yourself digital, no-budget filmmaking approaches. We were also about the same age, and it seemed like we made pretty much the same movie, the only difference being his film was more about people discovering sexuality-relationships in their early transformation into adulthood, whereas mine was discovering sex, boys and your body during your transition to teen-hood and tragically through rape and by means of a serial killer. But the style, the improv nature, the graphic content, the age of the filmmaker, the type of camera, the minimal location, etc., was all the same, so I felt after reading up on his film (and definitely after viewing it) that mine would be accepted where his film had been. (He was also getting tons of acclaim on *Film Threat* at the same time, which might have been where he heard of me.) So, after I got rejected by SXSW, which basically made Joe's career (and now he's huge), I got very, very discouraged. Very fucking discouraged. I watched his career grow as I was still struggling to get my first feature even screened. I reluctantly tried the horror festivals (never feeling like it was a horror film, surely not a slasher or gore one), and had no luck there as well.

Could you expand on the lack of exposure within the horror community in terms of festival and convention participation and/or screenings?

I've never done a horror convention as I never considered myself to be a horror filmmaker and I never thought I'd be accepted into that crowd. Although now I feel like maybe I could possibly do them as the horror community has shown me 100 times more support than the art house community but I've also never even had enough money to throw at attending a convention. I'm not sure how these other starving artists do it, but I think most have some sort of budget from somewhere and aren't making $10 movies like me. Or they have real jobs. I need one of those.

I think that's when I, myself, started realizing the film was a hard sell as it didn't really fall into any category. There was no blood, so it wasn't horror, the sex was too realistic and depraved to be sexploitation, and the movie was too sexual and horrific to be an art house film like mumblcore (even though it is basically mumblecore to the very definition of mumblecore). I got some major support by a very select few during this time: Doug from *Film Threat* as mentioned, Chad Clinton Freeman from Pollygrind (*APSK* didn't play there 'cause Chad hadn't started the festival yet but he constantly campaigned the films along with Doug and later screened many of my other films at the festival), and finally Felix Vasquez from *Cinema-Crazed*.[6] These three guys really kept it going, I believe. I got reviews from others in between, but these guys would continuously support the film and review it, post about it and gave me lots of hope. They all were coming to it with a fresh eye having not known me or having any connection to me before that so I knew that it was honest film critic opinion. But after a couple years, it wasn't enough and I think I actually did give up on screenings. The only one I ever got at this point was by a festival in Long Beach which pretty much I think was screening everything that was entered, and it was geared towards action films. I got a midnight showing on Sunday after everything was over, and in a conference-type room with chairs and a screen. They helped generate a lot of talk for the film, but I of course only had a few people show. And that was it until I got Greg's message.

The DVD release actually almost never happened. When Greg contacted me, *Grindhouse* [Quentin Tarantino and Robert Rodriguez, 2007] was about to come out and had a ton of hype. Everybody thought it was going to be a huge hit. So the first *APSK* was going to be a double feature with another film to ride off of the *Grindhouse* release. But then *Grindhouse* came out and tanked big time, so Greg cancelled his Grindhouse-style releases. He said he might not be able to release my film now, and asked if this little $45 movie could sell. I told him, "The title alone will sell this movie, trust me." I saw the response when I announced the film, and I knew that the title was how I got as far as I did. I told him people will not be able to help their curiosity, just like he couldn't help pulling it out of the trash. So he trusted me, took a chance on releasing it solo, and it was a huge hit.

Now that the film was generating significant interest, did you anticipate (or push for) a theatrical screening for the trilogy?

I knew Greg was releasing a lot of his films theatrically, and I wanted the reviews which come with theatrical releases (i.e., *L.A. Times*, etc.). So, I begged for a theatrical release. But now I was asking for a bit much. He only agreed to do it if I paid for it. I didn't have money. Fortunately, a family member of mine was making a great living off of selling dope at the time. There was plenty of money to go around, so we cut a deal, and I had my theatrical release. (Note: This person later got busted and lost everything and now has a real, and awful, day job, a wife and several kids, and can barely make ends meet.)

Unfortunately, though, midnight shows were no longer getting any of these notable places to cover them for reviews, so that whole bit was out. I finally got a full theatrical week booked with my fourth film, *Warning!!! Pedophile Released* [2009], which did indeed receive an amazing *L.A. Times* review (but nobody came to see it). *APSK1* and *2* showed theatrically in Los Angeles for the midnight slots only (in 2007 and 2008). They were later invited to screen at a festival in South Africa (*APSK1*, I believe this was 2008), at a nice theater through a festival in Paris (*APSK1*—this wasn't until 2015) and at a small theater through a festival in Switzerland (*APSK1* and *2*, just a few months before Paris in late 2014). The Swiss fest was in Lausanne, and they actually screened *APSK1* and *2* there for a full week, along with my other films *The Girl Who Wasn't Missing* [2011] and *My Name Is "A" by Anonymous* as a whole retrospective on my films. These were all invite screenings, which was great, since I was used to submitting and only being rejected. I guess it's just taken a lot of time for these films to slowly ease their way in through word of mouth. They also were presented as a lecture at a university in the UK, around 2011 or 2012, by Dr. Steve Jones and in a couple of books by him as well, and amazingly, about a dozen other books that I know of. Quite a surprise after all of the rejection.

The reactions seem 50–50. At Lausanne they were 50–50. I wasn't at Paris but I heard the same thing, 50–50 love-hate it. As far as my first real experience, it was at the *APSK1* Laemmle midnight showing. I felt at the time like it was mostly hated as many people quickly left afterwards and wouldn't say anything to the camera; my brother was attempting to interview people for reactions and nearly everyone declined. Before it started, in the lobby many people were talking it up, so by how quickly they took off, I felt like they were greatly disappointed. But then one guy who had talked me up before the screening then left right away afterwards without saying anything and went home and wrote an amazing review about it. Some porn star stayed afterwards for a long time waiting to talk to me about it in a very enthusiastic and affecting way. A couple high school guys who I thought would be disappointed that they didn't get a titillating sexploitation movie actually attended both screenings and said they were deeply affected by it and made a joke about wanting a trilogy, strangely enough. I made a few new filmmaker friends and future collaborators, lost a couple of friends who had attended and were offended, so a very mixed bag. Surprisingly though, not one person walked out (out of about 70 people; every single person actually stayed until after the credits were completely done and the screen went black). I also heard that we had a big attendance for a midnight screening as they told me the average was about five, ten people, aside from Tommy Wiseau's *The Room* [2003], which we were up against. Jonah Hill, Paul Rudd and all types of people were there that evening. It was also opening weekend of *Superbad* so it was the breakout weekend of Jonah Hill, and we were trying to get him and his friends to leave *The Room* for *APSK*. They didn't, and now I star in a film with Wiseau which opened during the time this whole gang was making a movie about Wiseau—strange world.[7]

The most wild reactions, though, were the days leading up to the screening. Laemmle is a chain indie theater, with around eight theaters total in the L.A. area. Even though we were only showing at the Sunset 5 Laemmle, we were allowed to put up our posters in Encino, Downtown, Fallbrook, Santa Monica and at least one other. They were being really supportive. On top of that, they let me flood the Sunset 5 with something like five posters, including two on standees in the lobby. We also had at least two, three posters up at other theaters. At first it worked out because I got along with the different theater managers, and my girlfriend's friend was a projectionist at the Fallbrook one, so we used every connection we had. But then, apparently, the other employees at the Fallbrook theater were "offended" by the title or idea of the film. So offended that they took out the posters and trashed them. We went to the theater and indeed found them crumbled beyond repair in the trash. And remember each poster cost us more than the budget of the actual film, and I was spending every last dime we had been given for the theatrical budget from the drug money. Other employees, who claimed to be "offended," when told they would have to repay us, suddenly found our posters at their own residence. So they were stealing the ones that they did not trash. We thought that was settled until this actress, Lesley Ann Warren (from such sex-fueled films as *Color of Night* [Richard Rush, 1994] and *Secretary* [Steven Shainberg, 2002]), complained about the posters, yet again "offended," claiming that her rights as a woman were being taken from her by having to view such images. Because she's known, and has an Academy Award or nomination or whatever, that's what got us into deep shit. At that point the theater had it and all of the theaters outside of the Sunset had to remove all of our promotional materials. Because the Sunset was playing the film and we paid for it, they had to keep one up poster but they made us remove all of the lobby promotion we had up until the night of the screening. Total bullshit. On top of that, there was a mistake in our *LA Weekly* ad and the poster ad for it had no theater or show times listed for the movie, so who knows how much better we might have made out if we actually were not trashed and banned of our promotions (which was about 40 times the cost of the film in total) and if we had had our info listed on our ad. But, we still did okay (seven to 14 times better than the average midnight showing there, according to Laemmle).

Rocket Video[8] had seen the promotions and invited me to do a DVD signing with them. Other people, like the critic for *LA Xpress* (the *LA Weekly* equivalent to porn), was so "outraged" by the film that he refused to review it and threatened to picket the screening if we didn't pull the film. Fun times, now that I think about it. We don't get that kind of controversy much any more. I remember it a lot as a kid, even people picketing tame stuff like *Total Recall* [Paul Verhoeven, 1990] and *Basic Instinct* [Verhoeven, 1992] when they came out. I miss that.

I noticed, in the A Boy, a Girl & a Camera *documentary[9], a wanted poster for APSK in the style of* Blair Witch. *Were you consciously evoking this film in the promotion? How did this type of marketing come about?*

That poster is what got actress Lesley Ann Warren all crazy. I don't recall *Blair Witch*'s marketing approach since I was so affected by the film before any marketing had happened, but I do know that however they marketed it, I paid attention due to all of the curiosity I had after finding out I had been tricked and I'm pretty sure I might have taken that idea from them since I wanted people to have that same feeling I did of "Holy shit, did I just watch something real?" Originally, when I was sending out the film, I also had no credits, like the copy I viewed of *Blair Witch*, as I was just sending out a VHS tape with "evidence" (a condom and tissue) and no actresses credited. But reviewers started complaining that they couldn't credit people so I added them when I added music. I used a similar approach with *Warning!!! Pedophile*

Released, handing out flyers which simply stated in big bold letters "*Warning!!! Pedophile Released*" and the film premiere date in tiny print underneath along with a picture of a five-year old Dakota Fanning as I released her first film (a 20-minute short) before each showing of *Pedophile*. I figured that would surely cause a lot of talk, though it instead simply scared people away. That approach was even more misunderstood than the film. But when you find something important to say, and use exploitation to promote and lure people in to try and say this important thing, there's never any rhyme or reason to the response you're going to get. It's better to be rich and have $50,000,000, hire a superstar and let them say something important without the trash and schlock temptation for a bait and switch.

How did Cinema Epoch pick up and distribute the film(s)?

After I had pretty much given up hope on the first film getting distributed, I got an email from Gregory Hatanaka, the president of Cinema Epoch, in early 2007 saying that he saw the film and loved it. But I hadn't submitted it to Cinema Epoch as they were a new company I had not yet heard of. It turned out I had sent it to Greg through another company he was working for in acquisitions. Greg didn't like the way that that they were handling acquisitions so he left to start his own distribution company. *Amateur Porn Star Killer* he found in the trash before he left. Apparently people were throwing films out before he could look at them, hence one of the reasons he decided to leave. So this interview exists because somebody decided to look through the trash and found my movie dumped there. I believe it was the month before *APSK* was set to hit DVD that Greg said he would distribute a sequel if I wanted to go make it right away and have it out within six months so I agreed, and as *APSK2* was coming out we decided to sign a deal for the third. I figured I had found a home for these films, and decided to make it a trilogy and just push them out.

More recently, your work has been part of a retrospective entitled Banned, Exploited & Blacklisted. *How did this come about?*

I can't recall exactly. I believe somebody had said those words to me about my work, that people exploited me to show that I was being exploitative, back when I was trying to make my human trafficking film and people said I was a monster for wanting to make a film about a trafficking victim even though my reason for wanting to make it was because I thought that sex trafficking was a sad and frightening thing which needed to be talked about more often. This was in 2009 when I announced plans after four years of trying to find a story—and this was right before there suddenly started to become this trend of making films about trafficking, and most of those actually are exploitative thrillers. This was around when *Warning!!! Pedophile Released* got me banned, causing all of my films to get blacklisted from multiple outlets, so then my friend took these pics of me and I don't know who actually came up with the label and title but we ended up with the poster for *Banned, Exploited & Blacklisted*. And then nothing came of it. But eventually a distributor asked me if I had a collection of shorts I could give them so I said, "Why don't I just give you this film poster-title and my shorts, trailers, behind-the-scenes clips, etc., dating back from when I was a kid to my most current work plus some of the controversy-critical acclaim-hater-death threats remarks in between and then you'll have basically a much larger collection of my stuff, and more like a retrospective?" So that was that.

Continuing with the theme of publicity, exposure and distribution, the Internet can be seen as a positive place for low-budget filmmakers such as mumblecore. What has been your Internet experience in terms of the marketing and promotion opportunities for the APSK *films?*

Well, pretty much no places that would praise and cover these mumblecore films would bat an eye at my stuff. I must have sent IndieWire (which along with SXSW defined the mumblecore movement) close to a thousand press releases over the past 12, 13 years—however long they've been around—zero mentions by them ever, even having an indie film, three indie films, which beat the indie film (film period) record of lowest budgeted films ever made. So, zero support there and countless hours, days, weeks of effort thrown at them and other places like them.

We'd have websites (Facebook, MySpace accounts) just disappear without warning after months, even years of building friends and fan bases. I've received more death threats, hundreds of times more death threats, via the Internet than I ever did by bullies at school (and that was pretty fucking bad). I have YouTube videos over and over disappear, even self-help ones I make to try and help people suffering from abuse or self-abuse get flagged, while my films in their uncensored form get ripped off and uploaded by people other than me and never taken down no matter how many hits they get. I've had millions (literally millions) of illegal downloads (and here I am still having to borrow money just to put gas in my car sometimes). So, yeah, the Internet has endless scumbags, "keyboard gangsters" ruining the art world. Pussy little fucks who couldn't amount to shit or have the balls to do anything in their lives get behind a keyboard and use their bitch little fingers like bullets, tearing shit up. I hate the Internet.

Then again it has moments of being useful, like people such as yourself contacting me via Internet, and I have noticed once I got rid of *Alter Ego Cinema*, made up a whole new site, a more professional and conservative one, that I've had less trouble. Less hits, but less trouble, though the hits-response that I do get seem to be more meaningful for the most part.

Seven. Hardcore Horror Production   171

How did your awareness of technological innovations, such as the DIY, "look at me" filmmaking of social media platforms such as YouTube, develop as the trilogy progressed? Did it change your approach to the material?

    I believe the only thing that changed was my knowledge of people having zero attention span in this day and age. Many people (who ripped off the film via the internet) I saw complained about *APSK2* not having any nudity and I was like, what the fuck, it shows penetration let alone tons of nudity. I was so pissed, not that people turned off the film ten minutes in, but that they did so and made "hater" remarks about something that was clearly not true at all. So I put tons of sex in the beginning of *APSK3* because of that. Only I fucked myself as Sony was manufacturing the *APSK* [discs] at the time and dropped Part 3 after I did that so we had to find somebody else to make the DVDs. So the only outcome learning about people's short attention spans got me was banned. I still, to this day, watch only VHS, DVD and go to the theater. I practically despise the Internet. I merely do what I have to with it (like having a Facebook, or Twitter—which I really fucking hate and see no point in, YouTube, website, etc.). But I don't watch YouTube videos (aside from a few relaxing ASMR [autonomous sensory meridian response] ones), I don't keep up on other faux snuff films. I still have never seen anyone else's faux snuff features—until just this year, I had to watch some shorts for the anthology that I put together. I don't even have the Internet, I get it when I get coffee. So I don't think it's affected me or changed my approach other than those first few minutes of *APSK3*. I believe the only other thing I learned, which is basically what I just talked about, was using nudity, sex, etc., to grab attention and promote the films. But I already knew that worked regardless of the Internet as that's how I came up with the title. But I made something like 100 mini 10- to 30-second trailers of *APSK 1* and *2* and would title them tons of different sexual things like "girl strips," "girl takes a shower," "young couple have sex," etc., and then after a few seconds of watching a clip like this cut to Michiko being punched or Kai being choked and then cut to the title and release date. Those got a shit tons of hits but were almost always flagged, sometimes within two minutes, but they'd have 5K, 10K hits in those couple minutes, and then I'd just keep uploading, re-uploading, etc., etc. But did that really help me or not? I don't know. They got several million hits overall, but do hits translate to sales? Or even enough curiosity to seek it out on a torrent site? Not necessarily. People's attention spans are too fucking short unless you have a link right then and there, something which takes zero work or research or brain space on their part. I give up on people like that.

Eight

"I'll pay you in cash to slip this thread into the purge"
Navigating Fandom in Hardcore Horror

Operating as a bridge between the alternative production practices of hardcore horror and fandom is Lucifer Valentine's excursion onto horror forums and message boards to promote *Slaughtered Vomit Dolls*. In 2005 when Valentine began frequenting horror forums, it represented a relatively novel approach in its utilization of the non-traditional new media forms of online marketing and promotion. It also clearly demarcated the cultural and performative dimension of fandom and notions of subcultural capital, distinction and connoisseurship that will become of crucial importance as we proceed with a specific analysis of the fandom of hardcore horror. To illustrate the complex, often fraught relationship between filmmaker and fan, a representative example will be given of Valentine's engagement with horror fans on *Rue Morgue* magazine's forum The Mortuary, which started in 2005 and continued intermittently until 2010 when a particularly hostile thread was closed by a moderator for contravening forum (and therefore fan) conduct and etiquette.

The Mortuary forum thread for *Slaughtered Vomit Dolls* provides clear concepts and socio-cultural dimensions of how audiences-fans interact with the hardcore horror subgenre. In particular, the notion of fandom as production rather than simply reception is given space and attention in terms of how it is narrated and constructed by the posters on the thread. Fandom as production has an important part to play in defining the fan community and is illustrated via the connoisseurship, distinction, authenticity and the accumulation of cultural capital of the fan. The main thread relating to *Slaughtered Vomit Dolls* contains 417 posts which took place from November 2005 to March 2006.[1] The thread quickly became acrimonious when attention was brought to the actions of Valentine, who asked one of the *Rue Morgue* staff members to interview him about the film. Despite being rejected, Valentine continued in his pursuit, citing bafflement at why a respected horror magazine would refuse to support independent horror filmmakers in this way. Valentine's response does seem to exhibit a certain naiveté concerning how many responses for coverage a magazine like *Rue Morgue* tends to get and the precise rules and limitations placed on accepting any particular request. Indeed, in mishandling a rejection, as Valentine does in this case, the reputation of the filmmaker can be adversely affected. However, rather than focusing on the strict policing of forum etiquette and the exacting protocols of the magazine over granting coverage to filmmakers, it is instead worth pursuing why such a reaction was articulated and how it links to the fundamental principles of fandom.

John Fiske has talked persuasively about how we should understand fandom "in terms of productivity, not of reception."[2] With regards to horror fans, it is not simply about watching the films but also about the performative aspect of what they do with their fandom. Fiske outlines three categories of production—semiotic, enunciative, and textual—which takes place at the interface between the object of fandom and of the fan themselves. Semiotic productivity "consists of the making of social identity and of social experience"[3] and is particularly interior in that it consists of an intense engagement with a text in terms of forming or reinforcing a self and social identity. When this essentially private aspect of fandom is made public, either verbally, written or through appearance, it becomes enunciative. Although taking in social interaction and forming social relationships that have a high cultural value to the fan, the production of enunciative fandom is limited to the restricted spaces of fan communities such as the forum, fanzine and convention. The final category, textual productivity, is when fans produce and circulate texts among their fan groups, such as fan fiction and fan videos. The investment in these categories, in turn, provides the fan with the accumulation of cultural capital derived from connoisseurship in the fan area, distinction in terms of knowledge and insight, and the status of being an authentic fan.

Members of the Mortuary forum engage in both the semiotic and enunciative productivity in their appreciation of horror cinema. It shapes their outsider identity, which is positioned against the mainstream and/or dominant culture as well as facilitating fan talk along the contours of discrete social formations and groupings. The third category of textual production is defined within The Mortuary as the process of the film review. A number of posters on the *Slaughtered Vomit Dolls* thread work for *Rue Morgue* in the capacity of critic and others produce work for horror sites such as terroraustralis.net and slasherama.com.[4] The production of horror films or fan versions of famous and respected horror texts are less evident due to economic precepts and issues surrounding technical aptitude and access to materials and production facilities. Those members who have filmmaking experience and produce films of their own tend to do so for a love of the genre and not solely (or at all) for profits and economic return. Valentine entered The Mortuary not as a fan of horror but as a textual producer looking to utilize the forum as an alternative means to promote and distribute his film. His initial purpose on the site was for the economic advancement of *Slaughtered Vomit Dolls*. In doing so, he transgressed the oppositional nature of the subordinate culture of The Mortuary by forcing a dominant capitalist approach on a fandom associated with cultural tastes "produced outside and often against official cultural capital."[5] Therefore, the negative response he received was based on two interlocking issues. Firstly, Valentine as a textual producer attains arguably the highest accolade of fandom and certainly it is a marker of a distinctive and authentic fan. Yet this was achieved without engaging with either a semiotic or enunciative production of fandom within any of the message boards of The Mortuary. Valentine did not discuss any reasons for being a film or horror fan and did not participate in other threads unconnected to his own work. The attainment of what many fans would consider that of an authentic fan is achieved without providing any evidence of fan practice, especially in terms of how it has contributed to concepts of self-identity and social interaction and experience. Secondly, in bypassing the first two categories in favor of textual production, Valentine privileges the technical, artistic and economic aspects of production which most resemble that of the official culture, while conterminously failing to provide any acknowledgment of fan behavior, identification and social interaction. That Valentine circumvented fan involvement only exacerbated the view that his presence represented an inauthentic fan and an agent of dominant capitalist interests.

Valentine's first post was a straightforward promotional junket for the film with release dates and a link to the website where people could view the trailer. The response was curious yet insistent with a number of posters asking Valentine for more narrative and thematic details of the film. Poster Robert Black put it succinctly when he replied, "I'm sick and tired of shock for shock's sake, and *Dolls* looks like another one of those. I do hope I'm wrong. Put it in the context of a fleshed-out narrative, experimental, symbolic or conventional, and you have me. Tell us about the story Mr. Valentine."[6] The tone of the responses in these early exchanges was that of an invested fan attempting to learn more about the film and Valentine's approach to horror. Valentine responds with limited and brief details about the film and as a consequence, the message board becomes increasingly hostile as a number of posters accuse him of being a "publicity whore"[7] and of contravening forum protocol by spamming the board with a blatant promotion of the film and his website.

The argument continued for a significant period of time and demarcates Valentine as an inauthentic fan in relation to The Mortuary members, particularly with regards to how he espouses dominant culture in his intent on serving economic self-interests. In these interchanges, the fan identity of the posters can be read as a "performative politics of identity in which the authentic self wishes to differentiate him or herself from the inauthentic other."[8] Later in the thread, the conversation turns back to resentment and anger with posters pointing out the high-end price ($34.95) of the *Slaughtered Vomit Dolls* DVD.[9] The pricing example again highlights the division between the economic principles of the filmmakers and a disenfranchised fan who is priced out of participating in the viewing of the film and in their investment within horror fandom due to the perceived avarice of Valentine. Furthermore, the lack of fan activity throughout by Valentine, in a social and cultural space *defined* by fannish participation, engendered direct ripostes as to why he was unwilling to partake in enunciative productions of fandom. For example, Uberdemon posted that Valentine referred to his intent to post on other threads, engage in wider discussions about horror and become a member of the community, but yet points out that Valentine only posts on threads connected to him or his films and only then on the topic of self-promotion and distribution opportunities. Uberdemon adds, "I do not see how you can become members of a message board when you ONLY POST IN YOUR OWN THREAD! ... I would like to see you guys on this forum still but in other threads as well."[10]

The *Slaughtered Vomit Dolls* thread featured two specific instances when Valentine achieved an almost parity with the other members by engaging in fan tropes such as connoisseurship, distinction and cultural capital. After Valentine's request for an interview by *Rue Morgue* was quickly and resolutely rejected by staff members, he eventually offered the Mortuary members the chance to view online screeners of the film and to post reviews in the thread and on their respective websites should they be affiliated with any. The tone dramatically improved as members Rovin, Skullatory and Robert Black posted reviews.[11] Perhaps inadvertently, Valentine had now aligned his participation on the thread along the axis of connoisseurship—distinction—(sub)cultural capital which is a dominant structuring element in much horror fandom studies. For Hills, "'connoisseurship' emerges as *the* master trope in fan struggles against other 'inauthentic' consumers and policing authorities"[12] and manifests itself in a cultural and social distinction-belonging marked by a knowledge which is embodied and objectified. In this case, the review provides the fan an opportunity to engage in all three categories of fan productivity and as such position themselves as authentic and distinctive fans. The second example is when Valentine, producer No One Body and star Ameara Le Vey provided more detailed responses to the questions asked about the film and its production processes. For the members asking the questions, it enabled the chance to attain cultural capital through embodied knowledge of behind-the-scenes information connected to the film in terms of its production history, directorial intention, special effects and thematic and representational strategies. In these cases, the cultural capital attained through the question and answer format with the filmmakers "confers status on its owner in the eyes of the relevant beholder."[13] The rarity and distinction of the information and knowledge can, therefore, be taken up and displayed through the various horror communities of which the member has affinities.

Valentine's method of exploiting horror forums does provide a further example of hardcore horror filmmakers deploying alternative and innovative methods surrounding the production, marketing and distribution of their films. Without a clear distribution network with which to release *Slaughtered Vomit Dolls,* Valentine attempted to enlist the help of the horror community which he thought would be receptive to his methods and his approach to horror encapsulated by the first entry in his vomit gore series. However, his early insistence on using the message board to primarily promote the film and his subsequent expression of dismay over what he perceived as *Rue Morgue*'s disinterest in supporting independent horror films fractured a cohesive affiliation with fan activity. He did not engage in the categories of fan production outlined by Fiske and instead positioned himself more in alliance with dominant culture due to the focus on economic precepts, which is often at odds with fan accumulation of cultural capital. However, it must be noted that commodification is still an active part of hardcore horror fandom despite the often hostile responses to Valentine's promotional strategies linked to his films. To provide a distinctive fan identity, the form of objectified fandom via links to and specific descriptions of a film-DVD collection is often attached to the posts of contributors to the threads.[14] Here the poster may try and distance themselves away from "inauthentic" culture by stressing their practices and strategies as "collection" rather than consumption and thus an exchange of the obscure rather than the overtly commercial, but there are nonetheless dedicated and ongoing consumption practices in place.[15] It is important to briefly account for this nuance as Valentine was often marked by other posters as an inauthentic or even a non-fan due to his perceived forays into the "mainstream" realm of consumer capitalism, despite the reality that many fans would have also engaged in consumption practices within, rather than being totally resistant to, various media forms and examples of commodity exchange. The disavowal of the "mainstream" and commercial activities is, of course, still vitally important for the authentic fan and it was only when the discussion prompted opportunities for members to properly engage in fandom and fan productivity that a consensus or parity was temporarily reached. The thread was eventually closed by a *Rue Morgue* moderator as it was adjudged to have contravened too many of forum rules. The last post was Plasma's succinct "I'll pay you in cash to slip this thread into the purge,"[16] reinforcing how a large number of members had asked moderators to intervene and close the thread. The chief reason was the aspect of spamming in terms of promoting *Slaughtered Vomit Dolls* and the website where a PayPal order system was set up. As the thread progressed, many also complained about the conversation between Valentine and Le Vey which took the form of an uninterrupted private message between the two. When Valentine returned to The Mortuary in 2010 to talk about and promote *ReGOREgitated Sacrifice*, further incidences of inauthentic fandom took place (spamming, little semiotic and enunciative productivity) and the thread was closed quickly by moderators.[17] The case accentuates the difficulties in moving outside of sanctioned and legitimate processes for the marketing and distribution of hardcore horror.

In exploring alternative strategies in the case of Valentine has meant moving into other spheres and communities that have distinct and heavily policed codes and conventions. Valentine did not account for the ways fandom was articulated and practiced within The Mortuary and as a result garnered responses that were of a hostile and negative nature. Yet despite the difficulty in effectively participating in fandom within the forum, Valentine and *Slaughtered Vomit Dolls* did generate a notoriety which afforded them a sizable amount of free publicity that brought Valentine to the attention of Unearthed Films. Furthermore, the bridge between alternative production practices and fan reception of hardcore horror delineates the principle foundations of horror fandom and foreshadows their use, development and contestation as we move toward how fans interact with the films of hardcore horror.

"I don't know if I really want to watch this?"[18]: *Hardcore Horror and Fandom*

The Valentine case study must be tempered with the caveats that the thread took place between members and filmmakers and that the posters may not necessarily have been fans of extreme or hardcore horror. Nonetheless, the fan practices articulated in response to Valentine's attempt to publicize his films align with fan behavior in threads dedicated to hardcore horror film examples and which are discussed by horror fans, many of whom are fans of extreme or underground horror. The fan communities that will be addressed primarily continue with the verbal enunciative fandom of the Mortuary message boards and will also be combined with YouTube examples which provide both visual and verbal fan productivity. In approaching the performative and productive nature of fandom through visual and verbal representations, it will be possible to account for how hardcore horror fandom engages in "policing the boundaries of film genres"[19] relating to horror in the 21st century. Primarily, such an approach will utilize Matt Hills' work on the pleasures of horror in terms of connoisseurship and affect of horror cinema. Following Hills' work will mean refuting "pathologizing notions of fandom [which] have dominated public discourse" that maps the fan out as either obsessive or hysterical in their celebration of "silly pleasures."[20] Looking at the social and cultural context of hardcore horror fandom beyond totalizing assumptions of the fan will identify the crucial elements of self-identity and social interaction and how subsequent fan practice can provide important additions to contemporary discourses over the use and affect of horror. That is, looking at hardcore horror fandom, not in terms of canonizing or elevating the films, but in making sense of the social identity and communicative interaction of the fan community surrounding this often overlooked and marginal subgenre of horror.

As one would expect, there are clear similarities between horror fans in general and those specifically engaged in hardcore horror fandom. In fact, there should be a certain sense of reluctance in creating a division between "mainstream" fans and "hardcore" fans as the boundary between them is not fixed with a great deal of movement existing between the two spheres. One key example emerging from the Mortuary message boards is how hardcore horror (of which the *August Underground* trilogy receive by far the most attention) is received due to its position with regards to both mainstream and canonical horror film examples. Despite one or two champions of hardcore horror, most members were dismissive in terms of criticizing the films as being tedious, of poor quality, and overly sensational. The *August Underground* films constituted the most popular examples of hardcore horror whether in dedicated threads or in more general discussions over what constituted the "sickest" or "most extreme" horror film. The single most used descriptor for Vogel's faux-snuff movies was that they were "boring"; thenewboss succinctly states that the original entry "bored the hell out of me" while El Capitan reinforces the negative viewing position articulated by many members when he says, "I found it to be extremely boring, pointless, mindless, drivel."[21] In these two cases, as well as being replicated in the majority of members, the reaction to the film was predicated on its lack of formal conventions and weak narrative exposition. The absence of "quality" markers was extenuated in how members compared the cinematic "lack" of *August Underground* with the aesthetic and cultural worth assigned to respected and legitimate extreme horror such as *The Texas Chain Saw Massacre*, *Cannibal Holocaust* and *Henry: Portrait of a Serial Killer*. Robert Black validated Toetag's authentic effects work in saying that it was "very effective" but that it provided an almost unanchored feature in that the film also needed "assured direction and emotional context to be entirely effective."[22] Here, the deliber-

Eight. "I'll pay you in cash to slip this thread into the purge"

Mass murderers and celebrity. Peter (Fred Vogel) fashions his own line in killer couture (*August Underground's Penance*, Toetag Pictures).

ately amateur quality of *August Underground* was simply received as just that rather than an attempt to engage in debates over screen violence and the representation and dissemination of such acts that had begun to form an unsettling part of the media landscape in the new millennium. Ultimately, the *August Underground* films, despite the extreme and disturbing nature of their content, were undermined due to their perceived lack of narrative, character identification and evidence of established (and accepted) formal design.

Their connection to the mainstream and the subordinate position the Mortuary members place the films of *August Underground* would seem to suggest a fandom closer to the dominant center of sanctioned, canonical and commercial horror cinema. Indeed, as Fiske has pointed out, "There is a complex, often contradictory relationship of similarities between fan and official cultural capital."[23] In the case of the Mortuary threads dedicated to *August Underground*, the expressions of fandom do not necessarily 'cross over' to the most marginal examples of hardcore horror. For example, one of the principal distinctions of fandom is that of the authentic fan categorized by "the tactics of distinction" which "all revolve around claims to authenticity—of being a true fan."[24] Although mainstream or commercial horror may be devalued as "inauthentic" by some sections of the horror community, in the case of fan responses to hardcore horror it exists as an expression of distinction and cultural capital. The markers of "ownership" and "discovery" which can validate authentic fandom are not often in place on the *August Underground* threads, primarily because established and mainstream texts cannot be claimed culturally in the way alternative or underground examples can. Yet validation of formal aesthetics, narrative strategies, emotional connection and an affective charge is always connected through examples from mainstream or classic horror texts. Therefore, in embracing the amateur, low-fi nature of hardcore horror, its lack of a coherent storyline, and distancing techniques would signal a less than secure fan position with regards to more established and revered horror films such as *Texas Chain Saw Massacre* and *Cannibal Holocaust*. In this case, the marginal status of hardcore horror is positioned as inauthentic due to how far it diverges from the codes and conventions of "quality" horror texts. Aspects of hardcore horror are validated, such as effects work and their affective quality, because they align with examples found in the films championed and debated within the forum thread. What the fan response to hardcore horror highlights on The Mortuary is that an understanding and reception of films like *August Underground* are formed through a fan position associated with established and well-known horror texts. It suggests a more complex and fractured consensus and moves away from the dichotomy of mainstream-inauthentic vs. alternative-authentic. Church has pointed out with regards to extreme horror ("sick films") fandom:

> While a sense of opposition to the "mainstream" horror viewer remains the utmost distinction drawn by "sick film" fans, the workings of subcultural capital become more intricate (and sometimes contradictory, indistinct and idiosyncratic) in the finer lines drawn between other horror fans attempting to gain access to the nebulously defined "sick film" niche.[25]

Thus, hardcore horror provides grist to the mill that "genre terms are ... fundamentally unstable and ambiguous and resistant to any essential definition."[26] Fan practice in the example of The Mortuary does not necessarily break down (sub)cultural divisions but rather shows further ruptures in a "world increasingly categorized by cultural fragmentation"[27] and how the horror genre is re-appropriated in new ways.

Distinction in terms of valuing aspects of horror found in celebrated and respected horror texts is further exemplified via the manifestations of knowledge, connoisseurship and discovery by horror fans. A relevant example permeating The Mortuary's various hardcore horror threads is that of member The Gore-met. Throughout the message boards discussions, he is established as a prominent fan through multiple articulations of insider knowledge and connoisseurship. He is also a *Rue Morgue* writer, providing another layer of fan distinction. For Hills, connoisseurship is an integral facet in establishing oneself as a true or authentic fan and in enabling the attainment of "social and cultural distinction/belonging"[28] within the fan community. Such a fan identity is underscored by a knowledge that is both embodied and objectified. Here, Hills is adapting Sarah Thornton's work on club culture and subcultural capital.[29] In applying Thornton's work on dance cultures to horror fandom, it can be seen that the notion of objectified subcultural capital is expressed primarily in the form of an extensive and well-constructed horror film collection and embodied as "being in the know." For The Gore-met, displays of fandom which provide examples of embodied knowledge are integral to their status as an authentic fan and how this, in turn, is read and accepted by other fans. The Gore-met is candid about his reaction to *August Underground*: "I wasn't kidding when I wrote that I had to turn the tapes off and walk away several times."[30] Yet the disclosure of being unable to continue watching the film without a break was not responded to in a negative manner commensurate with that of an inauthentic fan who finds horror films "too much" or who is "scared" by their content. Primarily, the reason being is that The Gore-met clearly articulates a distinctive fandom engendered by providing "knowledge" on the forum. On another *August Underground* thread, The Gore-met posts an early entry talking about how Toetag used a quote from his review ("A malignant, seething hatework that may be the most abhorrent masterpiece to ever slither from the underground"[31]) for the *Mordum* DVD cover. Later, they specifically mention meeting with Fred Vogel and attending horror conventions where they met other Toetag filmmakers. The Gore-met also displays his embodied knowledge, and an example of textual fan production, when they interject in a disagreement over Vogel's promotional intentions for the *August Underground* films and how he may have used the murder of his cousin as a way to promote *Penance*. At this point, The Gore-met reproduces an unexpurgated transcript from an interview they did with Vogel where he talks about his cousin's murder. The Gore-met concludes that the story is unfounded: "I've looked Fred in the eye. I don't believe he'd bullshit me."[32]

In the case of The Gore-met, embodiment does not just refer to a wide range of knowledge concerning horror film texts but also additional behind-the-scenes knowledge such as directorial intention, production history and interviews with the key personnel connected to Toetag. Further examples can be found from the visual cues found on message boards such as avatars, signatures, the number of posts, evidence of long-term fandom and if the member has moderator status. All of these embodied elements create (sub)-cultural capital through a sense of rarity (members with a very high number of posts), proximity to the beginning (start date of member corresponds to start date of the website) and insider knowledge (obscure or clever avatar symbol and/or signature).[33] With regards to The Gore-met, they are a long-standing member of The Mortuary as well as being a paid writer for their parent magazine *Rue Morgue*. They have 7093 posts on a wide range of horror threads starting in 2003, the year the online forum was created, and continuing until 2015. Their forum avatar is of *Doctor Butcher M.D.* (Marino Girolami, 1980)[34] and, of course, a play on the meaning of gourmet as a connoisseur of discerning taste. The Gore-met's signature displays a link to their YouTube channel and to a low-budget, self-directed horror film called *Zombie Dawn*. In these cases of embodied fandom by The Gore-met, the fan practice of exclusivity and knowledge is enacted so that it confers the status of an authentic and distinctive fan, especially with regard to how other members view them. The perception of a fan as authentic and true by others within the social and cultural community is of crucial importance in generating and ossifying (sub)cultural capital. In doing so, cultural capital is predicated along the contours of community distinctions and the formation of hierarchal fan identities and behavior. To this end, Thornton points out, "[d]istinctions are never just assertions of equal difference; they usually entail some claim to authority and presume the inferiority of *others*."[35]

Thornton frames the attainment of (sub)cultural status as providing an overarching distinction that creates a hierarchy within the fan community by marking out the figure of the "Other" that their fan identity can be constructed against. Therefore, a relationship of "them" vs. "us" is formed along the contour of the authentic and inauthentic fan and the underground vs. the mainstream. Hills also comments that this is a central part of horror fandom and issues of connoisseurship.[36] Yet in the Mortuary threads addressing hardcore horror in general, and the *August Underground* films in particular, they contain very little, if any, construction of the figure of the Other; that is the "'ordinary' viewer"[37] or the mainstream and commercial horror fan. This is a key difference between previous studies of horror fandom and fan practice associated with the hardcore horror community. It may be because it is so far removed from the construct of the "mainstream" that (sub)cultural identity is secure and is not perceived to be under any threat. Such a position is given credence by the way in which the Other is evoked the closer you get to the perceived mainstream. For example, online film reviewers of *August Underground* tend to cite the sanitized and homogenous product of Hollywood (horror) as a negative opposition to the authentic and underground status of hardcore horror—in part due to the inclusion in their respective websites of a variety of film entries across the spectrum of horror and non-horror cinema.[38] In these examples, the meaning of fandom is perhaps under threat or in conflict as there is more evidence of opposing definitions, in terms of general cinema and horror films, within the social and cultural sphere of the review website. Here, the reviewer has to reinforce their distinctive position by manufacturing a power dynamic between the mainstream and the alternative to recoup any lost (sub)cultural capital that the reader might perceive due to their interest and knowledge in other film genres and practices. Equally, due to the "increasing fragmentation of culture in contemporary society,"[39] the concept of alternative or subcultural communities and fandom becomes problematic. According to David Chaney, the "notion of subculture as a name for one type of cultural diversity is no longer relevant."[40] In the context of an increasing cultural pluralism, the practices of a subcultural group becomes more general and therefore "the varieties of modes of symbolization and involvement are more common in everyday life."[41] The ensuing fragmentation of culture, where boundaries are weaker and more fluid, produces heterogeneity in fan practices whereby there is less prevalence of a dominant or parent group to oppose.

Another area in which fan response to hardcore horror provides a more complex and contested landscape from other studies undertaken in horror fandom is that to do with the aspect of affect in watching horror. Church has persuasively argued of the importance of affective anticipation of watching extreme films and how the reputation of a film like *August Underground* can shape viewing positions and fan response as viewers may "approach the text with the primary expectation of being shocked and disgusted."[42] The strong affective charge of horror and/or fear is a potential threat to an authentic fan identity with Hills speaking at length on how "the act of being scared is predominantly located on the side of non-fandom"[43] and is thus downplayed or disavowed in fan discourse lest it is connected to inauthenticity. Jancovich also reiterates the importance for fans of not being affected by horror in that it would be inappropriate to admit to being frightened.[44] In both cases, the authors conclude that the persuasive nature of affect, which is generated through various mechanisms such as anticipation and reputation even before the viewer has watched the film, is effectively moderated by foregrounding knowledge. In doing so, (sub)cultural capital and status are left intact. In the Mortuary threads, fan response does reflect Hills and Jancovich's assertion that affect is sublimated into other areas connected to knowledge or is mitigated through critical and intellectual distance. For example, on the various *August Underground* threads, members talk about their reaction to the film in terms of affect. Atomagevampire positions *August Underground* as an endurance test: "I've made it about 5 minutes into it and it's the most hardcore thing I've ever seen."[45] According to brainbug, a viewer would need a "strong stomach" in that "you feel dirty and maybe a little ill during the first 5 or 10 minutes, which is something I haven't felt for a long time while watching a film."[46] The Gore-met, who has already acknowledged how difficult it is to view the first film in one continuous sitting, reiterates the film as an affective encounter: "You don't so much watch these films as experience them."[47] However, rather than develop these initial reactions to the film in terms of how they may have felt physically or psychologically afterward, the discussion instead deviates toward the reasons why horror fans would watch such disturbing and graphic material and hardcore horror's relationship with incidences and experiences of real-life death and violence.

Member Nekromantik was one of the first posters to explicitly surmise directorial intent for the *August Underground* films by saying that they "made us truly think about the cinematic violence and gore that we sit back and laugh at every day."[48] Indeed, the disavowal of affect along the lines of abject reactions such as fear, disgust, horror and being scared toward a more reflective engagement over the reasons of watching horror was continued by a number of other members over a range of threads. The Gore-met posts about how the films made them "realize [I'm] not as jaded as I think"[49] whereas Stuart Feedback Andrews questions whether Vogel's films are "legitimate mediations on violence or simply such voyeuristic perversions."[50] Being scared by a horror film, even one as "real" as *August Underground*, foregrounds a lack of knowledge and/or detailed information about the film and supposes a non-fan or casual viewer of horror. In the cases cited above, the fans read the films in an "educated" manner so that a defensive and self-effacing position can be attained to dispel the notion that "the fan may actually experience fear in response to a horror text."[51] Instead, the fans "use an accumulation of knowledge to evade the emotional experience of [horror films]" so that they can impress upon them "their own area of expertise."[52] In the threads, particularly "The Sickest Film Ever Made," a reflective account is given in terms of how discussions about fans' "enjoyment" of extreme horror moves across to discussions about real-life violence. In these cases, posters recount specific experiences of witnessing automobile accidents, shootings, previous or current jobs in hospitals and as part of news teams. By recounting personal stories, the overriding theme to emerge is that which is articulated by member Matt: "[H]ardcore horror can't affect you like real life."[53] What follows is the practice of distinction as posters regale the board with graphic and gruesome accounts of their experiences with real death. The focus of affect has been deflected to unverifiable accounts of 'real' incidences of death that get more extreme as the thread progresses and culminates with a relatively newcomer to the forum, AbraCadaver, overextending their influence (and thus depleting their cultural capital by trying "too hard") by suggesting that they have seen examples of "real-life horror that would make you vomit."[54] Running coterminous to these expressions of authenticity and distinction is a sub-discussion about non–U.S. extreme horror and covers topics such as illegal pornography, scat films and Japanese hardcore. The discussion once again deflects the affect hardcore horror might provide for the viewer in favor of who can suggest the more explicit and obscure title. The concepts of "ownership" and "discovery" are again linked to expressions of distinction and the authentic fan that was established in the posters' own recollections of involvement with real death. The thread has now established itself along more familiar and secure boundaries of authentic and distinct articulations of fandom and indicates that the affect and pleasures of horror are "narrated and discursively constructed in various ways by horror fan cultures."[55]

The diverse practices of horror fandom can be seen on the Mortuary message boards with the various approaches to horror that the fans take. Some, such as Jovanka Vuckovic, have singled out *August Underground*'s "brilliant ... verisimilitude to real gore"[56] while brainbug cites *Mordum*'s two achievements, "[i]ncredibly realistic special effects in most scenes, especially the disturbing self-castration and the two gushing throat slits," and an "[a]uthentic feel to the sick proceedings."[57] The focus of the violence and special effects links to more masculinist conceptions of the formal and aesthetic properties of horror as evidenced by studies carried out by Bolin and Sanjek.[58] Other members concentrated on markers of "quality" horror demonstrated by high production values, authorial presence, set design, acting, emotional connection and narrative. The focus on formal criteria by members such as Robert Black when he talks about the necessity for extreme cinema to provide "assured direction and emotional context" along with the gore, and Robo Cack who complained that *August Underground* "had no real story, the acting sucked for the most part and the camera they used seemed to be broken"[59] aligns with Brigid Cherry's analysis of female horror fans. For Cherry, female fans tended to seek out "thought-provoking"[60] horror rather than films with extreme or excessive representations of violence and gore. While this may hint at evidence that fandom around hardcore horror is that of "gendered interpretive communities," it does not suggest a concretizing of gender differences but rather that members of The Mortuary engage in a complex, intertwining and contested fandom that continues to "demarcate and valorize their preferences via debates over horror's aesthetics."[61] The Mortuary forum shows that fans approach hardcore horror in discursive ways to forge fan identities and social networks. This practice is often discriminatory and also territorial. There is very little movement across forums to different sites. Therefore, if we are to briefly conclude with a look at the affect of hardcore horror on fans at the Bloody Disgusting forum, we can address how fandom is also predicated on a social context in terms of the practices of fandom that emerge.

In operation since 2001, Bloody Disgusting is another well-established horror forum. If we continue to use the *August Underground* films as the archetypal examples of hardcore horror and affective fan response, then on the Bloody Disgusting message boards we see a much more pronounced and frequent acknowledgment of how the films made the members feel, which is often in opposition to the evasive practices put in place on the Mortuary threads. Although the term "scared" is never mentioned, fans' typical responses are along the lines of "I felt sick on several occasions," "I found [*Mordum*] disgusting," "it's very hard to watch," "exceptionally disturbing in its realism," "I lasted 5 mins ... that stuff is just too fucked up for my liking," "*Mordum* really disturbed me. So I doubt I could make myself go back to these movies," "I had to turn off after 35 minutes because my stomach was nauseous and I wanted to scrub my eyes with bleach" and finally resorts to physical violence-affect with "I'll punch Fred Vogel in the face for that [*Mordum*] if I ever meet him."[62] The responses highlight a very strong, almost primal response to the films and, while providing a reflective account of their experiences, the ensuing discussions did not attempt to "intellectualize" the affective charge of the films, as per The Mortuary, but provided a literal reading based on the physical sensations of watching. Although the posters did not articulate directly that they were fearful or scared by the films, reactions such as feeling sick, being disgusted and having to turn the film off and refusing to watch again should reduce the status of connoisseurship (as responding as a non-fan would do) and hence be inappropriate for producing a distinct fan (sub)cultural identity.

However, the Bloody Disgusting threads highlight that these reactions are instead valued and seen as the desired response. Fans who admit to these reactions to the films are bestowed with a status of increased authority and legitimacy. Primarily, this is connected to Vogel's commitment to making an authentic and realist document, with the intention to genuinely confuse viewers over the exact provenance of the material and whether or not it contained scenes of real death. Fans who aligned themselves with Vogel's approach understood that strong responses of fear, dread and horror were exactly the desired affective qualities of the film. *August Underground* is *not* meant to be viewed in the same way as horror films directed toward the mainstream, where being scared is denied so as to not expose yourself as an inauthentic fan. *August Underground* is a corrective to both the generally sanitized content of mainstream horror *and* to its safe affective spectatorship. Thus, viewers declaring that they were unaffected by what they saw were, in fact, conflating the films with more mainstream and commercial horror. In failing to acknowledge the distinction between the two spheres, viewers inadvertently marked themselves out as lacking connoisseurship and knowledge with regards to the representational strategies of the films. Fans that clearly expressed the affective qualities caused by the *August Underground* trilogy often continued by relating it to the authenticity of the diegetic violence and how it connected to their experiences of "real-life" scenes of violence. Mortuary Members also did this but reductively as a way to provide distinction and authenticity to their status as fans rather than examining how both examples exerted affective resonances on their engagement with media texts. Therefore, rather than crudely positioning themselves in opposition to the mainstream, the fans situate themselves as more active on the affect of horror and as Hills has pointed out, the fan instead "acts upon horror"[63] rather than the horror simply acting upon them. Ultimately, this produces (sub)cultural capital in that authority and even mastery over the texts is enacted, providing a clear distinctive identity for the (authentic) fan. The divergence of fan practices within The Mortuary and between this forum and Bloody Disgusting highlights the lack of consensus within fandom and how social and cultural context is an important structuring factor in fan identity and interaction. As we move into visual representations of fandom, we can examine the textual productivity of fan expressions in terms of how they add another valuable and discursive layer within horror fandom.

Videos of Affinity in Hardcore Horror Fandom

YouTube has been the fastest growing site on the web since its inception in 2005 and was sold to Google 12 months after its set-up for $1.65 billion. It is the prototypical and default site for video; during its first year it had 13 million unique visitors and in the range of a hundred million video clips.[64] The site promotes a "'empty' platform to be filled by the YouTube community with originally produced content of various kinds."[65] The community-driven content of YouTube spans the spectrum of professional- and business-orientated video to amateur videoblogging or vlogging, from highly commercialized practices to videos posted to friends as a more convenient format to that of email. Thus, YouTube emerges as an "industry, archive and a cultural form"[66] that is delineated through the axis of industry—community—commerce. Within its huge media platform and unprecedented accessibility, it also provides an integral medium of visual displays of fandom and articulations of textual production. The main format is the self-made video designed as a "narrowcast"[67] production to enable the formation of a social network and fan interaction based on similar likes, beliefs and interests.

One of the issues surrounding such a huge and multifaceted platform is the formation and sustainment of discrete yet interconnected communities, especially along the contours of fandom. The community is often regarded as one of the driving factors of YouTube, but "average" YouTubers do not see themselves, or indeed interact, within the larger community of users. The landscape of YouTube becomes one of limited community spaces that potentially problematizes the social interaction evident in fandom. However, there is a varied delineation of user-generated mechanisms that can address the fractured social realm of YouTube and formulate relationships and interactions within niche groupings. One such negotiation is found in Patricia G. Lange's term "videos of affiliation" which refers to "feelings of connection between people"[68] established through the video content delivery of YouTube.

Lange's work on "videos of affiliation" suggests a "labile field of connection"[69] between video uploaders and viewers in terms of how the videos and their content promote and maintain social interaction and communities within a large and dispersed social network such as YouTube. Affiliative connections are formed via the formation of an open communication channel so that an interaction is enabled "that gives viewers a feeling of being connected not to a video, but to a person who shares mutual beliefs or interests."[70] The communicative connection between people is often structured around an informal style, specifically targeted material, direct address, the involvement of the viewer in the community, and the centrality of the (fan) body in creating these mechanisms of affinity. The dynamic of videos of affiliation in terms of fandom is to continue, and expand upon, how notions of connoisseurship, distinction and (sub)cultural capital are exchanged within a visual space. Establishing a connection with other people is an integral part of fandom as it is with the user-generated content of reviews focusing on hardcore horror. Looking at how "[v]ideos of affinity can broaden one's social network by inviting self-interpellated viewers to participate in a video-mediated exchange"[71] can align the dispersed social identity and interaction contained with the platform of YouTube with the more discreet social networks of horror forums. In doing so, it will be possible to examine how the digital screen of YouTube impacts upon, continues and changes consumption and fan practices in the digital media age. Similar to the horror forums, YouTube content surrounding hardcore horror tends to focus on the *August Underground* films.

In terms of reviews of the films, there currently exist 53 user-generated videos which cover the period 2010 to 2015. Lucifer Valentine's vomit gore films constitute 41 videos which also cover that period. The *Amateur Porn Star Killer* films are less popular, with only three videos dating from 2010 to 2014. There are a number of videos which deal with the "most extreme" or "sickest" movies of all time and which contain comments on hardcore horror examples, but in terms of assuaging how disparate social communities form meaningful fan connections within niche areas, it is necessary to concentrate on videos specifically dealing with films such as *August Underground.*

The early examples of film reviews on *August Underground* and *Slaughtered Vomit Dolls* tended to take the form of an informal and private message performed directly to camera. The amateur or user-generated video established "feelings of connection" primarily because of the casual tone and the way that it purposefully selects an audience that potentially shares the same interests. Savini1979[72] represents one of the first fan reviews of *August Underground* and although they have a brief title page highlighting the name of their YouTube channel, it consists solely of the member speaking directly into the camera. Space is both private and domestic with a fairly nondescript appearance in that there is no visible marker or embodiment of fandom such

Eight. "I'll pay you in cash to slip this thread into the purge" 189

as film posters, DVD shelves or audio-visual equipment. Savini1979's review of *August Underground* is part of a larger body of horror fandom rather than specifically being of hardcore horror. Other reviews focus on *The Evil Dead*, the TV series *The Walking Dead* (American Movie Classics, 2010–) and horror movie artwork. Savini1979 often uploads videos thanking his subscribers for their support, runs competitions and organizes opportunities for people to buy items from his horror collection. His channel, with 1252 subscribers, adopts many of the organizational dynamics of the video of affiliation in how it fosters communicative networks through the direct involvement of subscribers. In the *August Underground* review, Savini1979 often makes reference to other community members and with the intent to make and upload future horror film reviews. Thus, Savini1979's review indexes a "present-focused perspective"[73] and a meaningful social affinity with other community members. Although concentrating on hardcore horror in the above example, the review exists with the interstices of his other work and the social connections formed throughout a larger network. Savini1979 uses mechanisms of social affinity to include and bring together all members despite their potentially disparate backgrounds in horror. He never alienates, dismisses or belittles viewers who might find *August Underground* too shocking and extreme and he is careful to say that the film is not for everybody "but if you want to see people fucked up, then this is for you."[74] Comments to the video are equally inclusive and positive with many praising the quality of the video and suggesting other films to review.

The community aspect of this particular YouTube channel is less discriminatory and more inclusive that what was evident from the horror forums, yet the affiliative qualities also display and strengthen fan practices and identity demonstrated in the forums. In the *August Underground* review, there are a number of references to him being a collector of horror and he says that although the film was "not really for me," it still provides an important addition to his collection due to the gore effects and shocking content. While the feminine marking of consumption is passed on to the commodity fetishism of collecting, the capital amassed through Savini1979's well-chosen horror film and memorabilia collection clearly highlights the objectified and embodied status of fandom and accumulation of capital. Certainly, Savini1979's collection is as much for the viewer ("eyes of the beholder") as it is for him and we see clear examples of its objectified nature in the sense of rarity it possesses with many personalized and limited edition items. It also delineates a fan embodiment in how the collection "proves" Savini1979 to be "in the know": a distinctive knowledge of the horror genre embodied through the meticulously selected and organized films, posters and horror ephemera. Distinction and knowledge are further demonstrated through various uploaded videos of Savini1979 visiting the horror festivals Celluloid

Screams and Sheffield Horror Film Fest where he provides behind-the-scenes footage, details of free giveaways ("swag") and footage of Q&A sessions of horror icons such as Catriona MacColl.[75] The videos provide a way for Savini1979 to cultivate a sense of inclusion and membership to his particular horror community where people are brought together via a broad interest in horror as well as an attraction to Savini1979. The channel also provides ample occasion to ossify a sense of fandom (from the often anonymous and strict hierarchal practices of horror fandom) through a visual delineation of an objectified and embodied cultural capital underscored by a distinctive and knowledgeable fan identity. Hardcore horror exists as a niche part of the amalgam of horror discussed within Savini1979's channel, yet its addition provides an illuminating presence in how it facilitates affiliative connections rather than a cascading binary of "them" vs. "us" or alternative horror vs. the mainstream. The interactional dynamics of hardcore horror in the example of Savini1979 offers another way of looking at the fandom of its films and how it navigates the categories of mainstream and alternative horror film fandom.

"Not for Everybody": Demarcating Vomit Gore Fandom

Early posters on the vomit gore films replicated the low-fi and informal aesthetics of the videos first posted around the *August Underground* films. In 2010, VeryCrudelyYours[76] posted multiple reviews which consisted of direct-to-camera address with nondescript interior locations. First he talks about problems with his camera and apologizes for the black-and-white picture. Criticnic[77] and Mrparka[78] also favor a straightforward address to the camera in familiar domestic settings such as the living room or front garden. The videos exemplify a decidedly non-professional quality and actively resist the pressure to make their work commercial and thus monetizable. In fact, the amateur or user-created videos place a certain emphasis on the authenticity of the uploader in regards to them posting reviews because they have a legitimate interest in the films or have been asked to do so by members of the community. Thus, they are not doing it merely to generate income and/or to generate quantifiable data, such as viewer clicks, likes and comments as a marker of success and "value." The personal nature of these reviews also attests to the importance in creating social affinity so that communication can be established within the social networks of hardcore and horror fandom. The users who upload the videos are careful to remain inclusive when talking about the vomit gore films while acknowledging that they are "not for everybody" as members such as Criticnic points out.[79] The lack of imposing a

Eight. "I'll pay you in cash to slip this thread into the purge" 191

hierarchal arrangement of spectatorship between those who can "take it" and those who will be offended and shocked is circumvented by posters demarcating the boundary between fans who prefer the more conventional horror elements of the story, acting and structure and those who prefer extreme horror and graphic violence and gore. The boundary is not framed as divisive but as an example of how horror is made up of a variety of genre users and fans. In the forums, this boundary was an example of mainstream influences dictating how horror fans received and made sense of hardcore horror where the films were rejected due to their perceived non-alignment with the conventions and aesthetics of quality horror films. As we move toward YouTube and its "delimited community spaces,"[80] the boundary becomes an inclusive mechanism for bridging gaps between variant communities and fans so that communicative lines can be brokered and maintained.

In the videos of Savini1979, it was clear that the member positioned themselves as a fan of authority and distinction through objectified and embodied displays of fandom. The importance of distinguishing yourself from the "'normal' cultural consumer"[81] is further developed through the rarity and inaccessibility of the original vomit gore films released through Lucifer Valentine's label Kingdom of Hell productions. xTheGoodBadUnusualx begins their review by establishing a clear affinity with their viewers through a personal address to the camera and via user-friendly statements that again the films "are not for everybody" yet "it's up to you to determine."[82] Practices of the authentic fan are enabled via the staging of the video in that the hosts' collection is prominently framed in the background. xTheGoodBadUnusualx displays the original Kingdom of Hell DVDs as a way of moving past the divisive content of the films and repositioning them as culturally valuable items. They outline the collecting aspect of their fandom and how it legitimizes the ownership of such maligned and controversial films. That is, they mention the personalized artwork hand-drawn by Valentine which accompanies each disc as well as certificates of authenticity, signed copies and the limited nature of their production, and conclude that they are "one-of-a-kind and as a collector I think that is highly motivating to buy stuff from [Valentine] knowing that he's going to send you a picture he drew.... That's what collectors look for."[83] The inaccessibility of the DVDs references the major recurrent aspects of hardcore horror fandom in that "it is not for everyone." Here, it is not the content that is only for the privileged few but the limited edition nature of the original vomit gore releases. In this case, the "not for everyone" label further situates the community as apart from the mainstream but also stresses the unobtainability and exclusivity of the films. Thus, the rarity and exclusivity of being in possession of these items highlights many aspects of distinction and of the authentic fan and "operates as a precious emblem of *insider* status."[84]

The notion of the fan as the collector of rare and exclusive versions of the films provides the distinction between the authentic and inauthentic fan. Although only evident implicitly in these videos, it does tend to normalize the fan and accept that the dominant expression of fan identity operates within these unwritten practices. The move from consumption to collecting anticipates Thornton's position that subculture is often coded as masculine while the mainstream is devalued as feminine. The demographic for the hardcore horror videos on YouTube is predominantly white, male and North American and thus would seem to reinforce the gender division between the subculture and the mainstream and normalize hardcore horror fandom as masculine and being carried out overwhelmingly by men. The process of commerce and commodity exchange is problematic for fans of niche markets due to the "rejection of the products of consumer capitalism"[85] exemplified by studio productions and the Hollywood mainstream. Thus, identifying as a consumer aligns the fan with the "passive, feminized consumption of 'mainstream cinema.'"[86] In this case, consumption becomes collecting to overcome the passive consumerist angle and situate an agency and "vision for their collection" whereby it becomes "an ensemble with a philosophy behind it."[87] Furthermore, the collecting of obscure items reinforces the fan's rejection of the commercial and thus recoups the anti-commercial endeavor of collecting. Collecting, or indeed hardcore horror fandom, does not put forth an essentialist position that it is inherently male. It is, as Thornton and Hollows would argue, more of a cultural construction "based on the rejection of the feminine" and which therefore may potentially "exclude 'real' women from some of the practices."[88] Certainly, hardcore horror, with its focus on sexualized violence, extreme gore and alternative production practices, can be classified as a niche area of horror which Brigid Cherry has shown can exclude female viewers due to the levels of violence, pornographic spectacle and sexist and misogynistic themes.[89] But this is not to say that women do not take an active part in the fandom of extreme horror as we have seen from Jovanka Vuckovic on the Mortuary forum and can be seen on other forums such as Wonderlust on the Bloody Disgusting message boards. Indeed, the cultural contingencies of (white, male) fan practices and filmic content may provide a barrier for other demographic groups to participate, but the social affiliation that circulates through the videos provides a more gender-inclusive set of mechanisms for participating in horror fandom.

Fangirl Sarah[90] is active in both *August Underground* and vomit gore fandom and provides a pertinent example of how videos of affiliation can facilitate connective lines while also establishing distinctive and authentic fandom. Fangirl Sarah often makes reference to her appearance in terms of talking about her hair color and what dye to use to get the best results to parading her dog before the camera and introducing it to the other members of her community. Such affiliative acts have created and maintained a distinct and strong community within the dispersive and labile social networks permeating through YouTube. Her channel has 4199 members and her videos on hardcore horror achieve between 2500 and 9000 views with significant comments generated below the line. Although some comments directly relate to her appearance rather than the content of the videos, they are never explicitly sexualized and are always subordinate to commenters who praise the videos and her analysis of the films. Fangirl Sarah also demonstrates an authentic fan identity in that she talks about how Lucifer Valentine contacted her and sent the vomit gore films to her for review.

Similar to xTheGoodBadUnusualx, she also presents the originally released discs on her videos and shows viewers the personalized content such as the hand-drawn pictures. The disclosure of her personal communication with Valentine emphasizes the cultural hierarchy within fandom as well as contributing to an authentic fan identity. The acts also facilitate successful interaction with others so that Fangirl Sarah is able to "assert [her] distinctive character and affirm that they are not anonymous members of an undifferentiated mass."[91] Jill Killington[92] and KHyacinthe[93] also show the clear utilization of affiliative mechanisms and the attainment of cultural capital through the display of authentic and distinctive fan practices. In a social platform such as YouTube which does not necessarily facilitate community-building or collaborative group productions, Jill Killington, KHyacinthe and others such as Goregrl[94] use a personal and spontaneous address to "interest delineated groups of people who wish to participate and remain connected socially"[95] in some way to their channels and social networks. Lange has pointed out how the "public access to intimate moments and the discourse surrounding the video artifacts on the Web allow social boundaries and pre-existing assumptions to be questioned and refashioned."[96] In turn, the personal fan identity can be converted into "more 'public' debates about social identities, ethics and cultural politics."[97] In terms of (hardcore) horror, such explorations of fandom can set in motion larger discussions about the cultural hierarchy of the various social groups and questions of ownership, belonging and authenticity which can recoup marginal fandom practiced by women and/or people of color.

Feelings of affinity surrounding the often personal communication of the fan's experience of a hardcore horror film are exacerbated by the centrality of the body in the communicative function of the fan video. Very few videos comprised of mediated communication include only a voiceover narration and no physical inclusion of a body. These videos, such as The theoasisking[98] and Save Mean,[99] have tended to be less successful both in terms of subscriptions and user views despite the narration carrying as much knowledge and insight about the films as videos using face-to-face communication. The presentation of the body is important in establishing affinity. In these cases, "the use of the body as a kind of trading currency in face-to-face communication indicates the social relational nature of what is often problematic in communication."[100] That is, the information of either the review, articulations of fan identity or developing and maintaining social connections can be driven via other mediated means (the written blog, podcast or voiceover narration), but the social desires of other community members to "see" who they are interacting with provides more opportunities for and a greater facilitation of connectivity and interaction between members. We have seen earlier from members such as Fangirl Sarah and Criticnic how a spontaneous and intimate interaction can "establish a personal, communicative effect."[101] The videos situate the self as distant via the technological apparatus of the camera and media platform of YouTube. Yet at the same time, the use of the body bridges that distance so that it is accessible to fans that are interested in the subject matter and share similar interests with the maker of the video. Fangirl Sarah regularly makes reference to her physical appearance and in one video "shared" her new puppy with her subscribers so as to interpellate them to both the content of the video and to "Sarah" as both an authentic fan and individual who subscribers may forge an affinity for.

As YouTube has developed from its inception in 2005, there has been ever more stress placed on the axis between community and commerce. The initial videos detailing hardcore horror fandom were exclusively made toward the "gift economy" rather than producing a video primarily for financial incentive and return. Henry Jenkins has discussed how the gift exchange of user-generated videos has been transformed into a monetized form through advertising revenue.[102] The impact on fan communities has been significant in that many have seen the social affiliation between the video producer and the wider social network threatened as the production activities become increasingly geared around commercial values rather than the niche, alternative fan spaces that their particular fandom may have embodied. In terms of hardcore horror, a distinct move toward more professional-looking videos and a constructed narrative format has changed the landscape from personal and casual reflections to more skit-based or gimmicky concepts. Furthermore, the presence of the body has equally been transformed with much more affectation, theatricality and performativity involved in the fan identity and behavior of the channel owner. Jill Killington offers a bridge between the early fan accounts and the more recent sketch show format of the reviews. She still provides affiliative acts through her direct and subjective address to camera, intimate and personal settings such as the bedroom, and an embodied and objectified form of fan distinction through her "alt" persona, insider knowledge and links to her website and Twitter account. The videos are of a high quality and show evidence of post-production in terms of editing and the

Eight. "I'll pay you in cash to slip this thread into the purge"   195

use of techniques such as inserts. There is a great deal of humor in her approach and for the videos on the vomit gore films she takes on the persona, complete with fake English accent, of a 19th-century gothic heroine. Jill's channel has 11,043 subscribers and 34,943 people viewed her video on *Slaughtered Vomit Dolls* which was uploaded in 2011. The professional and commercial values apparent in the video are mitigated through Jill's sincere and in-depth interaction with her social network. The problematic of a soulless, financially driven video is not received as such by her subscribers, who instead respond positively to the performativity of Jill and the jocular tone she adopts.

The development of a personal account to the "practice of self-staging and self-stylization"[103] of the more recent hardcore horror videos represents a growing trademark of contemporary digital culture. However, the increased theatricality and constructed nature of the videos and the uploaders has not undermined or ruptured the affiliative connections or the status of the fan as authentic and distinct. If anything, it has reinforced their cultural standing and increased the connectivity and interaction of their social networks. Emer Prevost[104] has 17,296 subscribers and provides "reaction and review" videos of horror films. In the videos for *August Underground* and *Slaughtered Vomit Dolls*, the views totaled 62,373 and 50,855 respectively, which represent the most-viewed hardcore horror fan videos. Prevost provides a very discriminatory fan identity and certainly references Fiske's notions that the boundary between what a fan likes and dislikes is sharply drawn.[105] His fierce critique of hardcore horror in that *August Underground* is "not even a film, just shit"[106] and that *Slaughtered Vomit Dolls* is the "worst film ever"[107] connects to forum members' reception in terms of how the films were adjudged next to the markers of conventional and/or quality horror. Prevost's cultural tastes and practices do not alienate fans of horror or even hardcore horror as the numerous quotes below the line attest to. In fact, his angry, polemical dismissal of hardcore horror engenders wider discussion among subscribers about the horror genre in general and the extreme and violent practices among some of its practitioners. Prevost's persona thus enables an ongoing fan discussion around horror as well as providing spaces for members to interact and contribute such as in below-the-line comments or by directly addressing Prevost with recommendations of future horror films to review. The channel thus provides a contrived, or at least exaggerated, fan identity but is received as such by its members. Prevost's knowledge of cult, exploitation and horror cinema is well established, which keeps the core elements of his fandom intact, while his flamboyant theatricality provides effective pathways into affiliative connections.

Other recent channels reviewing hardcore horror have developed the original low-fi and personal video toward a more professional standard which reflects the design and structure of popular YouTube channels such as the comedy skit format of Smosh.[108] Diamanda Hagan, Nyx Fears and Evil Steve at the Movies[109] all use a comedy-driven review structure in which an address to the camera is divided into clips of the film, comedic inserts and other supporting cast members. Often the host will affect a certain performativity of an exaggerated, over-the-top fan-critic to highlight, and render less threatening the extreme content and controversial nature of hardcore horror. The dismissive attitude conveyed by these channels connects to the recurring thread through hardcore horror reception in that they delineate the lack of "proper" conventions of filmmaking such as narrative and identifiable characters as a major factor in their negative appraisal of the films. The increased opportunities to embody and objectify fandom through the use of horror clips, set design in which posters, DVDs and horror memorabilia is carefully staged and presented in how it acts to ossify a distinctive and authentic fan.

Hardcore horror fandom provides a complex and contested landscape in terms of how it fits within the large sphere of the horror genre in the 21st century. While notions of the authentic and distinctive fan are clearly operating along the same axis as that expressed in more mainstream horror fandom, issues over the affect of horror present a more nuanced and disparate example peculiar to the outlier status of hardcore horror. The social and cultural context is of vital importance in how fandom is articulated and in how fan communities are formed and maintained. Visual articulations of fandom highlight how social affiliation is essential in establishing social networks and in contributing to their successful preservation. The "videos of affiliation" can also work to generate and reinforce more traditional forms of fandom such as connoisseurship as well as facilitating spaces for marginal fan identities to contribute and engage with.

Perhaps the most crucial factor to emerge is how the marginal strand of hardcore horror utilizes fan practices associated with the dominant culture and mainstream horror production. Dick Hebdige has discussed how "the tensions between dominant and subordinate groups can be found reflected in the surfaces of subculture"[110] which finds itself in dispute and constantly (re)defining its borders and practices. From the exaltations of "quality" horror as a marker against which hardcore horror was judged to the aping of the styles of the most popular YouTube channels in the videos of Diamanda Hagen, the dominant culture has been a structuring element of much of hardcore horror fandom. Indeed, to reiterate Fiske, there is a great deal of connection between fan and official culture as is evidenced by the fan practices, interactions and networks of hardcore horror. For fandom surrounding films such as *August Underground* and *Slaughtered Vomit Dolls*, the fan culture "is a form of popular culture that echoes many of the institutions of official culture, although in popular form and under popular control."¹¹¹ In the cases outlined above, fandom recoups the marginality of hardcore horror and invests within it a sense of identity, social belonging and prestige that has been withheld or denied in the most legitimate spaces of official or dominant culture.

Conclusion:
"It has no redeeming features whatsoever that I could discern"[1]—The Cultural Value of Hardcore Horror

The inclusion of hardcore horror into the wider discourse and cultural field of North American horror has contributed to a richer picture of the genre and its concomitant history and development in the 21st century. Fred Vogel's *August Underground* trilogy, Shane Ryan's *Amateur Porn Star Killer* series, Lucifer Valentine's vomit gore films (and others) have brought into focus the cultural value of hardcore horror and enabled new ways of thinking about the genre. With this in mind, *Hardcore Horror Cinema in the 21st Century* has sought to engage with the various strands of horror to account for and integrate the marginal film practices of Vogel et al. which have been situated as an outlier to mainstream horror and the majority of academic discourse. In some cases, hardcore horror offers an almost antithetical riposte to mainstream and commercial examples with how the films destabilize the boundary between the real and mimesis and in their protracted sequences of extreme horror. In other areas, the contours of hardcore horror have replicated and reinforced dominant practices, as in fandom which has been aligned along the axis of connoisseurship—distinction—(sub)cultural capital so integral to horror fandom in general. Additionally, hardcore horror often pushes against the political engagement connected within the larger umbrella of extreme film. *Salò* and *Cannibal Holocaust* sought to use reflective and symbolic practices alongside realist material to comment on issues such as the ethics of watching violent content. In contrast, hardcore horror can downplay the socio-political dimensions of extreme film in their pursuit of a realist horror.

For filmmakers like Fred Vogel, passing the film off as "real" *is* the central aim and tends to prioritize the spectacular arrangement of the violent material. Connected to this is an often unsettling and ethically troubling treatment of the actors from the intense physicality of Vogel's on-screen performance as serial killer Peter to Lucifer Valentine's filmic relationship with traumatized and abused young women. Thus, the complex, controversial and multi-varied narrative history of hardcore horror opens up a cultural and critical platform of 21st-century horror with which to properly incorporate marginal texts within the center ground. Not to invert the reductive binarism of the "inauthentic" mainstream with the "authentic" underground, but to shift the current dominant critical framework to accommodate what Lázaro-Reboll outlined as a "more inclusive cultural geography of horror." Including the films, the makers and the fans of hardcore horror is essential in bringing about an archaeology of the genre.

Yet, the schism between hardcore horror and mainstream forms still persist and are still evident. It would be reductive and perhaps too much of a move toward "legitimatizing" the extremity of the filmmaking practices of hardcore horror to flatten them out so that they fit unproblematically within more general conceptions of film. For example, the formal and narrative properties of classical Hollywood are resolutely withheld from the filmmaking practices of hardcore horror. Traditional elements of film style such as editing, sound, cinematography and the general *mise en scène* are rejected, as are the conventional formats of a clear resolution to the action, character development and causal narrative direction. Jones has indicated that such a disavowal of conventional film style is a "sign of anti-mainstream 'extremity'"[2] which not only situates the material as extreme but also the formal properties and style of the film. A double helix of extremity emerges which pushes hardcore horror further toward the liminal spaces of film practice. The films become reprehensible for the way in which they represent horror *and* in the way they do not adhere to the formal stylistics and conventions of mainstream or classical cinema. Fan articulation of the *August Underground* films often focused on their perceived lack of the essential principles of film form, which meant that it was categorically rejected on this premise by many horror fans. Furthermore, the rejection was often combined with a reaffirmation and restating of "quality" horror which *did* adhere to established and canonical tenets of film form and style. The reason to emerge as for why hardcore horror has been overlooked is therefore not just centered on the content but *is* also connected to the formal properties of the films. Clearly, the limited engagement with hardcore horror is a testament to the encompassing "difficulty" of the films in terms of reception and critical commentary. The absence of scholarly work attests to the problematic address of such films and is similarly evidenced by those scholars who have recently begun to explore hardcore horror through the marginal routes of pseudo-snuff, found footage and real violence within our visual media.

At the end of the recent expanded edition of *Killing for Culture*, David Kerekes interviews the editors of the anthology *Snuff: Real Death and Screen Media*. Initially, Kerekes talks about how the first volume of *Killing for Culture* was treated as illegitimate due to its "anti-academic flourish"[3] and that it was received as more of a prurient tabloid account than a serious attempt at cultural scholarship. The 2012 Snuff conference at Bournemouth University revived the cultural and critical interest in the mythology of snuff in which the exemplars of hardcore horror were included and discussed. Kerekes begins to ask about their rationale for staging a snuff conference before going on to ask if the organizers encountered any resistance from the academy. The responses presented a range of experiences from institutional support to being given explicit advice on how the pursuit of such a subject may impact negatively on career prospects and generate "unwanted media controversy."[4] In fact, one of the strands to emerge from the interview is that of justifying the subject of snuff (and indirectly extreme horror) as a pedagogically sound foundation for serious and legitimate scholarship and not simply only being about "blood, guts and gore."[5] As the *Snuff* anthology followed, the introduction by Neil Jackson provided critical space to delineate how the book was going to move away from sensationalist conceptions of snuff as violent, misogynistic pornography toward a fuller set of formal and thematic features which have seen snuff (fictions) permeate the cultural landscape from Hollywood through to the Internet. In the case of Kerekes and the editors of the *Snuff* anthology, the focus on extreme material does engender skeptical and resistant attitudes to how the work will be received both internally and externally. Additionally, positions have formed that have undermined the work on the basis of it being "illegitimate" and not worthy of academic attention and critical review. Scholarship in this area has thus replicated wider popular approaches which have rejected the films as both unpalatable and threatening representations of extreme violence, and because of this perception, state that they do not qualify as films (as worthy of study) due to their lack of "proper" formal and thematic qualities.

The Internet, digital technologies and socio-cultural contingencies ossified the subgenre of hardcore horror through the early 2000s to the present. While there are some North American filmmakers still engaged in extreme representations of horror, many have either moved toward more mainstream productions or in new genre directions. Stephen Biro continues to be involved with underground horror through his distribution company Unearthed Films and in the *American Guinea Pig* series. In 2015, he produced the second installment, *Bloodshock*, which was directed by effects artist Marcus Koch. Koch has worked in various low-budget horror films over almost 20 years and has been involved in the special effects work on the hardcore horrors *Amerikan HoloKaust*, *Slow Torture Puke Chamber* and *Bouquet of Guts and Gore*. *Bloodshock* continues the intense and extreme violent tableaux of the first entry as it features a minimalist aesthetic in the representational strategy of very graphic, realistic and protracted scenes of violence. Yet, the film is deliberately stylized in that it switches from black-and-white to color (for the climactic, surrealist sequence) and provides a greater characterization between the torturer and victim. The sense of realist horror is thus mitigated by the formal disruption of the *mise en scène* and a performativity more aligned to conventional acting. Koch intended to make *Bloodshock* an "endurance test" for the viewer and to make them question "Should I be watching this? What kind of person am I for even wanting to watch this?"[6] The approach from Koch and producer Biro, who had significant creative input in the film, would suggest a continuation of the criteria of hardcore horror despite its lapses into a self-conscious and conventional filmic structure.

Lucifer Valentine returned to his vomit gore films in 2015 with *Black Mass of the Nazi Sex Wizard*. It acts as a prequel, though continues the multidimensional reality and overlapping synchronicity of the first three films in delineating Angela as a type of "everywoman" destined to act out and repeat the horrific manifestations of her traumatic life. The film features numerous instances of affective acts such as vomiting, urination and sadomasochistic play. In this respect, *Black Mass* continues the thematic strand of the vomit gore films which used an affective-performativity to disrupt and destabilize feminine archetypes and ideals such as the princess and the Barbie doll. It is a horrifying and disturbing film which forcibly confronts the viewer with borderline unpalatable sequences of violence and horror. The outcome is another depressing and unsettling film about female identity as formed through prolonged suffering and trauma. Many archetypes of Angela (now played by performance artist Sister S) are ritualistically destroyed in a grotesque and destructive manner and again offer an engagement with female identity in which a more independent and coherent form can emerge. However, the film withholds any concrete sense of Angela moving past her trauma into a more stable and in-control identity by receding back into a "lost girl" archetype which is categorized as the personification of neglect, abuse and abandonment. Similar to the first three vomit gore films, *Black Mass* clearly underlines the essential criteria of hardcore horror and positions Angela to transcend her experiences and restrictive identity only to have her retreat back (or continue) in her repetitive pattern of suffering and trauma.

The horror anthology *Shane Ryan's Faces of Snuff* (various directors, 2016) is a collection of found footage pseudo-snuff vignettes constructed around the premise that the various scenes have been compiled from the Internet and amateur, unofficial sources. It shares a lineage with the first infamous shock compilation videos such as *Faces of Death* and the recent horror anthologies *The ABCs of Death* and *V/H/S* (both various directors, 2012). *Faces of Snuff* offers a relevant concluding film in the discussion of extreme horror as it has been put together and produced by a key member of the subgenre, is the most recent release (the official release date was December 2016) and provides a further example of the "illegitimate" status of hardcore horror. When Ryan began to commission filmmakers to submit an entry for the anthology, he expected to receive a wide range of submissions from which to pick the most effective and realistic. But he found that very few established low-budget or independent horror filmmakers wanted to be part of the enterprise despite guaranteed distribution. According to Ryan, filmmakers "shied away from participating in a snuff anthology"[7] even though they often worked in extreme horror and had drawn on influences such as *August Underground* and *Amateur Porn Star Killer*. Ryan's experience is further testament to the troubling extremity of hardcore horror and connects back to the lack of academic address and the recent controversial inroads into extreme horror. Potential filmmakers were reluctant to become involved in the project due to the graphic content associated with the pseudo-snuff film but more so because of the reputation "snuff" has in terms of a perceived lack of cultural worth or value. Filmmakers instead contributed to zombie and grindhouse anthologies which were being made conterminously with *Faces of Snuff*. Ryan had to use unknown and often first-time filmmakers for many of the segments and provided various inserts of his own work to increase the graphicness of the material. The reluctance of the filmmakers links back to the actors who refused to participate or to continue in hardcore horror productions and the movement from other pioneers into mainstream horror and cinema. Fred Vogel is currently in post-production with *The Final Interview* (2017), an independent drama addressing the media fascination with a Death Row killer. Eric Stanze has recently worked as cameraman and second unit director for the high-profile horror films of Jim Mickle such as *Stake Land* (2010) and *We Are What We Are* (2013).

The extremity of hardcore horror allows filmmakers to operate without restrictions, particularly with regards to film form. The properties of formal construction, film style and representational strategies define the conventions of mainstream cinema and facilitate normative viewing positions and expectations. It is transgressed in hardcore horror, meaning that a potent, threatening, marginal and ultimately authentic film emerges that challenges our viewing proclivities and acceptance of what a film is or should be. Hardcore horror is a volatile entity and it confronts, challenges, problematizes and redraws the boundaries of how we watch and think about horror. In this case, hardcore horror demands to be positioned as an outlier configuration of horror, but one that, contradictorily perhaps, needs to be brought into and included within the center. As Jack Sargeant recently commented in the *Senses of Cinema* dossier on American extreme cinema, not to justify them "because they shouldn't be justified," but because their inclusion opens up new critical space and shows that the horror genre (and extreme film more generally) is "contingent, negotiable and fluid."[8] A critical account of the "archeology" of hardcore horror advances the cultural field of horror and refigures the genre in terms of its producers and users. Perhaps they have no "redeeming features," perhaps they should "defy a critical space"[9] and perhaps the critic or academic should resist any attempt to justify their position, but they can provide an important, if disturbing and abhorrent, addition to an appreciation and understanding of the contemporary North American horror film.

Chapter Notes

Introduction

1. Louis Althusser, 1971. "Ideology and Ideological State Apparatuses (Notes Toward an Investigation)," *Lenin and Philosophy and Other Essays*. Translated from the French by Ben Brewster, 2001. New York: Monthly Review Press pp. 85–126.
2. When talking about cinema in general, the term "mainstream" refers primarily to big-budget, Hollywood studio productions operating through wide exhibition patterns and extensive marketing campaigns. Within the horror genre, the term "mainstream" is used as a term for a more conventional and commercial example of horror film production, which might still be considered non-mainstream compared to Hollywood productions of superhero and high concept action films.
3. Carol Clover, 1992. *Men, Women and Chainsaws: Gender in the Modern Horror Film*, Princeton, NJ: Princeton University Press, p. 187.
4. Sconce, Jeffrey, 1995. "'Trashing' the Academy: Taste, Excess, and an Emerging Politics of Cinematic Style," *Screen*, Vol. 36, No. 4, Winter, pp. 371–393. I am using the term in the context of "seeing anew" films which run alongside more mainstream material. That is, not judging them or interpreting them as we would a dominant text but with a set of criteria specific to the films under discussion, such as production practices, distribution and reception.
5. Steve Jones, 2013. *Torture Porn: Popular Horror After Saw*, Basingstoke: Palgrave Macmillan, p. 6.
6. *Ibid.*, p. 126.
7. *Ibid.*, p. 175.
8. Jones, 2013, p. 176.
9. Antonio Lazaro-Reboll, 2012. *Spanish Horror Film*, Edinburgh: Edinburgh University Press, p. 7.
10. *Ibid.*, p. 5.
11. *Ibid.*, p. 7.
12. Jones, 2013, p. 175.
13. Linnie Blake, 2008. *The Wounds of Nations: Horror Cinema, Historical Trauma and National Identity*, Manchester: Manchester University Press, p. 130.
14. David Ray Carter, 2010. "It's Only a Movie? Reality as Transgression in Exploitation Cinema," John Cline and Robert G. Weiner, eds., *From the Arthouse to the Grindhouse: Highbrow and Lowbrow Transgression in Cinema's First Century*, Lanham, MD: Scarecrow, p. 312.

Chapter One

1. Fred Vogel, 2005. Quoted in Matthew Dean Hill, "Underground: Twenty Questions with Fred Vogel—Director of *August Underground* and *August Underground's Mordum*," *Atrocities Cinema*, October, http://www.atrocitiescinema.com/interviews/fredvogel.html (10 May 2016).
2. For example see, James Aston and John Walliss, eds., 2013. *To See the Saw Movies: Essays on Torture Porn and Post–9/11 Horror*, Jefferson, NC: McFarland; Kevin, J. Wetmore, 2012. *Post–9/11 Horror in American Cinema*, New York: Continuum; Ian Conrich, ed., 2010. *Horror Zone*, London: I.B. Tauris; Stephen

Prince, ed., 2004. *The Horror Film*, New Brunswick, NJ: Rutgers University Press.

3. Figures from Box Office Mojo. For box office figures for the *Saw* franchise see, http://www.boxofficemojo.com/search/?q=saw, and for *Paranormal Activity* see, http://www.boxofficemojo.com/search/?q=Paranormal%20Activity (3 May 2016).

4. Mark Repp. 2015. "The 30 Most Extreme Movies of the 21st-Century So Far," *Taste of Cinema*, 14 May, http://www.tasteofcinema.com/2015/the-30-most-extreme-movies-of-the-21st-century-so-far/ (14 September 2016).

5. "Extreme Cinema: The 25 Most Disturbing Films of All Time," 2010. *Horror News*, 23 August, http://horrornews.net/6520/extreme-cinema-top-25-most-disturbing-films-of-all-time-part1/ (14 September 2016).

6. David Edelstein, 2006. "Now Playing at Your Local Multiplex: Torture Porn," *New York Times*, 28 January, http://nymag.com/movies/features/15622/ (3 May 2016).

7. Ibid.

8. Ibid.

9. Mike Hale, 2010. "Ending a Lethal Game and All Its Gory Details," *New York Times*, 29 October, http://www.nytimes.com/2010/10/30/movies/30saw.html?_r=0 (3 May 2016).

10. Peter Howell, 2009. "*The Last House on the Left*: Gruesome and Gratuitous," *The Toronto Star*, 13 March, http://www.thestar.com/news/2009/03/13/the_last_house_on_the_left_gruesome_and_gratuitous.html (3 May 2016).

11. Edelstein, 2006.

12. Peter Hartlaub, 2006. "*Saw III* Could Be Breaking Point for Many Fans," *San Francisco Chronicle*, 29 October, http://www.sfgate.com/bayarea/article/Saw-III-could-be-breaking-point-for-many-fans-2467514.php (3 May 2016).

13. Andrew Tudor, 1989. *Monsters and Mad Scientists: A Cultural History of the Horror Movie*, Oxford: Blackwell, pp. 211–224; Isabell Cristina Pinedo, 1997. *Recreational Terror: Women and the Pleasures of Horror Film Viewing*, Albany: State University of New York Press; 2004. "Postmodern Elements of the Contemporary Horror Film," Stephen Prince, ed., *The Horror Film*, Piscataway: Rutgers University Press; Cynthia Freeland, 2005. "Realist Horror," Thomas Wartenberg and Angela Curran, eds., *The Philosophy of Film: Introductory Text and Reading*, Oxford: Oxford University Press, 260–269.

14. Annette Kuhn, and Guy Westwell, 2015. "Extreme Cinema (Ordeal Cinema)," *A Dictionary of Film Studies*, Oxford: Oxford University Press [online].

15. Ibid.

16. Tanya Horeck and Tina Kendall, 2011. "Introduction," *The New Extremism in Cinema: From France to Europe*, Edinburgh: Edinburgh University Press, p. 1.

17. Asbjørn Grønstad, 2012. *Screening the Unwatchable: Spaces of Negation in Post-Millennial Art Cinema*, Basingstoke: Palgrave Macmillan, p. 3.

18. Ibid., p. 3.

19. Matt Frey, 2016. *Extreme Cinema: The Transgressive Rhetoric of Today's Art Film Culture*, New Brunswick: Rutgers University Press, p. 1.

20. Grønstad, 2012, p. 1.

21. Ibid., p. 2.

22. See Chi-Yun Shin, 2008. "The Art of Branding: Tartan 'Asia Extreme' Films," *Jump Cut*, Vol. 50, http://www.ejumpcut.org/archive/jc50.2008/TartanDist/. Chuck Kleinhans, 2009; "Cross-Cultural Disgust: Some Problems in the Analysis of Contemporary Horror Cinema," *Jump Cut*, Vol. 51, http://www.ejumpcut.org/archive/jc51.2009/crosscultHorror/index.html; Joan Hawkins, 2009 "Culture Wars: Some New Trends in Art Horror," *Jump Cut*, Vol. 51, http://www.ejumpcut.org/archive/jc51.2009/artHorror/index.html (3 May 2016).

23. Chuck Kleinhans, 2008. "Horror's New Terrain," *Jump Cut*, Vol. 50, http://www.ejumpcut.org/archive/jc50.2008/horrorintro/index.html (3 May 2016).

24. Ibid.

25. Ibid.

26. Ponder, Julian, 2006. "'To the Next Level': Castration in *Hostel II*," *Irish Journal of Gothic and Horror Studies*, Issue 4, http://irishgothichorrorjournal.homestead.com/hostel2castration.html (3 May 2016).

27. Ibid.

28. See Steve Jones, 2010. "Time Is Wasting: Con/Sequence and S/Pace in the *Saw* Series," *Horror Studies*, Vol. 1, No. 2, pp. 225–240; Donald L. Anderson, 2013. "How the Horror Film Broke Its Promise: Hyperreal Horror and Ruggero Deodato's *Cannibal*

Holocaust," *Horror Studies*, Vol. 4, Issue 1, pp. 109–126; Shaun Kimber, 2014. "Transgressive Edge Play and *Srpski Film/A Serbian Film*," *Horror Studies*, Vol. 5, No. 1, pp. 107–126.
  29. Jones, 2013, *p*. 2.
  30. *Ibid.*, p. 2.
  31. Phil Russell, 2013. *Beyond the Darkness: Cult, Horror and Extreme Cinema*, [S.n.]: Bad News Press, p. 7.
  32. *Ibid.*
  33. See also Jinhee Choi and Mitsuyo Wada-Marciano. 2009. *Horror to the Extreme: Changing Boundaries in Asian Cinema*, Hong Kong: Hong Kong University Press, for an approach to more commercial and populist Asian extreme cinema.
  34. Mikita Brottman, and John Mercer, 2014. "Subverting Senses, Circumventing Limits: An Introduction to the Launch Issue of the Cine-Excess eJournal," *Cine-Excess eJournal*, Issue 1, http://www.cine-excess.co.uk/subverting-senses-circumventing-limits.html (3 May 2016).
  35. Jenny Barrett, 2014. "More than Just a Game: Breaking the Rules in *The Bunny Game*," *Cine-excess eJournal*, Issue 1, http://www.cine-excess.co.uk/more-than-just-a-game.html (3 May 2016).
  36. David Kerekes and David Slater, 2016. *Killing for Culture, From Edison to Isis: A New History of Death on Film*, London: Headpress, p. 539.
  37. Marina Warner, 2016. Quoted in Kerekes and Slater, *Killing for Culture*, p. 539.
  38. Kerekes and Slater, 2016, p. 539.
  39. *Ibid.*
  40. Alexandra Heller-Nicholas, 2014. *Found Footage Horror Films: Fear and the Appearance of Reality*, Jefferson, NC: McFarland, p. 3.
  41. *Ibid.*, p. 7.
  42. *Ibid.*, p. 9.
  43. *Ibid.*, p. 6.
  44. Neil Jackson, 2016. "Introduction, Shot, Cut, and Slaughtered: The Cultural Mythology of Snuff," Neil Jackson, Shaun Kimber, Johnny Walker and Thomas Joseph Watson, eds., 2016. *Snuff: Real Death and Screen Media*, London: Bloomsbury, p. 2.
  45. *Ibid.*, p. 14.
  46. *Ibid.*, p. 16.
  47. Jones, 2013, p. 171.
  48. *Ibid.*, pp. 170–186.
  49. Freeland, 2005, p. 262.
  50. *Ibid.*, p. 264.
  51. *Ibid.*, p. 267.
  52. Jake Tapper, 2005. "Court Deals Blow to U.S. Anti-Porn Campaign," *ABC News*, January 24, http://abcnews.go.com/Nightline/LegalCenter/story?id=433956andpage=1 (8 August 2017).
  53. Nina Whett, 2002. "*Forced Entry*—Reviewer Rated…" *Adult Industry News*, May 26, http://ainews.com/Archives/Story4518.phtml (24 March 2016).
  54. Jones, 2013, p. 152.
  55. There have been a few high profile cases recently where men convicted of serious sexual assaults on women have been treated with leniency by the judiciary and the media. See the 2015 case of Brock Turner and accusations of a lenient Judiciary: https://www.washingtonpost.com/national/judge-in-stanford-sexual-assault-case-faces-recall-over-brock-turners-sentence/2017/06/26/6e5c0046-5a7e-11e7-a9f6-7c3296387341_story.html?utm_term=.e34c7bdb7d18. For general overview on media/social media reporting of sexual violence: Nickie Philips, 2016. *Beyond Blurred Lines: Rape Culture in Popular Media*, Lanham, MD: Rowman and Littlefield.
  56. Linda Williams, 2008. *Screening Sex*, Durham: Duke University Press, p. 132.
  57. Brenda Crossman, 2007. *Sexual Citizens: The Legal and Cultural Regulation of Sex and Belonging*, Redwood City: Stanford University Press, p. 56.
  58. Misha Kavka, 2016. "The Affective Reality of Snuff," Neil Jackson et al., eds., *Snuff: Real Death and Screen Media*, London: Bloomsbury, pp. 47–61.
  59. Vivian Sobchack, 2004. "The Charge of the Real: Embodied Knowledge and Cinematic Consciousness," *Carnal Thoughts: Embodiment and the Moving Image Culture*, Berkeley: University of California Press, pp. 258–285.
  60. *Ibid.*, p. 261.
  61. Kavka, 2016, p. 50.
  62. David Church, 2009. "Of Manias, Shit, and Blood: The Reception of *Salò* as a 'Sick Film,'" *Participations*, Vol. 6, No. 2, p. 340.

Chapter Two

  1. Kerekes and Slater, 2016, p. x.
  2. *Ibid.*

3. Charles Musser, 1994. *The Emergence of Cinema: The American Screen to 1907*, Berkeley: University of California Press, p. 1.
4. *Ibid.*, p. 42.
5. *Ibid.*, p. 20.
6. *Ibid.*, p. 21.
7. Étienne Gaspar Robertson, 1831. *Mémoires récréatifs, scientifiques et anecdotiques*, 2 vols., Paris: Chez l'auteur et Librairie de Wurtz, p. 278.
8. Musser, 1994, pp. 43–45.
9. *Orange* (NJ), *Chronicle*, 3 March, p. 5.
10. Musser, 1994, p. 53.
11. Tino Balio, 1995. *Grand Design: Hollywood as a Modern Business Enterprise, 1930–1939*, Berkeley: University of California Press, p. 298.
12. Jon Towlson, 2014. *Subversive Horror Cinema: Countercultural Messages of Films from Frankenstein to the Present*, Jefferson, NC: McFarland, p. 9.
13. *Ibid.*, p. 6.
14. *Ibid.*
15. Alison Peirse, 2013. *After Dracula: The 1930s Horror Film*, London: I.B. Tauris, p. 26.
16. Towlson, 2014, p. 31.
17. Tudor, 1989, p. 29.
18. Towlson, 2014, p. 21
19. Rachel Adam, 2001. *Sideshow USA: Freaks and the American Cultural Imagination*, Chicago: University of Chicago Press, p. 64.
20. Towlson, 2014, p. 29.
21. Peirse, 2013, p. 7.
22. *Ibid.*, p. 36.
23. Harry Benshoff, 2000. "Blaxploitation Horror Films: Generic Reappropriation or Reinscription?," *Cinema Journal*, Vol. 39, No. 2, Winter, p. 47.
24. Peirse, 2013, p. 2.
25. Susan Sontag, 2004. "Imagination of Disaster," Sean Redmond, ed., *Liquid Metal: The Science Fiction Film Reader*, London: Wallflower Press, pp. 40–47.
26. *Ibid.*, p. 47.
27. Michael Lee, 2003. "Ideology and Style in the Double Feature *I Married a Monster From Outer Space* and *Curse of the Demon*," Gary Rhodes, ed., *Horror at the Drive-in: Popular Essays on Americana*, Jefferson, NC: McFarland, p. 67–68.
28. *Ibid.*, p. 67.
29. *Ibid.*, p. 68.
30. *Ibid.*, p. 76.
31. Eric Schaefer, 1999. *Bold! Daring! Shocking! True!: A History of Exploitation Films, 1919–1959*, Durham: Duke University Press, p. 285.
32. *Ibid.*, p. 288.
33. *Ibid.*
34. Mikita Brottman, 1997. *Offensive Films: Toward an Anthropology of Cinéma Vomitif*, Westport, CT: Greenwood Press, p. 78.
35. Jonathan Crane, 2004. "Scraping Bottom: Splatter and the Herschell Gordon Lewis Oeuvre," Stephen Prince, ed., *The Horror Film*, Piscataway: Rutgers University Press, p. 156.
36. Herschell Gordon Lewis, 1986. Quoted in Juno and Pauline, "Interview: Herschell Gordon Lewis/Part 1," V. Vale and Andrea Juno, eds., *Incredibly Strange Films*, San Francisco: Re/Search Publications, p. 23.
37. *Ibid.*, p. 24.
38. *Ibid.*
39. *Ibid.*, p. 23.
40. Brottman, 1997, *p.* 77.
41. *Variety*, 6 May 1964. As cited by David Friedman and Don De Nevi, 1990. *A Youth in Babylon: Confessions of a Trash-Film King*, Amherst, NY: Prometheus, p. 357.
42. For example, David Friedman would conduct an impromptu vox pop with people milling about the drive-in during and after *Blood Feast* was showing, See Herschell Gordon Lewis and David Freidman, 2000. "DVD Commentary," Herschell Gordon Lewis (Director), *Blood Feast* [DVD], USA: Something Weird Video.
43. Crane, 2004, p. 159.
44. Lewis and Freidman, "DVD Commentary."
45. Lewis, "Interview," p. 26.
46. Lewis and Freidman, "DVD Commentary."
47. Amos Vogel, 1974. *Film as A Subversive Art*, London: Weidenfeld and Nicolson, p. 192.
48. *Ibid.*
49. Crane, 2004, p. 159.
50. Linda Williams, 1990. *Hard Core: Power, Pleasure and the "Frenzy of the Visible,"* Los Angeles: University of California Press, p. 36.
51. Xavier Mendik, 2002. "'Gouts of Blood': The Colourful Underground Universe of Herschell Gordon Lewis," Xavier Mendik and Steven Jay Schneider, *Underground U.S.A.:*

Filmmaking Beyond the Hollywood Canon, London: Wallflower, p. 188.
52. Brottman, 1997, p. 85.
53. *Ibid.*, p. 86.
54. *Ibid.*
55. See Tudor, 1989, pp. 211–244. Tudor defines paranoid horror as a break in the 1970s with secure horror of the classical Hollywood period which reflected the socio-political changes in the wake of events such as the war in Vietnam and the Watergate scandal. Characteristics include: a breakdown of oppositions (internal/external; good/bad; self/other), a lack of agency of central institutions, unsuccessful narrative resolution, and the primacy of disorder.
56. Crane, 2004, p. 163.
57. Gregory Waller, 1987. "Introduction," Gregory Waller, ed., *American Horrors: Essays on the Modern American Horror Film*, Urbana: University of Illinois Press, p. 4.
58. Jackson, 2016. "Introduction, Shot, Cut, and Slaughtered," p. 9.
59. *Ibid.*
60. *Ibid.*, p. 2.
61. Heller-Nicholas, 2014, p. 64.
62. Kerekes and Slater, 2016, p. 25.
63. *Ibid.*, p. 5.
64. The providence of *Faces of Death* is Japanese though it passes itself off as an American Production. It is included here due to its widespread success in America where it became one of the country's leading video rentals, as well as, of course, being a key aesthetic influence for future North American extreme horror.
65. Kerekes and Slater, 2016, p. 204.
66. Mark Goodall, 2006. *Sweet and Savage: The World Through the Shockumentary Film Lens*, London: Headpress, p. 126.
67. *Ibid.*, p. 123.
68. Kerekes and Slater, 2016, p. 215.
69. Shaun Kimber, 2011. *Henry: Portrait of a Serial Killer*, Basingstoke: Palgrave Macmillan, p. 7.
70. *Ibid.*
71. Kerekes and Slater, 2016, p. 68.
72. Kimber, 2011, p. 100.
73. Kerekes and Slater, 2016, p. 70.
74. Jackson, 2016. "Introduction, Shot, Cut, and Slaughtered," pp. 12–13.
75. Hill, 2005 (07 July 2017).
76. Mark Jones and Gerry Carlin, 2016. "Unfound Footage and Unfounded Rumors: The Manson Family Murders and the Persistence of Snuff," Jackson et al., *Snuff*, p. 184.
77. Kimber, 2011, p. 103.
78. Kerekes and Slater, 2016, p. 240.
79. *Ibid.*, p. 250.
80. Towlson, 2014, p. 180.
81. Eric Stanze, 2005. "Making of Scrapbook," in Eric Stanze (Director), *Scrapbook*, [DVD], USA: Wicked Pixel Cinema.
82. Fred Vogel, 2005. "DVD Commentary," Vogel, Fred (Director), *August Underground* [DVD], USA: Toe Tag Pictures.
83. Hill, 2005 (07 July 2017).

Chapter Three

1. Deborah Shaw and Armida De La Garza, 2010. "Introducing Transnational Cinemas," *Transnational Cinemas*, Vol. 1, Issue 1, p. 4.
2. Vincent Canby, 1977. "Film Festival: 'Salò' Is Disturbing…," *New York Times*, 1 October, http://www.nytimes.com/movie/review?res=9904E7D8163AE334BC4953DFB667838C669EDE (10 July 2017).
3. Richard Brody, 2016. "*Salò, or the 120 Days of Sodom*," *The New Yorker*, 29 April, http://www.newyorker.com/goings-on-about-town/movies/Salò-or-the-120-days-of-sodom (10 July 2017).
4. "*Salò/120 Days of Sodom*," 2017. BBFC, http://www.bbfc.co.uk/case-studies/Salò120-days-sodom (10 July 2017).
5. Steven Biodrowski, 2008. "*Salò* (1975)—Borderland Review," *Cinefantastique*, 27 August, http://cinefantastiqueonline.com/2008/08/borderland-Salò-1975/ (10 July 2017).
6. Michael Thomson, 2000. "*Salò, or the 120 Days of Sodom* (1975)," *BBC*, 17 October, http://www.bbc.co.uk/films/2000/10/17/Salò_1975_review.shtml (10 July 2017)
7. "Extreme Cinema: Top 25 Most Disturbing Films of All Time—Part 2," 2010. *Horror News Net*, 23 August, http://horrornews.net/6527/extreme-cinema-top-25-most-disturbing-films-of-all-time-part2/ (10 July 2017).
8. Richard Trejo, 2013. "Truly Disturbing's Top 10 MOST DISTURBING Movies of All Time," *Truly Disturbing*, 27 May, http://www.trulydisturbing.com/2013/05/27/disturbings-top-10-disturbing-movies-time/ (10 July 2017).

9. Brody, 2016.
10. Jonathan Rosenbaum, 2013. "*Salò, or the 120 Days of Sodom*," *The Chicago Reader*, http://www.chicagoreader.com/chicago/Salò-or-the-120-days-of-sodom/Film?oid=1068097 (10 July 2017).
11. John Waters, 2010. "Why You Should Watch Filth," *Big Think*, 10 September, http://bigthink.com/videos/why-you-should-watch-filth (10 July 2017).
12. Naomi Greene, 1992. *Pier Paolo Pasolini: Cinema as Heresy*, Princeton, NJ: Princeton University Press, p. 204.
13. Stephen Synder and Pier Paolo Pasolini, 1980. *Pier Paolo Pasolini*, Boston: Twayne, p. 165.
14. Greene, 1992, p. 207.
15. Naomi Green, 2011. "*Salò*: Breaking the Rules," *Criterion*, 4 October, https://www.criterion.com/current/posts/511-Salò-breaking-the-rules (10 July 2017).
16. *Ibid.*, p. 199.
17. *Ibid.*
18. *Ibid.*, p. 198.
19. *Ibid.*, p. 206.
20. Lisa Coulthard, 2011. "Interrogating the Obscene: Extremism and Michael Haneke," Horeck and Kendall, eds., *The New Extremism*, p. 183.
21. Greene, 1992, p. 216.
22. Lisa Blackman and Couze Venn, eds., 2010. "Affect," *Body and Society*, 16:1.
23. Kavka, 2016, p. 52.
24. Heller-Nicholas, 2014, p. 25.
25. Kerekes and Slater, 2016, p. 52.
26. F. Gere, 1981. "*Cannibal Holocaust* (Review)," *Cahier du Cinema*, 326: 63 July/August, p. 63.
27. Ian Grey, 2001. "Blood Feast: *Cannibal Holocaust* Returns and Here's Hoping You've Finished Your Lunch," *Baltimore City Paper*, August 29; Andrew Devos, 2010. "The More You Rape Their Senses, the Happier They Are," Robert Weiner and John Cline, eds., *Cinema Inferno: Celluloid Explosions from the Cultural Margins*, Lanham, MD: Scarecrow, p. 89.
28. Kerekes and Slater, 2016, p. 51.
29. Kavka, 2016, p. 52.
30. Mikita Brottman, 1998. *Meat Is Murder!: An Illustrated Guide to Cannibal Culture*, London: Creation, p. 149.
31. *Ibid.*, p. 150.
32. *Ibid.*, p. 149.
33. Kerekes and Slater, 2016, p. 49.
34. Kerekes and Slater, 2016, p. 51.
35. Mark Jones and Gerry Carlin, 2016. "Unfound Footage and Unfounded Rumors: The Manson Family Murders and the Persistence of Snuff," Neil et al., eds., *Snuff: Real Death and Screen Media*, p. 184.
36. Kerekes and Slater, 2016, p. 72.
37. Heller-Nicholas, 2014, p. 36.
38. *Ibid.*, p. 36.
39. Jay McRoy, 2008. *Nightmare Japan: Contemporary Japanese Horror Cinema*, Amsterdam: Rodopi, p. 2.
40. See http://www.blumhouse.com/ for details of the production company, Blumhouse mainly produce low to mid budget horror films such as, *Insidious* (James Wan, 2010), *The Purge* (James DeMonaco, 2013), and most recently *Get Out* (Jordan Peele, 2017).
41. Kerekes and Slater, 2016, p. 485.
42. *Ibid.*, p. 331.
43. *Ibid.*, p. 486.
44. McRoy, 2008, p. 24.
45. *Ibid.*, p. 32.
46. *Ibid.*, p. 35.
47. *Ibid.*, p. 42.
48. *Ibid.*, p. 30.
49. Freeland, 2005, p. 263.
50. McRoy, 2008, p. 105.
51. Anton Bitel, 2017. "Is This the Most Extreme 108 Minutes in the History of Japanese Cinema?," *Little White Lies*, 3 February, http://lwlies.com/articles/destruction-babies-extreme-japanese-cinema/ (10 July 2017).
52. V&R Planning are a very *outré* Japanese adult video production company which were formed in 1986 and are based in Tokyo. The company specializes in transgressive *vérité* productions such as scat porn and death videos. See Kerekes and Slater, 2016, pp. 244–247.
53. David Hoenigman, 2009. "If You Want Blood (You've Got It): An Interview with Koji Shiraishi," *3:AM Magazine*, 29 November, http://www.3ammagazine.com/3am/if-you-want-blood-you%E2%80%99ve-got-it-an-interview-with-koji-shiraishi/ (10 July 2017).
54. "*Grotesque*," 2009. *BBFC*, http://www.bbfc.co.uk/case-studies/grotesque (10 July 2017).
55. *Ibid.*
56. Blake, 2008, p. 27.

57. Vogel, 1974, p. 263.
58. *Ibid.*
59. David Kerekes, 1994. *Sex Murder Art: The Films of Jörg Buttgereit*, London: Headpress, p. 89.
60. Blake, 2008, p. 26.
61. *Ibid.*, p. 37
62. *Ibid.*, p. 41.
63. *Ibid.*, p. 28.
64. Barbara Creed, 1986. "Horror and the Monstrous-Feminine: An Imaginary Abjection," Screen 27 (1), p. 47.
65. Kristeva, Julia, 1982. *Powers of Horror: An Essay on Abjection*, New York, Columbia University Press, p. 3.
66. Sélavy, Virginie, 2015. "Jörg Buttgereits *Nekromantik*'s, or Sadean Shock of the Body," *Nekromantik 2 Anatomy of Desire Booklet*, London: Arrow Video, p. 15.
67. Kerekes, 1994, p. 27.
68. *Ibid.*, p. 30.
69. Kerekes, 1994, p. 87.
70. *Ibid.*, p. 88.
71. Knut Hichethier, 1993. "Report Regarding the Feature Film *Nekromantik 2* (1993)," *Nekromantik 2 Anatomy of Desire Booklet*, p. 53.
72. Richard Taylor, 2016. "Bending Reality: The World of Marian Dora—A Severed Cinema Interview," *Severed Cinema*, 6 May, http://severed-cinema.com/marian-dora/bending-morality-the-world-of-marian-dora-a-severed-cinema-interview (10 July 2017).
73. Ray Casta, 2011. "*Melancholie der Engel*—Shock DVD Entertainment," *Severed Cinema*, 11 April, http://severed-cinema.com/m-reviews/melancholie-der-engel-shock-dvd-entertainment (13 July 2017).
74. Kristeva, 1992, p. 4.
75. Blake, 2008, p. 27.
76. Kerekes, 1994, p. 43.
77. Taylor, 2016.
78. Kerekes and Slater, 2016, p. 89.
79. Dejan Ognjanović, 2014. ""Welcome to the Reality Studio": Serbian Hand-Held Horrors," Linnie Blake and Xavier Aldana Reyes,, eds., *Digital Horrors: Haunted Technologies, Network Panic and the Found Footage Phenomenon*, London: I.B. Tauris, p. 80.
80. Linnie Blake and Xavier Aldana Reyes, 2015. "Introduction: Horror in the Digital Age," *Ibid.*, pp. 8–9.
81. Kerekes and Slater, 2016, p. 91.

82. Mark Featherstone and Beth Johnson, 2012. "'Ovo Je Srbija': The Horror of the National Thing in *A Serbian Film*," *Journal for Cultural Research*, Vol. 16, Issue, 1, p. 63 (abstract).
83. Kerekes and Slater, 2016, p. 91.
84. A.O. Scott, 2011. "Torture or Porn? No Need to Choose," *New York Times*, 12 May, http://www.nytimes.com/2011/05/13/movies/a-serbian-film-directed-by-srdjan-spasojevic-review.html?smid=tw-nytimesmoviesandseid=auto (10 July 2017).
85. badhead, 2010. "Mark Kermode—*A Serbian Film*," *YouTube*, 13 December, https://www.youtube.com/watch?v=KLiwki7-dSEandt=2s (10 July 2017).
86. *Ibid.*
87. Kimber, 2014, p. 111.
88. *Ibid.*, p. 121.
89. Alan Jones, 2010. "The Nightmare of Truth," *A Serbian Film Blu-ray Sleeve Notes*, London: Revolver Entertainment.
90. "*A Serbian Film—Srpski Film*," 2010. *BBFC*, http://www.bbfc.co.uk/case-studies/serbian-film-srpski-film (10 July 2017).
91. Kimber, 2014, p. 117.

Chapter Four

1. "*Murder Set Pieces*," 2008. *BBFC*, http://www.bbfc.co.uk/releases/murder-set-pieces-1970 (13 July 2017).
2. *Ibid.*
3. Blake and Reyes, 2015, p. 1.
4. Blake, 2008, p. 130.
5. David Ray Carter, 2010. "It's Only a Movie? Reality as Transgression in Exploitation Cinema," in John Cline and Robert G. Weiner, eds., *From the Arthouse to the Grindhouse: Highbrow and Lowbrow Transgression in Cinema's First Century*, Lanham, MD: Scarecrow, p. 312
6. Blake and Reyes, 2015, p. 3.
7. Jorge Palacios, 2015. "NSFW: Interview With Filmmaker Eric Stanze," *Dirge Magazine*, 21 July, http://www.dirgemag.com/interview-the-dark-stylings-of-eric-stanze/ (26 August 2016).
8. Jeremy Wallace, "The Making of *Scrapbook*."
9. Jeremy Tucker, 2011. "INTERVIEW: Director Eric Stanze Spills His Guts on 'Ratline,'" *insideSTL*, September 14, http://insides

tl.com/interview-director-eric-stanze-spills-his-guts-on-ratline-2/1942609 (10 May 2016).

10. Eric Stanze, "DVD Commentary," in Stanze, E (Director), *Scrapbook*, [DVD].

11. Todd Telvin, "Making of *Scrapbook*."

12. Daniel Myrick and Edwardo Sánchez, the filmmakers behind *The Blair Witch Project* also engaged in a similar approach in order to create an authentic and intense environment of horror. See, Heller-Nicholas, "Productive Masochism: "Method Filmmaking" and Authorship," *Found Footage Horror Films*, pp. 95–99.

13. Emily Haack, "DVD Commentary," in E. Stanze (Director), *Scrapbook*, [DVD].

14. *Ibid*.

15. Todd Telvin, "Making of *Scrapbook*."

16. Emily Haack, *ibid*.

17. Eric Stanze, quoted in Josh Samford, 2014. "An Interview with Eric Stanze," in *Rogue Cinema*, http://www.roguecinema.com/an-interview-with-eric-stanze-by-josh-samford.html (5 May 2016).

18. Before the completed film was completed and officially screened, Biondo died tragically in an on-set accident on his latest film and thus missed ever seeing a final cut of the film he had worked on for so long.

19. Eric Stanze, personal communication, email, 20 April 2016.

20. "Year End Issue," (2002. January/February). *Rue Morgue*, Issue #25.

21. Claire, 2004. "*Scrapbook*—Filth or Horror?," *Cult Movie Forums*, February 5, http://www.cultmovieforums.com/forum/threads/scrapbook-eric-stanze-1999-merged.2842/ (10 May 2016).

22. Chainsawfodder, 2004. "*Scrapbook* (2000)," *The Mortuary*, 26 September, http://the-mortuary.com/showthread.php?t=5546andhighlight=scrapbook (10 May 2016).

23. Church, 2009, p. 348.

24. *Ibid*., p. 343.

25. *Ibid*., p. 346.

26. Kavka, 2016, p. 61.

27. *Ibid*., p. 59.

28. Smokedragon, 2004. "What Is the Goriest, Most Actual Horrifying Horror Movie on DVD?," *DVD Talk*, Post #30, 11 May, http://forum.dvdtalk.com/archive/t-363440.html (8 August 2017).

29. This quote is by NancyLovesFreddy and taken from the *Bloody Disgusting* forum thread, "Most Shocking or Disturbing Movie Ever" from 2010. The Forum site has now been revamped and updated and as yet a thread archive has not been included. For details see, http://bloody-disgusting.com/forums/ (8 August 2017).

30. wlj, 2007. "The Sickest Horror Movie Ever Made," *DVD Talk*, Post #12, 8 February, http://forum.dvdtalk.com/7630583-post12.html (8 August 2017).

31. Jovanka Vuckovic, 2001. "Too Real for Comfort: An Outsiders Perspective," in Fred Vogel (Director), *August Underground* [DVD].

32. *Ibid*.

33. *Ibid*.

34. The quote was taken from the front cover of *Rue Morgue*, 2003. #31, January/February.

35. *Rue Morgue* quote taken from the DVD cover, Fred Vogel (Director), 2003. *August Underground: Mordum* [DVD], USA: Toetag Pictures, http://toetag.biz/product/august-undergrounds-mordum-dvd// (26 August 2016).

36. Steve Jones, 2011. "Dying to be Seen: Snuff-Fiction's Problematic Fantasies of 'Reality,'" *Scope: An Online Journal of Film and Television Studies*, Issue 19, October, p. 7.

37. Fred Vogel, "DVD Commentary," Fred Vogel (Director), *August Underground* [DVD].

38. Steve Jones, 2011. "Dying to be Seen," p. 10.

39. Tony Simonelli, 2001. "Too Real for Comfort: An Outsiders Perspective," in Fred Vogel (Director), *August Underground* [DVD].

40. These two quotes are by Wonderlust and Riaxion respectively and taken from the now deleted *Bloody Disgusting* forum thread, "Most Shocking or Disturbing Movie Ever" from 2010. See footnote 29 for details.

41. Heller-Nicholas, 2014, p. 87.

42. Shane Ryan, 2014. "Amateur Porn Star Killer DVD commentary," in Shane Ryan (Director), *Amateur Porn Star Killer: The Complete Collection* [DVD], USA, Mongolian Barbecue.

43. Shane Ryan, personal communication, email, 10 July 2016.

44. Shane Ryan quoted in Craddock, John, 2011. "Shane Ryan," *Horror Fan Reviews*, http://horrorfansreview.tripod.com/shane-ryan-interview.htmll (11 May 2016).

45. Horeck and Kendall, 2011. "Introduction," *The New Extremism in Cinema*, p. 8.

46. Neil Jackson, 2016. "Introduction, Shot, Cut, and Slaughtered: The Cultural Mythology of Snuff," Neil Jackson et al., eds., *Snuff: Real Death and Screen Media*, p. 3.
47. *Ibid.*, p. 5.
48. Kerekes and Slater, 2016, p. 416.
49. *Ibid.*, pp. 521–522.
50. See Eliza Gale, 2012. "An Inteview [sic] with Actor/Director/Writer Shane Ryan," *elizagalesinterviews*, 21 June, https://elizagalesinterviews.com/2012/06/21/in-inteview-with-actordirectorwriter-shane-ryan/ (11 May 2016).
51. *Ibid.*
52. *Ibid.*
53. *Ibid.*
54. Rini Gates, "A Boy, a Girl a Camera," Ryan, Shane (Director), *Amateur Porn Star Killer: The Complete Collection* [DVD].
55. Glenn Cochrane, "A Boy, a Girl a Camera."
56. MTV, quoted in *Mad Sin Cinema*, http://www.madsincinema.com/amateur-porn-star-killer.html (26 August 2016).
57. Anthony Spadaccini, "A Boy, a Girl a Camera."
58. Taken from the "About Us" page from the Cinema Epoch website. See, http://www.cinemaepoch.com/about_us.html (14 July 2016).
59. Steve Jones, 2016. "A View to a Kill: Perspectives on Faux-Snuff and Self," Neil Jackson et al., eds., *Snuff: Real Death and Screen Media*, p. 291.
60. Kerekes and Slater, 2016, p. 78.
61. Necromagikal, 2011. "Interview: Lucifer Valentine (*Slow Torture Puke Chamber, ReGORGEgitated* [sic] *Sacrifice*)," *Horror News*, 10 October, http://horrornews.net/42170/interview-lucifer-valentine-slow-torture-puke-chamber-regorgegitated-sacrifice/ (14 July 2016).
62. Lucifer Valentine, 2011. "Epilogue," Lucifer Valentine (Director), *The Vomit Gore Trilogy* [DVD], USA/Canada: Unearthed Films.
63. *Ibid.*
64. *Ibid.*
65. *Ibid.*
66. *Ibid.*
67. *Ibid.*
68. *Ibid.*
69. *Ibid.*
70. Necromagikal, 2011.
71. *Ibid.*
72. Jesus magGot, 2010. "Lucifer Valentine," *Maggot Films*, 7 October, http://maggotfilms.com/2010/10/07/jesus-interviews-lucifer-valentine/ (14 July 2016).
73. Valentine, "Epilogue."
74. Matt, 2015. "Interview with Lucifer Valentine…," *Matts Rotten Review*, 6 August, http://mattsrottenreviews.tumblr.com/post/126006603043/interview-with-lucifer-valentine (26 August 2016).
75. Valentine, "Epilogue."
76. "Pictures Painted in Hell—My Interview with Lucifer Valentine," 2012. *Video Star*, 5 April, http://videostarforever.blogspot.co.uk/2012/04/quality-time-with-lucifer-valentine.html (26 August 2012).
77. Greigh Johanson, 2012. "Lucifer Valentine," *Goregasmic Cinema*, September, http://goregasmiccinema.blogspot.co.uk/2012/09/lucifer-valentine.html (26 August 2016).
78. 'History of Vomit Gore," Valentine, Lucifer (Director), *The Vomit Gore Trilogy* [DVD].
79. *Ibid.*
80. Matt, 2015 (26 August 2016).
81. The Gore-met, 2010. "Lucifer Valentine," #6, *The Mortuary*, 7 July, http://themortuary.com/showthread.php?t=28578 (5 September 2016).
82. See *The Mortuary* thread "WHY won't Rue-Morgue Review Slaughtered Vomit Dolls?" which started 27 November 2005: http://themortuary.com/showthread.php?t=12117and highlight=august+underground (26 August 2016).
83. Cremasterfan, 2006. "*Slaughtered Vomit Dolls* (2006): Don't Waste Your Time, It's Rubbish!," *Internet Movie Database (IMDb)*, 18 July, : http://www.imdb.com/title/tt0811073/board/nest/48541588?ref_=tt_bd_1 (5 September 2016).
84. "Voice Memos," Lucifer Valentine (Director), *The Vomit Gore Trilogy* [DVD].
85. Jude Felton, 2012. "QandA with *The Bunny Game*'s Adam Rehmeier," *The Lair of Filth*, 21 August, http://www.thelairoffilth.com/2012/08/q-with-bunny-games-adam-rehmeier.html (26 August 2016).
86. Jason, 2011. "Horrorphilia Podcast #55 w/ Adam Rehmeier Director of *The Bunny Game*: Reviews of *Valhalla Rising, Pin, Macabre* and *Seven Days*," *Horrorphilia*, 31 January, http://www.horrorphilia.com/horror

philia-podcast-55-w-adam-rehmeier-director-of-the-bunny-game-reviews-of-valhalla-rising-pin-macabre-and-seven-days/ (5 September 2016).
87. Luci Herbert, 2012. "Interview—Bunny Game Director Adam Rehmeier," *Ave Noctum*, 16 July, http://www.avenoctum.com/2012/07/interview-bunny-game-director-adam-rehmeier/ (14 July 2016).
88. Oliver Maxwell Kupper, 2011. "*The Bunny Game*: An Interview with Adam Rehmeier," *Autre*, 21 October, http://www.pasunautre.com/interviewsmain/2011/10/21/interview-the-bunny-game (15 September 2016).
89. Jason Meredith, 2012. "*The Bunny Game*," *Cinezilla*, 6 January, http://cinezilla.blogspot.co.uk/2012/01/bunny-game.html (15 September 2016).
90. Mark Everleth, 2012. "Movie Review: *The Bunny Game*," *Underground Film Journal*, March 26, http://www.undergroundfilmjournal.com/movie-review-the-bunny-game/ (5 September 2016).
91. "*The Bunny Game*," 2011. *British Board of Film Classification (BBFC)*, 12 November, http://www.bbfc.co.uk/releases/bunny-game-1970 (5 September 2016).
92. Andy Copp, 2012. "Talking to THE BUNNY GAME Directer [sic] Adam Rehmeier," *Exploitation Nation*, 29 June, http://exploitationnation2.blogspot.co.uk/2012/06/talking-to-bunny-game-directer-adam.html?zx=233721ecbebb95f3 (5 September 2016).
93. Joel Black, 2002. *The Reality Effect: Film Culture and the Graphic Imperative*, New York: Routledge, p. 10.
94. Herbert, 2012. "Interview—Bunny Game Director Adam Rehmeier," *Ave Noctum*.
95. *Ibid*.
96. Asbjørn Grønstad, 2012. *Screening the Unwatchable*, p. 38.
97. Anton Bitel, 2015. "Review: Hate Crime (2013)," The Horror Show, 27 May, http://blog.thehorrorshow.tv/review-hate-crime-2013/ (11 May 2016).
98. Vogel, 1974, p. 9.
99. "*Hate Crime*," 2015. *BBFC*, 2 March, http://www.bbfc.co.uk/releases/hate-crime-vod (5 September 2016).
100. The next installment, *American Guinea Pig: Bloodshock* (Koch, 2015), was released in 2016 after funding via Indiegogo again. Directed by Marcus Koch who was responsible for the SFX in the "vomit gore" films and produced by Unearthed Films CEO, Stephen Biro.
101. Fredric Jameson, 1992. "Postmodernism and Consumer Society," Peter Brooker, ed., *Modernism/Postmodernism*, New York: Longman, p. 168.
102. *Ibid*., p. 169.
103. *Ibid*., p. 169.
104. *Ibid*., p. 167.
105. *Ibid*., p. 166.
106. Black, 2002, p. 1
107. Heller-Nicholas, 2014, p. 92.

Chapter Five

1. Excerpts of this chapter first appeared in: James Aston, 2015. "Nightmares Outside the Mainstream: *August Underground* and Real/Reel Horror," Linnie Blake and Xavier Aldana Reyes, eds., *Digital Horror*, pp. 137–148 (reprinted with permission).
2. Christopher Williams, 1980. *Realism and the Cinema: A Reader*, London: BFI, p. 1.
3. Julia Hallam and Margaret Marshment, 2000. *Realism and Popular Cinema*, Manchester: Manchester University Press, p. 3.
4. Jay David Bulter, 2005. "Preface," Geoff King, ed., *The Spectacle of the Real: From Hollywood to Reality TV and Beyond*, Bristol: Intellect, p. 9.
5. Black, 2002, p. 1.
6. Hallam and Marshment, 2000, p. 14.
7. Williams, 1980, p. 3.
8. *Ibid*., p. 2.
9. Hallam and Marshment, 2000, p. 8.
10. Williams, 1980, p. 36.
11. See Leo Braudy, Gerald Mast and Marshal Cohen, eds., 1992. *Film Theory and Criticism: Introductory Readings*, fourth edition, New York: Oxford University Press, pp. 3–114.
12. MacCabe, Colin, Quoted in, Williams, 1980, p. 157.
13. Hallam and Marshment, 2000, p. 12.
14. "Film and Reality," Braudy et al., *Film Theory and Criticism*, p. 7.
15. Keith Jenkins, 1995. *On "What Is History?": From Carr and Elton to Rorty and White*, London: Routledge, p. 18.
16. Black, 2002, p. 4.
17. *Ibid*., p. 8.

18. *Ibid.*
19. Heller-Nicholas, 2014, *p. 7.*
20. *Ibid.*, p. 7.
21. *Ibid.*, p. 8.
22. Cynthia Freeland, 2005. "Realist horror," p. 263.
23. Hallam and Marshment, 2000, p. 11.
24. I am referring to the initial bootleg release and not the official 2006 DVD release.
25. Fred Vogel, 2001. "DVD Commentary," Fred Vogel (Director), *August Underground* [DVD].
26. Freeland, 2005, p. 269.
27. *Ibid.*, pp. 264–267.
28. Hill, 2005.
29. Kimber, 2011, p. 102.
30. Hill, 2005.
31. Mikita Brottman, 2004. "Mondo Horror: Carnivalizing the Taboo," Stephen Prince, ed., *The Horror Film*, New Brunswick, NJ: Rutgers University Press, p. 168.
32. *Ibid.*
33. *Ibid.*.
34. Brottman, 2004, p. 169.
35. Fred Vogel, personal communication, email, 2013.
36. See the featurette "'Too real for Comfort': An Outsider's Perspective," *August Underground* DVD.
37. Fred Vogel, "DVD Commentary," Fred Vogel (Director), *August Underground* [DVD].
38. Despite *Mordum*'s fictional representation of violence, the film was still considered so obscene and troubling that Vogel was arrested after he attempted to cross the border into Canada for the Rue Morgue Festival of Fear in 2005.
39. Hill, 2005.
40. Fred Vogel, "DVD Commentary," Fred Vogel (Director), *August Underground* [DVD].
41. Kerekes and Slater, 2016. *Killing for Culture*, p. 75.
42. Neil Jackson, 2016. "Introduction, Shot, Cut, and Slaughtered: The Cultural Mythology of Snuff," p. 16.
43. See thealiveness, 2013. "INTERVIEW (Part 1): Shane Ryan, Filmmaking as Bloodsport," *Fugitive Cinema*, 3 June, https://fugitivecinema.wordpress.com/2013/06/03/interview-part-1-of-2-shane-ryan-filmmaking-as-bloodsport/ (5 September 2016).
44. Robert Fure, 2008. "Exclusive: Director Shane Ryan of Amateur Porn Star Killer Talks Ultra-Low Budget, Great Music and No Excuses," *Film School Rejects*, 1 November, https://filmschoolrejects.com/exclusive-director-shane-ryan-of-amateur-porn-star-killer-talks-ultra-low-budget-great-music-and-37d894822a9c#.f58hnyj7u. (5 September 2016).
45. Maria San Filippo, 2011. "A Cinema of Recession: Micro-Budgeting, Microdrama, and the 'Mumblecore' Movement," *Cineaction* 85, http://www.cineaction.ca/wp-content/uploads/2014/04/issue85sample1.pdf (15 September 2016).
46. Ginette Vincendeau, 2011. "*Fat Girl:* Sisters, Sex, and Sitcom," *The Criterion Collection*, 3 May, https://www.criterion.com/current/posts/495-fat-girl-sisters-sex-and-sitcom (5 September 2016).
47. *Ibid.*
48. *Ibid.*
49. See Laura Mulvey, 1999. "Visual Pleasure and Narrative Cinema," Leo Braudy and Marshall Cohen, eds., *Film Theory and Criticism: Introductory Readings*, New York: Oxford University Press, pp. 833–44; Annette Kuhn and Guy Westwell, 2015. "Imaginary/Symbolic," *A Dictionary of Film Studies*, Oxford: Oxford University Press, [online].
50. Vera Dika, 1987. "The Stalker Film, 1978–81," Gregory A Waller, ed., *American Horrors: Essays on the Modern American Horror Film*, Urbana: University of Illinois Press, p. 88.
51. *Ibid.*
52. *Ibid.*, p. 89.
53. Steve Jones, 2016. "A View to a Kill: Perspectives on Faux-Snuff and Self," p. 291.
54. Black, 2002, p. 8.
55. See also *The Last Horror Movie* (Richards, 2003), in which the killer uses horror film rentals to select his victims.
56. Hallam and Marshment, 2000, p. 128.
57. *Ibid.*, p. 12.
58. Mark Astley, 2016. "Snuff 2.0: Real Death Goes HD Ready," Neil Jackson, et al., eds., *Snuff: Real Death and Screen Media*, p. 159.
59. Black, 2002, p. 111.

Chapter Six

1. Ronny, 2009. "Aiming High with Christies Whiles," *Film Bizarro*, December, http://www.filmbizarro.com/cristiewhiles.php (14 July 2016).

2. Kerekes and Slater, 2016, p. 81.
3. See http://www.musiquemachine.com/articles/articles_template.php?id=225 and Fred Vogel, "DVD Commentary," in Fred Vogel (Director), *August Underground* [DVD].
4. Roger Batty, 2011. "Blood, Guts and Vomit—The *August Underground* Trilogy Interview," *Musique Machine*, 27 April, http://www.musiquemachine.com/articles/articles_template.php?id=225 (14 July 2016).
5. *Ibid.*
6. "Caretaking the Monster: Making of Featurette," 2010. Adam Rehmeier (Director), *The Bunny Game* [Blu-Ray], USA: Death Mountain Productions.
7. Luci Herbert, 2012. "Interview—Bunny Game director Adam Rehmeier."
8. Shane Ryan, "DVD Commentary," in Shane Ryan (Director), *Amateur Porn Star Killer: The Complete Collection* [DVD].
9. Batty, 2011.
10. Mary Strine, Beverley Long and Mary Hopkins, quoted in, Marvin Carlson, 2004. *Performance: A Critical Introduction*, second edition, New York: Routledge, p. 1.
11. Carlson, 2004, p. 1.
12. *Ibid.*, p. 4.
13. *Ibid.*, p. 5.
14. *Ibid.*, p. 5.
15. See Susannah Clapp, 2014. "Hamlet Review—Maxine Peake Is a Delicately Ferocious Prince of Denmark," *The Guardian*, 21 September, https://www.theguardian.com/stage/2014/sep/21/hamlet-maxine-peake-royal-exchange-review-delicate-ferocity (18 September 2016).
16. *Ibid.*, p. 111.
17. Richard Schechner and Sara Brady, 2013. *Performance Studies: An Introduction*, third edition [eBook], New York: Routledge, p. 158.
18. Carlson, 2004, p. 112.
19. Colin Counsell and Laurie Wolf, eds., 2001. *Performance Analysis: An Introductory Course Book*, New York: Routledge, p. 141.
20. Schechner and Brady, 2013, p. 159.
21. Lucifer Valentine, 2011. "*ReGOREgitated Sacrifice*—Director's Commentary," Lucifer Valentine (Director), *The Vomit Gore Trilogy* [DVD].
22. *Ibid.*, p. 31.
23. Carlsson, 2004, p. 6.
24. *Ibid.*, p. 3.
25. Judith Butler, 1993. *Bodies That Matter*, New York: Routledge, p. 95.
26. Judith Butler, 1990. *Gender Trouble: Feminism and the Subversion of identity*, New York: Routledge, p. 173.
27. Schechner and Brady, 2013, p. 152.
28. Elena del Río, 2008. *Deleuze and the Cinemas of Performance: Powers of Affection*, Edinburgh: Edinburgh University Press, p. 5.
29. Río, 2008, p. 6.
30. *Ibid.*
31. Max Hardcore is a pornographic actor, producer and filmmaker. He is known for extreme gonzo pornography and in 2009 was sentenced to 46 months in jail for making and distributing obscene material. Many of his films feature scenes of vomiting and urination. See http://www.tampabay.com/news/courts/criminal/pornographer-sentenced-to-nearly-4-years-in-prison/838305 (20 September, 2016).
32. Río, 2008, p. 31.
33. *Ibid.*, p. 36.
34. Jones, 2013. p. 180
35. Río, 2008, p. 151.
36. Teague, Lewis, 2011. Quoted in, Jason, "Horrorphilia Hot Seat w/ *The Bunny Game* Actress Rodleen Getsic," *Horrorphilia*, 6 January, http://www.horrorphilia.com/horrorphilia-hot-seat-w-the-bunny-game-actress-rodleen-getsic/ (19 September 2016).
37. Erik Piepenburg, 2012. "Testing Horror's Threshold for Pain," *New York Times*, 16 September, http://www.nytimes.com/2012/09/16/movies/rodleen-getsic-in-the-horror-film-the-bunny-game.html (17 September 2016).
38. Río, 2008, p. 151.
39. Luce Irigaray, 1985. *This Sex Which Is Not One*, translated from the French by Catherine Porter with Carolyn Burke, Ithaca, NY: Cornell University Press, p. 184.
40. *Ibid.*, p. 187.
41. Río, 2008, p. 41.
42. *Ibid.*, p. 27.
43. Karolina Lambrou, 2015. "The Traumatised Body of the Performance Artist: Marina Abramović and Franko B.," Laura Colmenero-Chilberg and Ferenc Mújdricza, eds., *Facing Our Darkness: Manifestations of Fear, Horror and Terror*, Oxford: Inter-Disciplinary Press, p. 58.
44. Carlsson, 2004, p. 113.

presentation of the body is important in establishing affinity. In these cases, "the use of the body as a kind of trading currency in face-to-face communication indicates the social relational nature of what is often problematic in communication."[100] That is, the information of either the review, articulations of fan identity or developing and maintaining social connections can be driven via other mediated means (the written blog, podcast or voiceover narration), but the social desires of other community members to "see" who they are interacting with provides more opportunities for and a greater facilitation of connectivity and interaction between members. We have seen earlier from members such as Fangirl Sarah and Criticnic how a spontaneous and intimate interaction can "establish a personal, communicative effect."[101] The videos situate the self as distant via the technological apparatus of the camera and media platform of YouTube. Yet at the same time, the use of the body bridges that distance so that it is accessible to fans that are interested in the subject matter and share similar interests with the maker of the video. Fangirl Sarah regularly makes reference to her physical appearance and in one video "shared" her new puppy with her subscribers so as to interpellate them to both the content of the video and to "Sarah" as both an authentic fan and individual who subscribers may forge an affinity for.

As YouTube has developed from its inception in 2005, there has been ever more stress placed on the axis between community and commerce. The initial videos detailing hardcore horror fandom were exclusively made toward the "gift economy" rather than producing a video primarily for financial incentive and return. Henry Jenkins has discussed how the gift exchange of user-generated videos has been transformed into a monetized form through advertising revenue.[102] The impact on fan communities has been significant in that many have seen the social affiliation between the video producer and the wider social network threatened as the production activities become increasingly geared around commercial values rather than the niche, alternative fan spaces that their particular fandom may have embodied. In terms of hardcore horror, a distinct move toward more professional-looking videos and a constructed narrative format has changed the landscape from personal and casual reflections to more skit-based or gimmicky concepts. Furthermore, the presence of the body has equally been transformed with much more affectation, theatricality and performativity involved in the fan identity and behavior of the channel owner. Jill Killington offers a bridge between the early fan accounts and the more recent sketch show format of the reviews. She still provides affiliative acts through her direct and subjective address to camera, intimate and personal settings such as the bedroom, and an embodied and objectified form of fan distinction through her "alt" persona, insider knowledge and links to her website and Twitter account. The videos are of a high quality and show evidence of post-production in terms of editing and the of her community. Such affiliative acts have created and maintained a distinct and strong community within the dispersive and labile social networks permeating through YouTube. Her channel has 4199 members and her videos on hardcore horror achieve between 2500 and 9000 views with significant comments generated below the line. Although some comments directly relate to her appearance rather than the content of the videos, they are never explicitly sexualized and are always subordinate to commenters who praise the videos and her analysis of the films. Fangirl Sarah also demonstrates an authentic fan identity in that she talks about how Lucifer Valentine contacted her and sent the vomit gore films to her for review.

Similar to xTheGoodBadUnusualx, she also presents the originally released discs on her videos and shows viewers the personalized content such as the hand-drawn pictures. The disclosure of her personal communication with Valentine emphasizes the cultural hierarchy within fandom as well as contributing to an authentic fan identity. The acts also facilitate successful interaction with others so that Fangirl Sarah is able to "assert [her] distinctive character and affirm that they are not anonymous members of an undifferentiated mass."[91] Jill Killington[92] and KHyacinthe[93] also show the clear utilization of affiliative mechanisms and the attainment of cultural capital through the display of authentic and distinctive fan practices. In a social platform such as YouTube which does not necessarily facilitate community-building or collaborative group productions, Jill Killington, KHyacinthe and others such as Goregrl[94] use a personal and spontaneous address to "interest delineated groups of people who wish to participate and remain connected socially"[95] in some way to their channels and social networks. Lange has pointed out how the "public access to intimate moments and the discourse surrounding the video artifacts on the Web allow social boundaries and pre-existing assumptions to be questioned and refashioned."[96] In turn, the personal fan identity can be converted into "more 'public' debates about social identities, ethics and cultural politics."[97] In terms of (hardcore) horror, such explorations of fandom can set in motion larger discussions about the cultural hierarchy of the various social groups and questions of ownership, belonging and authenticity which can recoup marginal fandom practiced by women and/or people of color.

Feelings of affinity surrounding the often personal communication of the fan's experience of a hardcore horror film are exacerbated by the centrality of the body in the communicative function of the fan video. Very few videos comprised of mediated communication include only a voiceover narration and no physical inclusion of a body. These videos, such as The theoasisking[98] and Save Mean,[99] have tended to be less successful both in terms of subscriptions and user views despite the narration carrying as much knowledge and insight about the films as videos using face-to-face communication. The

45. *Ibid.*, p. 113.
46. Lambrou, 2015, p. 58–9.
47. Schechner and Brady, 2013, p. 158–59.
48. Rodleen Getsic, 2013. "My Monsterpiece: An Art Film," *Cine-Excess eJournal*, August, Issue 1, http://www.cine-excess.co.uk/my-monsterpiece.html (19 September, 2016).
49. Jason, 2011b.
50. BBFC News Release, 2011. "The British Board of Film Classification (BBFC) has rejected the DVD THE BUNNY GAME," BBFC, 12th October, http://www.bbfc.co.uk/news releases/2011/10/the-british-board-of-film-classification-bbfc-has-rejected-the-dvd-the-bunny-game/ (20 September 2016).
51. Barrett, Jenny, 2014.
52. *Ibid.*
53. *Ibid.*
54. Río, 2008, p. 30.
55. *Ibid.*, p. 148.

Chapter Seven

1. Iain Robert Smith, 2012. "King of the Porn Spoofs: An Interview with Michael L. Raso," Xavier Mendik, ed., *Peep Shows: Cult Film and the Cine-Erotic*, London: Wallflower Press, p. 135.
2. thealiveness, 2013. "INTERVIEW (Part 1): Shane Ryan, Filmmaking as Bloodsport," (29 July 2016).
3. Lompoc is a city in Santa Barbara County, California, United States.
4. Image Entertainment is a producer and distributor of film and television productions in North America: http://www.watchimage.com/ (2 September 2016).
5. MTI Home Video is a United States-based movie distributor in the direct-to-video market: http://www.mtivideo.com/. Maverick Entertainment specializes in "niche genre films that major studios often overlook. These genres include urban (inspirational, action, comedy), Latino. horror, erotic, and LGBT titles": http://www.maverickentertainment.cc/ (5 September 2016).
6. Cinema Crazed is a website "celebrating film culture and pop culture." See http://cinema-crazed.com/blog/ (5 September 2016).
7. The Tommy Wisseau/Shane Ryan film is *Samurai Cop 2: Deadly Vengeance* (Hantanka, 2016). *The Room* inspired movie is the yet unreleased *The Disaster Artist* (2017) directed by and starring James Franco with Zac Efron, Sharon Stone, and Seth Rogen.
8. Video and video game rental shop in Los Angeles. Noted for its obscure titles and knowledgeable staff. Now closed.
9. "A Boy, a Girl a Camera," Shane Ryan (Director), *Amateur Porn Star Killer: The Complete Collection* [DVD].

Chapter Eight

1. See thread, 2005–2006. "*Slaughtered Vomit Dolls*," 15 November—10 March, *The Mortuary*, http://the-mortuary.com/showthread.php?t=11972andhighlight=lucifer+valentine (12 September 2016).
2. John Fiske, 1992. "The Cultural Economy of Fandom," Lisa A. Lewis, *The Adoring Audience: Fan Culture and Popular Media*, London: Routledge, p. 37.
3. *Ibid.*
4. Both of these websites have now been discontinued.
5. Fiske, 1992, p. 32.
6. Robert Black, 2005. "*Slaughtered Vomit Dolls*," Post #13, 15 November, *The Mortuary* (12 September 2016).
7. Uberdemon, 2005. "*Slaughtered Vomit Dolls*," Post #32, 22 November (12 September 2016).
8. Jeroen de Kloet and Liesbet van Zoonen, 2007. "Fan Culture—Performing Difference," Eoin Devereux, ed., *Media Studies: Key Issues and Debates*, Los Angeles: SAGE, p. 326.
9. Examples can be found from posts #195–#208 on the "*Slaughtered Vomit Dolls*' thread.
10. Uberdemon, 2006. "*Slaughtered Vomit Dolls*," Post #404, 19 February (12 September 2016).
11. See "*Slaughtered Vomit Dolls*' thread. Review posts: Roven #76, Skullatory #77, Robert Black #151 (21 September 2016).
12. Matt Hills, 2005. *The Pleasures of Horror*, London: Continuum, p. 74.
13. Sarah Thornton, 1995. *Club Cultures: Music, Media and Subcultural Capital*, Cambridge: Polity Press, p. 11.
14. For an example see *Rue Morgue* member Kiss Fan, http://kiss-fan.filmaf.com/ owned (7 August 2017).
15. See, Joanne Hollows, 2003. "The Masculinity of Cult," Mark Jancovich, et al., eds.,

Defining Cult Movies: The Cultural Politics of Oppositional Taste, Manchester: Manchester University Press, pp. 35–53.

16. Plasma, 2006. "*Slaughtered Vomit Dolls,*" Post #417, 10 March (21 September 2016).

17. See madmax3000, 2010. "Lucifer Valentine," 7 July, *The Mortuary* (12 September 2016).

18. Amy Lynn Best, 2001. "Too Real for Comfort: An Outsiders Perspective," in Fred Vogel, (Director), *August Underground* [DVD].

19. Mark Jancovich, 2000. "A Real Shocker: Authenticity, Genre and the Struggle for Distinction," *Continuum: Journal of Media and Cultural Studies*, 14,1, p. 25.

20. H.J. de Kloet and E.A. van Zoonen, 2011. "Fan Culture—Performing Difference," Eoin Devereux, ed., *Media Studies: Key Issues and Debates*, p. 323.

21. thenewboss, 2005. "*August Underground* DVD," Post #21, 14 September, *The Mortuary*, http://the-mortuary.com/showthread.php?t=10534andhighlight=august+underground (8 August 2016); El Capitan, 2005. "*August Underground* DVD," Post #12, 9 December (8 August 2016).

22. Robert Black, 2004. "*August Underground*," #43, 13 May, *The Mortuary*, http://the-mortuary.com/showthread.php?t=3547andhighlight=august+underground (21 September 2016).

23. Fiske, 1992, p. 42.

24. de Kloet and van Zoonen, 2011, p. 326.

25. Church, 2009, p. 346.

26. Jancovich, 2000, p. 24.

27. Alan Bennett and Keith Kahn-Harris, 2004. "Introduction," Alan Bennett and Keith Kahn-Harris, eds., *After Subculture: Critical Studies in Contemporary Youth Culture*, Basingstoke: Palgrave Macmillan, p. 2.

28. Hills, 2005, p. 74.

29. Thornton, 1995.

30. The Gore-met, 2004. "*August Underground*," Post #14, 7 April (21 September 2016).

31. This is the full quotation used on the *Mordum* DVD and cited in Chapter 2.

32. The Gore-met, 2007. "*August Underground: Penance (2007),*" Post #113, 16 May, *The Mortuary*, http://the-mortuary.com/showthread.php?t=17877andpage=3andhighlight=august+underground (21 September 2016).

33. Two relevant examples of connoisseurship in practice would be Gore-met's member profile from *Rue Morgue*: http://www.themortuary.com/member.php?u=147 and Wonderlust's member profile from *Bloody Disgusting*: http://bloody-disgusting.com/legacy/member.php?u=108160 (10 October 2015).

34. *Doctor Butcher M.D.* is the American title. In the UK and Europe it was titled *Zombie Holocaust*.

35. Thornton, 1995, p. 15.

36. Hills, 2005, pp. 71–90.

37. Jancovich, 2000, p. 33.

38. For example see, Michael Scrutchin, 2002. "August Underground," *Flipside Archive*, 3 September, http://www.flipsidearchive.com/augustunderground.html; Daydreamer, 2012. "DVD Review: August Underground (Video 2001)," *Daydreamer—The Playground*, 17 April, http://daydreamer-theplayground.blogspot.se/2012/04/dvd-review-august-underground-video.html (Both 12 September 2016).

39. Bennett and Kahn-Harris, 2004, p. 15.

40. Chaney, David, 2004. "Fragmented Culture and Subcultures," in Bennett and Kahn-Harris, 2004, p. 36.

41. *Ibid.*, p. 37.

42. Church, 2009, p. 348.

43. Hills, 2005, p. 74.

44. Jancovich, 2000, p. 32.

45. Atomagevampire, 2004. "*August Underground*," Post #13, 27 February (21 September 2016).

46. brainbug, 2003. "*August Underground (2002),*" Post #1, 10 September, *The Mortuary*, http://the-mortuary.com/showthread.php?t=2311andhighlight=august+underground (21 September 2016).

47. The Gore-met, "*August Underground*," #14.

48. Nekromantik, 2004. "*August Underground*," Post #15, 7 April (21 September 2016).

49. The Gore-met, 2003. "*August Underground (2002),*" Post #6, 12 September (21 September 2016).

50. Stuart Feedback Andrews, 2004. "*August Underground*," Post #16, 7 April (21 September 2016).

51. Hills, 2005, p. 74.

52. Julian Hoxter, 2000. "Taking Possession: Cult Learning in *The Exorcist*," Xavier Mendik and Harper Graeme, eds., *Unruly Pleasures*, Guildford: FAB Press, p. 185.

53. Matt, 2004. "The Sickest Movie Ever

Made," Post #47, 5 November, *The Mortuary*, http://the-mortuary.com/showthread.php?t=6120andpage=7andhighlight=the+sickest+movie+ever+made (21 September 2016).

54. AbraCadaver, 2006. "The Sickest Movie Ever Made," Post #371, 26 October (21 September 2016).

55. Hills, 2005, p. 76.

56. Jovanka Vuckovic, 2004. "The Sickest Movie Ever Made," Post #10, 5 November (21 September 2016).

57. brainbug, 2005. "*August Underground's Mordum* (2003)," Post #19, 30 September, *The Mortuary*, http://the-mortuary.com/showthread.php?t=5034andhighlight=august+underground (21 September 2016).

58. Cited in Hills, 2005. They are: Goran Bolin, 2000. "Film Swapping in the Public Sphere: Youth Audiences and Alternative Cultural Publicities," *Javnost: The Public*, 7:2, pp. 57–74; and David Sanjek, 2000. "Fans' Notes: The Horror Film Fanzine," Ken Gelder, ed., *The Horror Reader*, London: Routledge, pp. 314–23.

59. Robo Cack, 2005. "*August Underground DVD*," Post #49, 27 September (21 September 2016).

60. Brigid Cherry, 1999. "Refusing to Refuse to Look: Female Viewers of the Horror Film," Melvyn Stokes and Richard Maltby, eds., *Identifying Hollywood's Audiences: Cultural Identity and the Movies*, London: BFI Publishing, pp. 195.

61. Hills, 2005, p. 76.

62. The Forum site has now been revamped and updated and as yet an archive thread has not been included. For details see, http://bloody-disgusting.com/forums/ (21 September 2016).

63. Hills, 2009, p. 89.

64. See Pelle Snickars and Patrick Vonderau, 2009. "Introduction," Pelle Snickars and Patrick Vonderau, eds., *The YouTube Reader*, Stockholm: National Library of Sweden.

65. Pelle, and Vonderau, 2009. "Introduction," *Ibid.*, p. 10.

66. *Ibid.*, p. 18.

67. Fiske, 1992, p. 39.

68. Bonnie A. Nardi, 2005. "Beyond Bandwidth: Dimensions of Connection in Interpersonal Communication," *Computer-Supported Cooperative Work* No. 14, pp. 347–354. Quoted in Patricia G. Lange, 2009, p. 71.

69. *Ibid.*, p. 71.

70. Lange, 2009, p. 83.

71. *Ibid.*, p. 84.

72. Savini1979's Channel, https://www.youtube.com/channel/UCYy_b_Qf2oiLNaQI6qP4HCg (21 September 2016).

73. Lange, 2009, p. 79.

74. Savini1979, 2010. "Savini1979's Horror Reviews Episode 15 *August Underground*," 13 January, *YouTube*, https://www.youtube.com/watch?v=scHi_ZnZ-6Eandlist=PLLSuQFaPbVeQCpV-g9FbZInW0c72rcT0_andindex=1 (21 September 2016).

75. See Thornton for a discussion on how subcultural capital can be both objectified and embodied. Thornton, 1995, pp. 11–12.

76. VeryCrudelyYours, 2010. "VeryCrudelyYours Reviews *Slaughtered Vomit Dolls*," 11 April, *YouTube*, https://www.youtube.com/watch?v=opVuswjqRWoandlist=PLLSuQFaPbVeSsvu4sa5qFVUcHncjtcGwAandindex=1 (21 September 2016).

77. CriticNic, 2010. "Week 9—CriticNic Reviews *Slaughtered Vomit Dolls*," 25 April, *YouTube*, https://www.youtube.com/watch?v=imIZ0Tl_BN8andlist=PLLSuQFaPbVeSsvu4sa5qFVUcHncjtcGwAandindex=3 (21 September 2016).

78. Mrparka, 2010Mrparka Review's "*ReGOREgitated Sacrifice*,'" 12 May, *YouTube*, https://www.youtube.com/watch?v=ZvDPpinaroQandlist=PLLSuQFaPbVeSsvu4sa5qFVUcHncjtcGwAandindex=4 (21 September 2016).

79. CriticNic, "Week 9—CriticNic reviews *Slaughtered Vomit Dolls*."

80. Snickars and Vonderau, 2009, p. 12.

81. Jancovich, 2002, p. 308.

82. xTheGoodBadUnusualx, 2012. "The Films of Lucifer Valentine," 18 August, *YouTube*, https://www.youtube.com/watch?v=6mUF3rZhoNIandlist=PLLSuQFaPbVeSsvu4sa5qFVUcHncjtcGwAandindex=19 (21 September 2016).

83. *Ibid.*

84. Jancovich, 2002, p. 319.

85. Janet Hollows, 2003, p. 46.

86. *Ibid.*

87. Remy Saisselin, quoted in Hollows, 2003, p. 46

88. Hollows, 2003, p. 46.

89. Brigid Cherry, 1999. "Refusing to Refuse to Look," pp. 187–203.

90. Fangirl Sarah's Channel: Gacktfangirl 2323 https://www.youtube.com/channel/UC66puntVbA4xXtL8f3-TazA (21 September 2016).
91. Thornton, 1995, p. 16
92. Jill Killington's Channel: https://www.youtube.com/user/TheJillkill (21 September 2016).
93. KHyacinthe's Channel: https://www.youtube.com/user/KHyacinthe (21 September 2016).
94. Goregrl's Channel: https://www.youtube.com/user/ShawnTizzle17 (21 September 2016).
95. Lange, 2009, p. 73.
96. Lange, Patricia, G. 2007. "The Vulnerable Video Blogger: Promoting Social Change Through Intimacy," *The Scholar and Feminist Online*, Volume 5, Number 2, http://sfonline.barnard.edu/blogs/lange_01.htm (13 September 2016).
97. Jean E. Burgess and John A. Banks, 2010. "User-Created Content and Online Social Networks," in Stuart D. Cunningham and Graeme Turner, eds., *The Media and Communications in Australia*, third edition, St. Leonard's: Allen and Unwin, p. 535.
98. theoasisking's Channel: https://www.youtube.com/user/theoasisking (21 September 2016).
99. Save Mean's Channel: https://www.youtube.com/channel/UCML_peD1_9hzrGr9ct66qzQ (21 September 2016).
100. Nardi, 2005, p. 115.
101. Lange, 2009, p. 79.
102. Henry, Jenkins, 2006. "Interactive Audiences? The "Collective Intelligence" of Media Fans," Henry Jenkins, *Fans, Bloggers and Gamers: Exploring Participatory Culture*, New York: NYU Press, pp. 134–151.
103. Kathrin Peters and Andrea Seier, 2009. "Home Dance: Mediacy and Aesthetics of the Self on YouTube," Snickars and Vonderau, eds., p. 188.
104. Emer Prevost's Channel: https://www.youtube.com/user/Hellsing920 (21 September 2016).
105. Fiske, 1992, pp. 34–37.
106. Emer Prevost, 2011. "'*August Underground's Mordum*' Reaction and Review," 21 April, *YouTube*, https://www.youtube.com/watch?v=6DuGAJCTFXsandlist=PLLSuQFaPbVeQCpV-g9FbZInW0c72rcT0_andindex=7 (21 September 2016).
107. Emer Prevost, 2011. "'Slaughtered Vomit Dolls' Reaction and Review," 28 June, YouTube, https://www.youtube.com/watch?v=RthbTQTplGMandindex=13andlist=PLLSuQFaPbVeSsvu4sa5qFVUcHncjtcGwA (21 September 2016).
108. Smoosh are an American web-based comedy duo that enjoyed remarkable popularity on YouTube with 22 million subscribers and 5,8 billion site visits. See http://smosh.wikia.com/wiki/Smosh_Wiki. https://en.wikipedia.org/wiki/Smosh#YouTube_success:_2006.E2.80.932012 (21 September 2016).
109. Diamanda Hagen's Channel: https://www.youtube.com/user/DiamandaHagan. Nyx Fears' Channel: https://www.youtube.com/user/BrutalMovieReview. Evil Steve at the Movies/GalloogaJoeProductions' Channel: https://www.youtube.com/user/balefulwerewolf (21 September 2016).
110. Dick Hebdige, 1979. *Subculture: The Meaning of Style*, London: Routledge, p. 2
111. Fiske, 1992, p. 33.

Conclusion

1. Dark Mark, 2012. "*August Underground's Mordum* (2003)," Post #65, 5 January (21 September 2016).
2. Jones, 2013, p. 177.
3. Kerekes and Slater, 2016, p. 588.
4. Johnny Walker, quoted in, *ibid.*, p. 589.
5. Thomas Watson, quoted in, *ibid.*, 590.
6. Steve Del Diablo, 2015. "Exclusive Interview with Director and Special FX Magician MARCUS KOCH from Florida," *The Daily Horror*, 29 January, http://www.thedailyhorror.com/newsblog/2015/01/29/exclusive-interview-with-director-and-special-fx-magician-marcus-koch-from-florida/. 29 September 2016.
7. Shane Ryan, personal communication, email, 10 July 2016.
8. Alexandra Heller-Nicholas and Jack Sargeant, 2016. "Introduction: American Extreme," *Senses of Cinema*, Issue 80, September, http://sensesofcinema.com/2016/american-extreme/introduction-american-extreme/ (29 September 2016).
9. *Ibid.*

Bibliography

Adam, Rachel. 2001. *Sideshow USA: Freaks and the American Cultural Imagination.* Chicago: University of Chicago Press.
Althusser, Louis. 2001. *Lenin and Philosophy and Other Essays.* Translated from the French by Ben Brewster. New York: Monthly Review Press.
Anderson, Donald L. 2013. "How the Horror Film Broke Its Promise: Hyperreal Horror and Ruggero Deodato's *Cannibal Holocaust*." *Horror Studies.* Vol. 4, Issue 1. pp. 109–126.
Aston, James, and John Walliss, eds. 2013. *To See the Saw Movies: Essays on Torture Porn and Post-9/11 Horror.* Jefferson, NC: McFarland.
Balio, Tino. 1995. *Grand Design: Hollywood as a Modern Business Enterprise, 1930–1939.* Berkeley: University of California Press.
Barrett, Jenny. 2014. "More than Just a Game: Breaking the Rules in the *Bunny Game*." *Cine-Excess EJournal.* Issue 1. http://www.cine-excess.co.uk/more-than-just-a-game.html (3 May 2016).
Batty, Roger. 2011. "Blood, Guts and Vomit—The *August Underground* Trilogy Interview." *Musique Machine.* 27 April. http://www.musiquemachine.com/articles/articles_template.php?id=225 (14 July 2016).
Bennett, Alan, and Keith Kahn-Harris, eds. 2004. *After Subculture: Critical Studies in Contemporary Youth Culture.* Basingstoke: Palgrave Macmillan.
Benshoff, Harry. 2000. "Blaxploitation Horror Films: Generic Reappropriation or Reinscription?." *Cinema Journal.* Vol. 39, No. 2. Winter. pp. 31–50.
Biodrowski, Steven. 2008. "Salo (1975)—Borderland Review." *Cinefantastique.* 27 August. http://cinefantastiqueonline.com/2008/08/borderland-salo-1975/ (10 July 2017).
Bitel, Anton. 2015. "Review: *Hate Crime* (2013)." *The Horror Show.* 27 May. http://blog.thehorrorshow.tv/review-hate-crime-2013/ (11 May 2016).
_____. 2017. "Is This the Most Extreme 108 Minutes in the History of Japanese Cinema?." *Little White Lies.* 3 February. http://lwlies.com/articles/destruction-babies-extreme-japanese-cinema/ (10 July 2017).
Black, Joel. 2002. *The Reality Effect: Film Culture and the Graphic Imperative.* New York: Routledge.
Blake, Linnie. 2008. *The Wounds of Nations: Horror Cinema, Historical Trauma and National Identity.* Manchester: Manchester University Press.
_____, and Xavier Aldana Reyes, eds. 2015. *Digital Horror: Haunted Technologies, Network Panic and the Found Footage Phenomenon.* London: I.B. Tauris.
Braudy, Leo, Gerald Mast and Marshal Cohen, eds. 1992. *Film Theory and Criticism: Introductory Readings.* Fourth Edition. New York: Oxford University Press.

Bibliography

British Board of Film Classification (BBFC). http://www.bbfc.co.uk/ (4 September 2017).
Brody, Richard. 2016. "Salò, or the 120 Days of Sodom." *The New Yorker*. 29 April. http://www.newyorker.com/goings-on-about-town/movies/salo-or-the-120-days-of-sodom (10 July 2017).
Brottman, Mikita. 1997. *Offensive Films: Toward an Anthropology of Cinéma Vomitif*. Westport, CT: Greenwood.
———. 1998. *Meat Is Murder!: An Illustrated Guide to Cannibal Culture*. London: Creation.
———. 2004. "Mondo Horror: Carnivalizing the Taboo." Prince, Stephen. ed. *The Horror Film*. New Brunswick, NJ: Rutgers University Press. pp. 167–188.
Brottman, Mikita, and John Mercer. 2014. "Subverting Senses, Circumventing Limits: An Introduction to the Launch Issue of the Cine-Excess Ejournal." *Cine-Excess EJournal*. Issue 1. http://www.cine-excess.co.uk/subverting-senses-circumventing-limits.html.
Butler, Judith. 1990. *Gender Trouble: Feminism and the Subversion of Identity*. New York: Routledge.
———. 1993. *Bodies That Matter*. New York: Routledge.
Canby, Vincent. 1977. "Film Festival: 'Salo' Is Disturbing…." *New York Times*. 1 October. http://www.nytimes.com/movie/review?res=9904E7D8163AE334BC4953DFB667838C669EDE (10 July 2017).
Carlson, Marvin. 2004. *Performance: A Critical Introduction*. Second Edition. New York: Routledge.
Casta, Ray. 2011. "Melancholie Der Engel—Shock DVD Entertainment." *Severed Cinema*. 11 April. http://severed-cinema.com/m-reviews/melancholie-der-engel-shock-dvd-entertainment (13 July 2017).
Cherry, Brigid. 1999. "Refusing to Refuse to Look: Female Viewers of the Horror Film." Melvyn Stokes and Richard Maltby, eds. *Identifying Hollywood's Audiences: Cultural Identity and the Movies*. London: BFI Publishing. pp. 187–203.
Choi, Jinhee, and Mitsuyo Wada-Marciano. 2009. *Horror to the Extreme: Changing Boundaries in Asian Cinema*. Hong Kong: Hong Kong University Press.
Church, David. 2009. "Of Manias, Shit, and Blood: The Reception of *Salò* as a "Sick Film."" *Participations*. Vol. 6, No. 2. pp. 340–372.
Cline, John, and Robert G. Weiner, eds. 2010. *From the Arthouse to the Grindhouse: Highbrow and Lowbrow Transgression in Cinema's First Century*. Lanham, MD: Scarecrow.
Clover, Carol. 1992. *Men, Women and Chainsaws: Gender in the Modern Horror Film*. Princeton, NJ: Princeton University Press.
Colmenero-Chilberg, Laura, and Ferenc Mújdricza, eds. 2015. *Facing Our Darkness: Manifestations of Fear, Horror and Terror*. Oxford: Inter-Disciplinary Press.
Conrich, Ian, ed. 2010. *Horror Zone*. London: I.B. Tauris.
Copp, Andy. 2012. "Talking to THE BUNNY GAME Director [Sic] Adam Rehmeier." *Exploitation Nation*. 29 June. http://exploitationnation2.blogspot.co.uk/2012/06/talking-to-bunny-game-directer-adam.html?zx=233721ecbebb95f3 (5 September 2016).
Counsell, Colin, and Laurie Wolf, eds. 2001. *Performance Analysis: An Introductory Course Book*. New York: Routledge.
Craddock, John. 2011. "Shane Ryan." *Horror Fan Reviews*. http://horrorfansreview.tripod.com/shane-ryan-interview.htmll (11 May 2016).
Crane, Jonathan. 2004. "Scraping Bottom: Splatter and the Herschell Gordon Lewis Oeuvre." Prince, Stephen. Ed. *The Horror Film*. Piscataway, NJ: Rutgers University Press. pp. 150–166.
Creed, Barbara. 1986. "Horror and the Monstrous-Feminine: An Imaginary Abjection." *Screen*. Vol. 27, No. 1. pp. 44–71.
Crossman, Brenda. 2007. *Sexual Citizens: The Legal and Cultural Regulation of Sex and Belonging*. Redwood City, CA: Stanford University Press.

Cunningham, Stuart D., and Graeme Turner, eds. 2010. *Nardi3rd Edition*. St. Leonard's: Allen & Unwin

Del Diablo, Steve. 2015. "Exclusive Interview with Director and Special FX Magician Marcus Koch from Florida." *The Daily Horror*. 29 January. http://www.thedailyhorror.com/newsblog/2015/01/29/exclusive-interview-with-director-and-special-fx-magician-marcus-koch-from-florida/. 29 September 2016.

Devereux, Eoin, ed. 2011. *Media Studies: Key Issues and Debates*. Los Angeles: SAGE.

Dika, Vera. 1987. "The Stalker Film, 1978–81." Waller, Gregory. A. Ed. *American Horrors: Essays on the Modern American Horror Film*. Urbana: University of Illinois Press. pp. 86–101.

Edelstein, David. 2006. "Now Playing at Your Local Multiplex: Torture Porn." *New York Times*, 28 January. http://nymag.com/movies/features/15622/ (3 May 2016).

Everleth, Mark. 2012. "Movie Review: *The Bunny Game*." *Underground Film Journal*. March 26. http://www.undergroundfilmjournal.com/movie-review-the-bunny-game/ (5 September 2016).

"Extreme Cinema: The 25 Most Disturbing Films of All Time." 2010. *Horror News*. 23 August. http://horrornews.net/6520/extreme-cinema-top-25-most-disturbing-films-of-all-time-part1/ (14 September 2016).

Featherstone, Mark, and Beth Johnson. 2012. "'Ovo Je Srbija': The Horror of the National Thing in *A Serbian Film*." *Journal for Cultural Research*. Vol. 16, No. 1. pp. 63–79.

Felton, Jude. 2012. "Q&A with the *Bunny Game*'s Adam Rehmeier." *The Lair of Filth*. 21 August. http://www.thelairoffilth.com/2012/08/q-with-bunny-games-adam-rehmeier.html (26 August 2016).

Filippo, Maria San. 2011. "A Cinema of Recession: Micro-Budgeting, Microdrama, and the "Mumblecore" Movement." *Cineaction* 85. http://www.cineaction.ca/wp-content/uploads/2014/04/issue85sample1.pdf (15 September 2016).

Fiske, John. 1992. "The Cultural Economy of Fandom." Lisa A. Lewis, ed. *The Adoring Audience: Fan Culture and Popular Media*. London: Routledge. pp. 30–49.

Freeland, Cynthia. 2005. "Realist Horror." Thomas E. Wartenberg and Angela Curran, eds. *The Philosophy of Film: Introductory Text and Reading*. Oxford: Oxford University Press. pp. 260–269.

Frey, Matt. 2016. *Extreme Cinema: The Transgressive Rhetoric of Today's Art Film Culture*. New Brunswick, NJ: Rutgers University Press.

Friedman, David, and Don De Nevi. 1990. *A Youth in Babylon: Confessions of a Trash-Film King*. Amherst, NY: Prometheus.

Fure, Robert. 2008. "Exclusive: Director Shane Ryan of Amateur Porn Star Killer Talks Ultra-Low Budget, Great Music and No Excuses." *Film School Rejects*. 1 November. https://filmschoolrejects.com/exclusive-director-shane-ryan-of-amateur-porn-star-killer-talks-ultra-low-budget-great-music-and-37d894822a9c#.f58hnyj7u (5 September 2016).

Gale, Eliza. 2012. "An Inteview [Sic] with Actor/Director/Writer Shane Ryan." *elizagalesinterviews*. 21 June. https://elizagalesinterviews.com/2012/06/21/in-inteview-with-actor-directorwriter-shane-ryan/ (11 May 2016).

Gere, F. 1981. "Cannibal Holocaust" (Review). *Cahier du Cinema*. 326: 63 July/August.

Getsic, Rodleen. 2013. "My Monsterpiece: An Art Film." *Cine-Excess EJournal*. Issue 1. August. http://www.cine-excess.co.uk/my-monsterpiece.html (19 September, 2016).

Goodall, Mark. 2006. *Sweet and Savage: The World Through the Shockumentary Film Lens*. London: Headpress.

Greene, Naomi. 1992. *Pier Paolo Pasolini: Cinema as Heresy*. Princeton, NJ: Princeton University Press.

_____. "Salò: Breaking the Rules." *Criterion*. 4 October. https://www.criterion.com/current/posts/511-salo-breaking-the-rules (10 July 2017).

Grey, Ian. 2001. "Blood Feast: *Cannibal Holocaust* Returns and Here's Hoping You've Finished Your Lunch." *Baltimore City Paper*. August 29.

Grønstad, Asbjørn. 2012. *Screening the Unwatchable: Spaces of Negation in Post-Millennial Art Cinema*. Basingstoke: Palgrave Macmillan.

Hale, Mike. 2010. "Ending a Lethal Game and All Its Gory Details." *New York Times*, 29 October. http://www.nytimes.com/2010/10/30/movies/30saw.html?_r=0 (3 May 2016).

Hallam, Julia, and Margaret Marshment. 2000. *Realism and Popular Cinema*. Manchester: Manchester University Press.

Hartlaub, Peter. 2006. "*Saw III* Could Be Breaking Point for Many Fans." *San Francisco Chronicle*. 29 October. http://www.sfgate.com/bayarea/article/Saw-III-could-be-breaking-point-for-many-fans-2467514.php (3 May 2016).

Hawkins, Joan. 2009 "Culture Wars: Some New Trends in Art Horror." *Jump Cut*. Vol. 51. Spring. http://www.ejumpcut.org/archive/jc51.2009/artHorror/index.html (3 May 2016).

Hebdige, Dick. 1979. *Subculture: The Meaning of Style*. London: Routledge.

Heller-Nicholas, Alexandra. 2014. *Found Footage Horror Films: Fear and the Appearance of Reality*. Jefferson, NC: McFarland.

Heller-Nicholas, Alexandra, and Jack Sargeant. 2016. "Introduction: American Extreme." *Senses of Cinema*. Issue 80. September. http://sensesofcinema.com/2016/american-extreme/introduction-american-extreme/ (29 September 2016).

Herbert, Luci. 2012. "Interview—Bunny Game Director Adam Rehmeier." *Ave Noctum*. 16 July. http://www.avenoctum.com/2012/07/interview-bunny-game-director-adam-rehmeier/ (14 July 2016).

Hichethier, Knut. 1993. "Report Regarding the Feature Film Nekromantik 2 (1993)." *Nekromantik 2 Anatomy of Desire Booklet*. London: Arrow Video. pp. 49–59.

Hill, Matthew Dean. 2005. "Underground: Twenty Questions with Fred Vogel—Director of *August Underground* and *August Underground's Mordum*." *Atrocities Cinema*. October. http://www.atrocitiescinema.com/interviews/fredvogel.html (10 May 2016).

Hills, Matt. 2005. *The Pleasures of Horror*. London: Continuum.

Hoenigman, David. 2009. "If You Want Blood (You've Got It): An Interview with Koji Shiraishi." *3: AM Magazine*. 29 November. http://www.3ammagazine.com/3am/if-you-want-blood-you%E2%80%99ve-got-it-an-interview-with-koji-shiraishi/ (10 July 2017).

Hollows, Janet. 2003. "The Masculinity of Cult." Mark Jancovich, Antonio Lazaro-Reboll, Julian Stringer and Andy Willis, eds. *Defining Cult Movies: The Cultural Politics of Oppositional Taste*. Manchester: Manchester University Press. pp. 35–53.

Horeck, Tanya, and Tina Kendall. 2011. *The New Extremism in Cinema: From France to Europe*. Edinburgh: Edinburgh University Press.

Howell, Peter. 2009. "*The Last House on the Left*: Gruesome and Gratuitous." *The Toronto Star*. 13 March. http://www.thestar.com/news/2009/03/13/the_last_house_on_the_left_gruesome_and_gratuitous.html (3 May 2016).

Irigaray, Luce. 1985. *This Sex Which Is Not One*. Translated from the French by Catherine Porter with Carolyn Burke. Ithaca, NY: Cornell University Press.

Jackson, Neil, Shaun Kimber, Johnny Walker and Thomas Joseph Watson, eds. 2016. *Snuff: Real Death and Screen Media*. London: Bloomsbury.

Jameson, Fredric. 1992. "Postmodernism and Consumer Society." Peter Brooker, ed. *Modernism/Postmodernism*. New York: Longman.

Jancovich, Mark. 2000. "A Real Shocker: Authenticity, Genre and the Struggle for Distinction." *Continuum: Journal of Media and Cultural Studies*. Vol. 14, No.1. pp. 23–35.

_____. 2002. "Cult Fictions: Cult Movies, Subcultural Capital and the Production of

Cultural Distinctions." *Continuum: Journal of Media and Cultural Studies*. Vol. 16, No. 2. pp. 306–322.
Jancovich, Mark, et al., eds. 2003. *Defining Cult Movies: The Cultural Politics of Oppositional Taste*, Manchester: Manchester University Press.
Jason. 2011a. "Horrorphilia Podcast #55 W/ Adam Rehmeier Director of the *Bunny Game*: Reviews of *Valhalla Rising, Pin, Macabre* and *Seven Days*." *Horrorphilia*. 31 January. http://www.horrorphilia.com/horrorphilia-podcast-55-w-adam-rehmeier-director-of-the-bunny-game-reviews-of-valhalla-rising-pin-macabre-and-seven-days/ (5 September 2016).
_____. 2011b. "Horrorphilia Hot Seat w/ the *Bunny Game* Actress Rodleen Getsic." *Horrorphilia*. 6 January. http://www.horrorphilia.com/horrorphilia-hot-seat-w-the-bunny-game-actress-rodleen-getsic/ (19 September 2016).
Jenkins, Henry. 2006. *Fans, Bloggers and Gamers: Exploring Participatory Culture*. New York: NYU Press.
Jenkins, Keith. 1995. *On "What Is History?": From Carr and Elton to Rorty and White*. London: Routledge.
Johanson, Greigh. 2012. "Lucifer Valentine." *Goregasmic Cinema*. September. http://goregasmiccinema.blogspot.co.uk/2012/09/lucifer-valentine.html (26 August 2016).
Jones, Alan. 2010. "The Nightmare of Truth." *A Serbian Film Blu-Ray Sleeve Notes*. London: Revolver Entertainment.
Jones, Steve. 2010. "Time Is Wasting: Con/Sequence and S/Pace in the *Saw* Series." *Horror Studies*. Vol. 1, No. 2. pp. 225–240.
_____. 2013. *Torture Porn: Popular Horror After Saw*. Basingstoke: Palgrave Macmillan.
_____. 2016. "A View to a Kill" Perspectives on Faux-Snuff and Self." Neil Jackson, et al., eds. *Snuff: Real Death and Screen Media*. London: Bloomsbury.
Kavka, Misha. 2016. "The Affective Reality of Snuff." Neil Jackson, et al., eds. *Snuff: Real Death and Screen Media*. London: Bloomsbury. pp. 47–61.
Kerekes, David. 1994. *Sex Murder Art: The Films of Jörg Buttgereit*. London: Headpress.
Kerekes, David, and David Slater. 2016. *Killing for Culture. from Edison to Isis: A New History of Death on Film*. London: Headpress.
Kimber, Shaun. 2011. *Henry: Portrait of a Serial Killer*. Basingstoke: Palgrave Macmillan.
_____. 2014. "Transgressive Edge Play and *Srpski Film/A Serbian Film*." *Horror Studies*. Vol. 5, No. 1. pp. 107–126.
King, Geoff, ed. 2005. *The Spectacle of the Real: From Hollywood to Reality TV and Beyond*. Bristol: Intellect.
Kleinhans, Chuck. 2008. "Horror's New Terrain." *Jump Cut*. Vol. 50. Spring. http://www.ejumpcut.org/archive/jc50.2008/horrorintro/index.html (3 May 2016).
_____. 2009. "Cross-Cultural Disgust: Some Problems in the Analysis of Contemporary Horror Cinema." *Jump Cut*. Vol. 51. Spring. http://www.ejumpcut.org/archive/jc51.2009/crosscultHorror/index.html (4 September 2017).
Kristeva, Julia. 1982. *Powers of Horror: An Essay on Abjection*. New York: Columbia University Press.
Kuhn, Annette, and Guy Westwell. 2015. "Extreme Cinema (Ordeal Cinema)." *A Dictionary of Film Studies*. Oxford: Oxford University Press.
Kupper, Oliver Maxwell. 2011. "*The Bunny Game*: An Interview with Adam Rehmeier." *Autre*. 21 October. http://www.pasunautre.com/interviewsmain/2011/10/21/interview-the-bunny-game (15 September 2016).
Lambrou, Karolina. 2015. "The Traumatised Body of the Performance Artist: Marina Abramović and Franko B." Laura Colmenero-Chilberg and Ferenc Mújdricza, eds. *Facing Our Darkness: Manifestations of Fear, Horror and Terror*. Oxford: Inter-Disciplinary Press. pp. 57–64.

Lange, Patricia. 2007. "The Vulnerable Video Blogger: Promoting Social Change Through Intimacy." *The Scholar and Feminist Online*. Volume 5. Number 2. http://sfonline.bar nard.edu/blogs/lange_01.htm (13 September 2016).

_____. 2009. "Videos of Affinity on YouTube." Pelle Snickars and Patrick Vonderau, eds. *The YouTube Reader*. Stockholm: National Library of Sweden. pp. 70–88.

Lazaro-Reboll, Antonio. 2012. *Spanish Horror Film*. Edinburgh: Edinburgh University Press.

Lewis, Herschell, Gordon (Director). 2000. *Blood Feast* [DVD]. USA: Something Weird Video.

magGot, Jesus. 2010. "Lucifer Valentine." *Maggot Films*. 7 October. http://maggotfilms.com/2010/10/07/jesus-interviews-lucifer-valentine/ (14 July 2016).

Matt. 2015. "Interview with Lucifer Valentine…." *Matts Rotten Review*. 6 August. http://mattsrottenreviews.tumblr.com/post/126006603043/interview-with-lucifer-valentine (26 August 2016).

McRoy, Jay. 2008. *Nightmare Japan: Contemporary Japanese Horror Cinema*. Amsterdam: Rodopi.

Mendik, Xavier, ed. 2012. *Peep Shows: Cult Film and the Cine-Erotic*. London: Wallflower Press.

Mendik, Xavier, and Steven Jay Schneider. 2002. *Underground U.S.A.: Filmmaking Beyond the Hollywood Canon*. London: Wallflower.

Meredith, Jason. 2012. "*The Bunny Game*." *Cinezilla*. 6 January. http://cinezilla.blogspot.co.uk/2012/01/bunny-game.html (15 September 2016).

Mulvey, Laura. 1999. "Visual Pleasure and Narrative Cinema." Leo Braudy and Marshall Cohen, eds. *Film Theory and Criticism: Introductory Readings*. New York: Oxford University Press. pp. 833–44.

Musser, Charles. 1994. *The Emergence of Cinema: The American Screen to 1907*. Berkeley: University of California Press.

Nardi, Bonnie A. 2005. "Beyond Bandwidth: Dimensions of Connection in Interpersonal Communication." *Computer-Supported Cooperative Work* no. 14. pp. 347–354.

Necromagikal. 2011. "Interview: Lucifer Valentine (*Slow Torture Puke Chamber, ReGORGEgitated* [Sic] *Sacrifice*)." *Horror News*. 10 October. http://horrornews.net/42170/interview-lucifer-valentine-slow-torture-puke-chamber-regorgegitated-sacrifice/ (14 July 2016).

Palacios, Jorge. 2015. "NSFW: Interview with Filmmaker Eric Stanze." *Dirge Magazine*. 21 July. http://www.dirgemag.com/interview-the-dark-stylings-of-eric-stanze/ (26 August 2016).

Peirse, Alison. 2013. *After Dracula: The 1930s Horror Film*. London: I.B. Tauris.

Philips, Nickie. 2016. *Beyond Blurred Lines: Rape Culture in Popular Media*. Lanham, MD: Rowman & Littlefield.

"Pictures Painted in Hell—My Interview with Lucifer Valentine." 2012. *Video Star*. 5 April. http://videostarforever.blogspot.co.uk/2012/04/quality-time-with-lucifer-valentine.html (26 August 2012).

Piepenburg, Erik. 2012. "Testing Horror's Threshold for Pain." *New York Times*. 16 September. http://www.nytimes.com/2012/09/16/movies/rodleen-getsic-in-the-horror-film-the-bunny-game.html (17 September 2016).

Pinedo, Isabell Cristina. 1997. *Recreational Terror: Women and the Pleasures of Horror Film Viewing*. Albany: State University of New York Press.

_____. 2004. "Postmodern Elements of the Contemporary Horror Film." in Stephen Prince, ed. *The Horror Film*. Piscataway: Rutgers University Press. pp. 85–117.

Ponder, Julian. 2006. "'To the Next Level': Castration in *Hostel II*." *Irish Journal of Gothic and Horror Studies*. Issue 4.

Prince, Stephen, ed. 2004. *The Horror Film*. New Brunswick, NJ: Rutgers University Press.
Redmond, Sean, ed. *Liquid Metal: The Science Fiction Film Reader*. London: Wallflower Press.
Rehmeier, Adam (Director). 2011. *The Bunny Game* [Blu-Ray]. USA: Death Mountain Productions.
Repp, Mark. 2015. "The 30 Most Extreme Movies of the 21st-Century So Far." *Taste of Cinema*. 14 May. http://www.tasteofcinema.com/2015/the-30-most-extreme-movies-of-the-21st-century-so-far/ (14 September 2016).
Rhodes, Gary, ed. *Horror at the Drive-In: Popular Essays on Americana*. Jefferson, NC: McFarland.
Río, Elena del. 2008. *Deleuze and the Cinemas of Performance: Powers of Affection*. Edinburgh: Edinburgh University Press.
Robertson, Étienne Gaspar. 1831. *Mémoires Récréatifs, Scientifiques Et Anecdotiques*. 2 vols. Paris: Chez l'auteur et Librairie de Wurtz.
Ronny. 2009. "Aiming High with Christies Whiles." *Film Bizarro*. December. http://www.filmbizarro.com/cristiewhiles.php (14 July 2016).
Rosenbaum, Jonathan. 2013. "Salò, or the 120 Days of Sodom." *The Chicago Reader*. http://www.chicagoreader.com/chicago/salo-or-the-120-days-of-sodom/Film?oid=1068097 (10 July 2017).
Rue Morgue. Toronto: Marrs Media. 1997–. https://rue-morgue.com/ (4 September 2017).
Russell, Phil. 2013. *Beyond the Darkness: Cult, Horror and Extreme Cinema*. [S.n.]: Bad News Press.
Ryan, Shane (Director). 2014. *Amateur Porn Star Killer: The Complete Collection* [DVD]. USA. Mongolian Barbecue.
Samford, Josh (2014). "An Interview with Eric Stanze." In *Rogue Cinema*. http://www.roguecinema.com/an-interview-with-eric-stanze-by-josh-samford.html (5 May 2016).
Schaefer, Eric. 1999. *Bold! Daring! Shocking! True!: A History of Exploitation Films, 1919–1959*. Durham: Duke University Press.
Schechner, Richard, and Sara Brady. 2013. *Performance Studies: An Introduction*. Third edition. New York: Routledge.
Sconce, Jeffrey. 1995. ""Trashing" the Academy: Taste, Excess, and an Emerging Politics of Cinematic Style." *Screen*. Vol. 36, No. 4. Winter. pp. 371–393.
Scott, A.O. 2011. "Torture or Porn? No Need to Choose." *New York Times*. 12 May. http://www.nytimes.com/2011/05/13/movies/a-serbian-film-directed-by-srdjan-spasojevic-review.html?smid=tw-nytimesmovies&seid=auto (10 July 2017).
Sélavy, Virginie. 2015. "*Jörg Buttgereits Nekromantik's, or Sadean Shock of the Body.*" *Nekromantik 2 Anatomy of Desire Booklet*. London: Arrow Video. pp. 11–19.
Shaw, Deborah, and Armida de la Garza. 2010. "Introducing Transnational Cinemas." *Transnational Cinemas*. Vol. 1, No. 1. pp. 3–6.
Shin, Chi-Yun. 2008. "The Art of Branding: Tartan 'Asia Extreme' Films." *Jump Cut*. Vol. 50. Spring. http://www.ejumpcut.org/archive/jc50.2008/TartanDist/ (4 September 2017).
Snickars, Pelle, and Patrick Vonderau, eds. 2009. *The YouTube Reader*. Stockholm: National Library of Sweden.
Sobchack, Vivian. 2004. *Carnal Thoughts: Embodiment and the Moving Image Culture*. Berkeley: University of California Press.
Stanze, Eric (Director). 2005. *Scrapbook*. [DVD]. USA: Wicked Pixel Cinema.
Stokes, Melvyn, and Richard Maltby, eds. 1999. *Identifying Hollywood's Audiences: Cultural Identity and the Movies*. London: BFI Publishing.
Snyder, Stephen, and Pier Paolo Pasolini. 1980. *Pier Paolo Pasolini*. Boston: Twayne.
Tapper, Jake. 2005. "Court Deals Blow to U.S. Anti-Porn Campaign." *ABC News*. January

24. http://abcnews.go.com/Nightline/LegalCenter/story?id=433956&page=1 (8 August 2017).

Taylor, Richard. 2016. "Bending Reality: The World of Marian Dora—A Severed Cinema Interview." *Severed Cinema*, 6 May. http://severed-cinema.com/marian-dora/bending-morality-the-world-of-marian-dora-a-severed-cinema-interview (10 July 2017).

Thomson, Michael. 2000. "Salò, or the 120 Days of Sodom (1975)." *BBC*. 17 October. http://www.bbc.co.uk/films/2000/10/17/salo_1975_review.shtml (10 July 2017).

Thornton, Sarah. 1995. *Club Cultures: Music, Media and Subcultural Capital*. Cambridge: Polity Press.

Towlson, Jon. 2014. *Subversive Horror Cinema: Countercultural Messages of Films from Frankenstein to the Present*. Jefferson, NC: McFarland.

Trejo, Richard. 2013. "Truly Disturbing's Top 10 MOST DISTURBING Movies of All Time." *Truly Disturbing*. 27 May. http://www.trulydisturbing.com/2013/05/27/disturbings-top-10-disturbing-movies-time/ (10 July 2017).

Tucker, Jeremy. 2011. "INTERVIEW: Director Eric Stanze Spills His Guts on "Ratline."" *Insidestl*. September 14. http://insidestl.com/interview-director-eric-stanze-spills-his-guts-on-ratline-2/1942609 (10 May 2016).

Tudor, Andrew. 1989. *Monsters and Mad Scientists: A Cultural History of the Horror Movie*. Oxford: Blackwell.

Vale, V., and Andrea Juno, eds. 1986. *Incredibly Strange Films*. San Francisco: Re/Search.

Valentine, Lucifer (Director). 2006–2010. *The Vomit Gore Trilogy* [DVD]. USA/Canada: Unearthed Films.

Vincendeau, Ginette. 2011. "Fat Girl: Sisters, Sex, and Sitcom." *The Criterion Collection*. 3 May. https://www.criterion.com/current/posts/495-fat-girl-sisters-sex-and-sitcom (5 September 2016).

Vogel, Amos. 1974. *Film as a Subversive Art*. London: Weidenfeld and Nicolson.

Vogel, Fred (Director). 2005. *August Underground* [DVD]. USA: Toe Tag Pictures.

Waller, Gregory, ed. *American Horrors: Essays on the Modern American Horror Film*. Urbana: University of Illinois Press.

Waters, John. 2010. "Why You Should Watch Filth." *Big Think*. 10 September. http://bigthink.com/videos/why-you-should-watch-filth (10 July 2017).

Wetmore, Kevin J. 2012. *Post–9/11 Horror in American Cinema*. New York: Continuum.

Whett, Nina. 2002. "Forced Entry—Reviewer Rated...." *Adult Industry News*. May 26. http://ainews.com/Archives/Story4518.phtml (4 September 2017).

Williams, Christopher. 1980. *Realism and the Cinema: A Reader*. London: BFI.

Williams, Linda. 1990. *Hard Core: Power, Pleasure and the "Frenzy of the Visible."* Berkeley: University of California Press.

_____. 2008. *Screening Sex*. Durham: Duke University Press.

Index

Numbers in **_bold italics_** indicate pages with illustrations

The ABCs of Death 202
Abramović, Marina 136; *Lips of Thomas* 149
affect 20–21, 26, 34, 39, 65, 72, 75, 77, 81; and hardcore horror 2, 27–28, 29, 98, 105–106, 133; and reception 73, 88, 89–90, 93, 180, 183–186; *see also* relevant film entries
All Night Long 69
Amateur Pornstar Killer (*APSK*) trilogy 6, 10, 198; and affect 94; *APSK* 4, 6, 27, 28, 81, 109, 155, 156, 159, 160, 161, 162, 163, 164, 170, 171, 202; *APSK II* 94, 97, 156, 162, 169, 171; *APSK II: Snuff Version* 155; *APSK III* 94, 156, 157, 162, 163, 171; as an archetype of hardcore horror 93–97; distribution and marketing 163–169, 170–171; and performance 135, 156–157; and production 160–163; and realism 61, 122–130, 131, 157–159, 159–160; as true horror 154–155
American Guinea Pig: Bloodshock 200–201
American Guinea Pig: Bouquet of Guts and Gore 10, 27, 101, 106–108, 132
American Independent Pictures (AIP) 37, 44
Amerikan Holokaust 81
archaeology of horror 6–7, 8, 9, 12, 55, 199
L'Arrivée d'un train en gare de la Ciolat/The Arrival of a Train at La Ciotat Station 111
August Underground trilogy 10, 15, 16, 25, 93, 198; and affect 81, 85–86; as an archetype of hardcore horror 88–93; *August Underground* 4, 6, 10, 55, 56, 60, 61, 64, 70, 74, 80, 83, 88, 95, 126, 202; *Mordum* 6, 90, 91, 92, 132, 181, 185; and opposition to Hollywood 52, 54; *Penance* 6, 91, 92, 121, 132, 133, **_179_**, 181; and performance 133, 135; and realism 109, 115–116, 116–122, 123, 127, 129, 130, 131; and reception 71, 178, 179, 181–182, 185–186, 188, 189, 190, 192, 195, 196, 199; and reputation 28

Bad Taste 53
Basket Case 53

Berg, Nick 93, 128
The Beyond 99
Biondo, Tommy 83, 85–86, 212n18
Biro, Stephen 101, 102, 108, 200, 201
Bite 99
Bitel, Anton 105, 106
Black, Joel 113, 114, 128
The Black Cat 36
Black Christmas 44–45
Black Mass of the Nazi Sex Wizard 6, 52, 97, 98, 100, 102, 201
The Blair Witch Project 5, 93, 115, 160, 212n12
Blake, Linnie 3, 72
Blood Feast 8, 9, 31, 38–44, 45, 54, 99, 208n42; and affect 40, 42–44
Bloody Disgusting 12, 185, 186, 187, 192
Blumhouse 66, 210n40
Bonnie and Clyde (1967) 111
Brain Dead 53
Breaking Her Will 81
Breillet, Catherine 19, 57, 125–126
Bressack, James Cullen 106
British Board of Film Classification (BBFC) 4, 23, 56, 57, 70, 78, 80, 81, 87, 104, 105, 106, 150
Browning, Tod 34, 35
The Bunny Game 10, 11, 23, 27, 78, 79, 106, 134, **_149_**, 151; and affective performativity 146–151; as an archetype of hardcore horror 103–105
Burden, Chris 136; *Shoot* 149
The Burning Moon 74
Butler, Judith 139
Buttgereit, Jorg 5, 71–77

Cannibal 74, 75
Cannibal Holocaust 5, 8, 9, 16, 21, 47, 55, 60–64, **_63_**, 73, 76, 178, 180, 198; and affect 62
Cherry, Brigid 3, 31, 85, 192
Church, David 28, 90, 180, 183

229

230　Index

Classification and Ratings Administration (CARA)　4, 15, 23, 49, 108, 119
Cloverfield　28, 29, 114
The Cohasset Snuff Movie　95
Cohen, Herman　37
The Conjuring　13
Corman, Roger　23, 37, 44
Coulthard, Lisa　60
Craven, Wes　44
Creed, Barbara　72

Death Scenes　48, 118
Deep Throat　45
Deleuze, Gilles　11, 137
del Río, Elena　11, 37, 140, 142, 145
Destruction Babies　70
The Devil's Experiment see *The Guinea Pig* Films
The Devil's Rejects　18
Diary of the Dead　114
Dnepropetrovsk Maniacs　24, 82
Dora, Marian　74–76, 94
Dracula (1931)　8, 9, 33, 35

8MM　123
Eisenstein, Sergei　111
Electrocuting an Elephant　30, 111
Emanuelle in America　47
The Evil Dead (1981)　53, 189
The Execution of a Chinese Bandit　30
The Execution of Mary, Queen of Scots　33
Executions　48, 53
The Exorcist (film)　99

Faces of Death　38, 47, 48, 52, 53, 118, 202, 209n64
Faces of Gore　53
fandom　12, 172–173, 196–197; and gendered communities 185–187, 192; *see also* Valentine, Lucifer; vomit gore
Fat Girl　19, 125–126
Fetus　81
15 Minutes　157–158
Fight Club　160
film threat　65, 163–164
Findlay, Michael　31, 45
Findlay, Roberta　31, 45
Fiske, John　95, 173, 176, 179, 195
Flowers of Flesh and Blood see *The Guinea Pig* Films
Forced Entry (2002)　26–27
Frankenstein (1931)　33, 34, 35
Freaks　34, 35
Freddy vs Jason　13
Freeland, Cynthia　18, 26, 49, 117–118, 121
Frei, Matt　19–20
Friday the 13th (2009)　126
Friday the 13th Part II　44

Getsic, Rodleen　11, 103–105, 134; affective performativity 146–151

Gilmore, Gregg　103, 134
The Gore Gore Girls　44
The Great American Snuff Film　115
Grindhouse (film)　166
Grønstad, Asbjørn　19, 20, 29
Grotesque　55, 70–71
The *Guinea Pig* Films　16, 71, 106, 108, 156, 166–169; *The Devil's Experiment* 67–70; *Flowers of Flesh and Blood* 67–68, **68**, 70, 120

Haack, Emily　83, 85, 86, 105
Halfway to Hell　38
Hallam, Julia　110
Hammer horror　44
Haneke, Michael　19, 57
Hardcore (film)　46
Hardcore, Max　26, 141, 216n31
hardcore horror: definition 29; lack of academic address 2–4, 18–22; pornography and 25–27
Hate Crime　10, 78, 105–106, 108
Haute Tension/Switchblade Romance　80
Hebdige, Dick　196
Heller-Nicholas, Alexandra　5, 6, 23, 24, 108, 114, 117
Henry: Portrait of a Serial Killer　5, 8, 46–52, **50**, 55, 93, 118, 122, 123, 178; and affect 51–52
Hideshi, Hino　5
Hills, Matt　12, 175, 178, 180, 181, 182, 183, 187
Hollywood horror: 1930s 33–36; 1950s 36–38; 1990s 52–54
Hostel franchise　17, 19, 22; *Hostel 3*, 21, 70; *Hostel II* 20–21
House at the Edge of the Park　23
The Human Centipede　23, 74

I Know What You Did Last Summer　115
I Married a Monster from Outer Space　37
I Spit on Your Grave (2010)　80
I Was a Teenage Frankenstein　37
I Was a Teenage Werewolf　37
Ichi the Killer　69
The Immoral Mr. Teas　37
Indiegogo　107–108, 214n100
The Invasion of the Body Snatchers　36
Irigaray, Luce　147
Irish Journal of Gothic and Horror Studies　21
Irreversible　16, 18, 19, 25
Islamic State/Isis　24, 30, 82, 95, 128, 130, 157
Island of Lost Souls　36

Jameson, Fredric　107
Jancovich, Mark　12, 183
Jenkins, Henry　194
Jimenez, Michiko　94, 124, 156 -157, 160, 161, 162, 171
Joan of Arc (1895)　111
Jones, Steve: definition of hardcore horror 25; hardcore horror 142, 143–144, 166, 199;

Index

Mordum 92; torture porn 4–5, 6, 7, 21, 22, 25, 26, 28
Jump Cut 20–21
Ju-on: The Grudge 66

Kavka, Misha 27, 28, 62, 90
Kerekes, David 4, 5, 23, 24, 30, 51, 64, 200
The Killing of America 38, 47, 48
Kimber, Shaun 51, 77, 78–79
Kinematoscope 31, 32, 33
Kissing on the Mouth (film) 164

Lanette, Kai 94, 157, 161–162, 171
Lange, Patricia 12, 193; videos of affiliation 187–188
The Last Exorcism 114
The Last House of the Left (1972) 44
The Last House of the Left (2009) 18
The Last House on Dead End Street 47
La Vey, Ameara 11, **29**, 97, 99, 100, 102, 105, **138**, **141**, **144**; affective performativity 137–146, 151; reception 175, 177
Lázaro-Reboll, Antonio 6–7, 12, 199
Lewis, Herschell Gordon 38, 39, 40, 41, 43, 44, 53, 98, 99
Likens, Hope 98, 99, 100, 101, 143, 145
Live Feed 81
Lolita Vibrator Torture 69

MacCabe, Colin 112, 115
Mad Love 36
the magic lantern 31–33
Magnotta, Luca 24, 82, 95, 128
Man Bites Dog 8, 55, 64–65, 67, 73
Maniac (2012) 80
Marchment, Margaret 110
Martyrs 16, 80
MASH (film) 111
Mau Mau (film) 38
McNaughton, John 48, 49
Melancholie der Engel/The Angel's Melancholia 16, 55, 74, 75–76
Mickle, Jim 202
Mondo film 5, 24, 47–48, 54, 118, 119, 122; *Mondo Cane* 38
The Mortuary 172–181, 183, 185, 186, 187, 192
Murder Set Pieces 9, 78, 80–81, 106
Musser, Charles 31
Muybridge, Eadweard 32, 33

My Name Is "A" by Anonymous 154, 155, 166
Naked Blood 69
Natural Born Killers 28, 158, 159
Nekromantik 16, 71–73, 76
Nekromantik II 72, 73
Nénette and Boni 145
New American Cinema 111
New French Extremism **17**, 19, 125
Nymphomaniac Vol. 1 20

Oldboy (2003) 19

Page, Betty 37
Paranormal Activity 13, 15, 115
Pasolini, Pier Paolo 56, 57, 58, 65
Pearl, Daniel 93, 128
Peeping Tom (1960) 96
performance art 136–137; studies 135–137
Peters, Allen 133–134
Pinedo, Isabel 18, 26
Platoon 159
The Pornographer 158
The Poughkeepsie Tapes 126

Quandt, James 16, 17

realism 5, 6, 9, 23–24, 25, 33, 38, 44, 45–46, 48; and hardcore horror 10–11, 27–29, 52, 75, 81, 90–91, 103, 155–156, 157–159, 186; theoretical approaches to 110, 112–113; in 21st century horror 113–116; *see also* affective performativity; *Amateur Porn Star Killer*; *August Underground*
realist horror 2, 18, 26, 49, 54, 62–64, 69, 73, 76, 77, 105, 198, 201
Red Room 69
The Redsin Tower 133
ReGOREgitated Sacrifice 6, 97, 97–98, 100, 142–143, **144**, 177
Rehmeier, Adam 103, 104, 105, 134, 146, 150
Renfro, Jeff 103, 104, 134, 150
Requiem for a Dream 163
The Return of the Living Dead 3 53
Ringu 66
Romero, George 44
The Room 167
Rossellini, Roberto 111
Rubber's Lover 69
Rue Morgue 12, 87, 91, 92, 102, 172, 173, 175, 176, 180, 181, 215n38
Russell, Phil 4, 22
Ryan, Shane 6, 11, 123, **125**, 201–202; on performing in *APSK* 135; 156–157; and the production practices of *APSK* 12, 94, 95–97, 127, 130, 153–154, 157–159, 160–165, 169, 170–171; and true horror 94–95, 154–155

S&man 28
Salò, or 120 Days of Sodom 8, 9, 16, 196; and affect 57, 60; the authentic and symbolic in 58–60, **59**, 61; reception 56–57
Sargeant, Jack 203
Saving Private Ryan 112, 113
Saw 3, 13, 18, 21, **22**, 70; franchise 3, 15, 17, 18, 19, 21, 22, 75
Schechner, Richard 139
Schrader, Paul 95, 124, 127, 128, 123
Scrapbook 10, 15, 54, 79, 89, 93, 95, 105, 136; as an archetype of hardcore horror 83–88, **84**, **87**
Scream 52, 53, 115
Seul contre tous 16, **17**
Shane Ryan's Faces of Snuff 201–202

Shortbus 19
Sheen, Charlie 66–67, 120
The Silence of the Lambs 52, 53, 85, 122
Slater, David 4, 5, 23, 24, 30, 51, 64
Slaughter 31, 45, 46
Slaughtered Vomit Dolls 4, 6, **29**, 56, 81, 99, 100, 101, **141**, 151, 172; affective performativity 137–142; reception 102, 172–177, 188, 195, 196
Slow Torture Puke Chamber 6, 44, 97, 98, 100, 143, 201
Snuff: aesthetics 6, 10, 11, 24, 28, 45, 51–52, 63, 114,115, 123, 155; and affect 27–28, 62, 90; in extreme cinema 19, 76; and found footage 5; and hardcore horror 5, 23–24, 44, 92–93, 106–107, 119–120, 121, 122, 123, 130, 151, 178; Hollywood and 123, 157–158; Internet and 24, 48, 53, 95, 128, 200, 201–202; mediation of death in fictional 46–48, 62; mythology 11, 95, 106, 123–124, 127–129; porno-horror hybridization 26–28; and pornography 46; pseudo- 16, 34, 67–69; *Snuff: Real Death and Screen Media* 4, 200; in *Videodrome* 1, 12
Snuff (film) 8, 24, 31, 44–46, 47, 48, 55, 63, 64, 95, 115
Snuff 102 95
Sobchack, Vivian 27
Society 53
Sontag, Susan 36–37
Soska Sisters 98, 100; as the Black Angels of Hell 98, 100, 143
Splatstick 53
Srpski Film/A Serbian Film 8, 9, 16, 21, 56, 76–79, 80
Stanze, Eric 52, 54, 83, 85, 86, 87, 88, 105, 108, 202
Stockholm Syndrome (film) 81

Tartan Asia Extreme 20, 23
Tetsuo 69
The Texas Chainsaw Massacre (1974) 44, 178, 180
The Thing (2011) 114
Thornton, Sara 12, 181, 182, 192

torture porn 3, 4, 17, 18, 19, 20, 21, **22**, 25, 70, 75, 80, 140
Towlson, Jon 34, 53
Traces of Death 53
Trouble Every Day 16
Tudor, Andrew 18, 26
Twentynine Palms 17

Valentine, Lucifer 6, 103, 105, 144, 146, 153, 191, 193, 199, 201; and filmmaking 101–103; and navigating fandom 172–177; and vomit gore 98–101;
Vertov Dziga 111
V/H/S 202
Videodrome 1, 2, 3, 12, 93; the program within the film 1, 2, 3, 6, 12, 13
Viennese Actionism 136, 148–149
Violent Shit 74
Vogel, Amos 41
Vogel, Fred 6, 24, 34, 54, 92, 93, 97, 135, 199, 202; and *August Underground* 116–117, 122, 133–134; and distribution approaches10–11, 67, 90–91, 119–120, 127, 130, 151, 181; and *Henry: Portrait of a Serial Killer* 52, 118; on *Mordum* and *Penance* 121, **179**, 186, 215n28
vomit gore 6, 11, 16, 27, 97–103, 108, 148, 201; affective performativity 137–146, 151; definition 98–100; and fandom 176, 188, 190–197

War of the Worlds (1953) 36
War Zone 163
Warning!!! Pedophile Released 166, 168–170
Werewolf in London 36
Whale, James 34
Whiles, Christie 132–133
Why Don't You Play in Hell 70
Williams, Christopher 110, 111

YouTube 11, 12, 24, 107, 161, 170, 171, 182, 196; and fan communities 187–189, 191, 193, 194; and fan demographics 192–193

Zedd, Nick 5

www.ingramcontent.com/pod-product-compliance
Lightning Source LLC
Chambersburg PA
CBHW051220300426
44116CB00006B/656